A VERY RUDE AWAKENING

A VERY RUDE AWAKENING

The night the Japanese midget subs came to Sydney Harbour

PETER GROSE

ALLEN&UNWIN

For my wife Roslyn, whose mother hid her under the kitchen table while all this was going on. And with special thanks to my publisher and lifelong friend Richard Walsh, whose mother threw him into the umbrella cupboard instead.

First published in 2007

Allen & Unwin
83 Alexander Street
Crows Nest NSW 2065
Australia
Phone: (61 2) 8425 0100
Fax: (61 2) 9906 2218
Email: info@allenandunwin.com
Web: www.allenandunwin.com

National Library of Australia
Cataloguing-in-Publication entry:

Grose, Peter, 1941–.
   A very rude awakening : the night the Japanese midget subs
   came to Sydney Harbour.

   Bibiography.
   Includes index.
   ISBN 978 1 74175 219 9 (pbk.).

   1. Midget submarines. 2. World War, 1939-1945 – Naval
   operations – Submarine. 3. World War, 1939-1945 – Naval
   operations, Japanese. 4. Sydney (N.S.W.) – History –
   Bombardment, 1942. I. Title.

940.545952

Internal design by Darian Causby
Illustrations and maps by Ian Faulkner (unless otherwise attributed)
Set in 12/16 pt Bembo by Midland Typesetters, Australia
Printed and bound in Australia by Griffin Press

10 9 8 7 6 5 4 3 2 1

Contents

Introduction

The Japanese midget submarine raid on Sydney Harbour is one of those events, like the assassination of President Kennedy or the death of Princess Diana, where everybody seems to remember what they were doing at the time. It is hard to find a Sydneysider who can't tell you where they were, or what their neighbours or parents or grandparents were doing, on the night their harbour became a battlefield.

The raid has been the subject of endless magazine articles, radio and television documentaries, and has featured in many books. Yet one story has remained largely untold: how did Sydney respond to the attack? The focus has always been on the Japanese raiders. Where did they come from? What exactly did they do?

The Japanese were not the only heroes that night. From the civilian nightwatchman in his rowboat who first raised the alarm, to the young Australian Navy lieutenant on his first night of command who fired the first effective depth charge (and crippled his own ship in the process), there were heroes aplenty among the defenders.

There were failures as well. The defences were slapdash, the command was erratic, and there was a lot of undisciplined gunfire, which happily did little damage beyond blasting chunks out of the venerable stonework of Fort Denison in mid-harbour. Some of the command decisions, like the order to commercial traffic on the harbour to keep moving as normal and fully lit, were plain barmy.

By the end of the night 27 men had died—19 Australian and two British sailors, and the six Japanese crew of the three midget submarines. All three submarines were sunk, only one by hostile action. The *Kuttabul*, a converted ferry used as a dormitory for junior seamen, lay partially submerged against the harbour wall, smashed by the torpedo which exploded beneath her.

There can be no doubting the courage of the Japanese sailors. But courage was not in short supply that night. Nor was incompetence, confusion and indecision. Luck, too, played its part, mostly favouring the defence.

I hope the reader will bear with me as I give the political and historical background, both Australian and Japanese, to the raid. In the 21st century we complain of the speed of change, as we adapt to a high-tech global village. Yet at the time of the midget submarine raid, the world must have appeared to the people of Australia to be spinning out of control. The certainties of white supremacy evaporated in the humiliation of Singapore's fall; the invincible British Empire suddenly looked frail and vulnerable; 160 years of Australian foreign policy were overturned in three weeks—a change that has lasted to this day, putting Australian soldiers on the streets of Iraq. It is impossible to understand the actions and reactions in Sydney on the night of 31 May and 1 June 1942, without first delving into this background.

Peter Grose,
March 2007

Part I

PREPARATION

Chapter I

There's a war on

Sydney was suffering an uncharacteristically foul night on Sunday, 31 May 1942. Winter would begin next day, and the golden beaches had long been abandoned. Throughout the day the south-west wind brought squally rain and biting cold to city and suburbs. The rain died back by evening, but the sky stayed thick with cloud, masking the full moon. In town the soldiers, sailors and airmen made the best of their leave at Sydney's traditionally boisterous theatres, nightclubs, restaurants, illegal gambling dens, and brothels. In 1942 entertainment was a seven-days-a-week affair. After all, there was a war on.

Sydney in 1942 would be unrecognisable to the citizens of that gleaming Emerald City today. The iconic Harbour Bridge was a mere 10 years old, and still something of a novelty. Men wore hats. Nice women wore gloves. Divorce was a source of shame. The tallest building in Sydney was the 13-storey AWA tower in York Street, whose art deco walls are today jostled to oblivion by the surrounding forest of skyscrapers stretching up to 300 metres. Sydney's civic architecture in 1942 was still low-rise colonial conventional, a triumphalist embodiment of British Empire solidity and bourgeois virtue rather than the soaring celebration of the imagination which is the Sydney Opera House today.

Australia's rich then were not stock-market wizards or property developers. They were the sheep and cattle barons, the so-called 'squattocracy' made up from old families of the colony. They owned huge tracts of land in the outback, overseen from graceful homesteads, and grew rich from the insatiable worldwide demand for Australian wool and beef. They kept splendid second homes in Sydney and Melbourne, and sent their sons and daughters to expensive boarding schools in the capital cities. Meanwhile, the wrought-iron balconied terrace houses of Sydney's Paddington and Surry Hills had to wait another 25 years to become fashionable. In 1942 they were slums.

It was a city of hypocrites. Pubs closed their bars at 6 pm. Sly grog shops flourished thereafter. The police were quick to ferret out obscene books and bawdy art exhibitions. Yet the city's vice squad seemed unable to pinpoint the location of brothels in Palmer Street and Chapel Street, near Kings Cross. Gambling other than via an on-course bookmaker was illegal. The classic Australian game of two-up, involving the tossing of two coins while punters bet on two heads or two tails, could be found in suburban backyards and bushland clearings everywhere. Thommo's Two-up School, which prudently shifted location every so often including a brief stint on a ferry, had been a household name for over 20 years. It managed to stay several steps ahead of a none-too-zealous police force throughout the war. The notorious Tilly Divine and Kate Lee ruled an underworld of prostitution, illegal drinking and illegal betting. Police demands were very reasonable. No doubt there were some honest vice squad coppers, but the rest offered blind-eye service at affordable prices.

Chicken was expensive. Men drank beer. Few families could afford a car. Luxury was a night out in the gilded splendour of the Hotel Australia in central Sydney where, so it was rumoured, *continental* food was served as well as the traditional steak, roast beef and lamb. Romano's nightclub nearby offered even more sophistication, with live entertainment to accompany a menu which could be navigated only with a smattering of French. Strip clubs had not yet been invented, but at the Tivoli Theatre showgirls appeared topless on stage, on the strict understanding that they stayed rigid and motionless in pursuit of their art.

Nevertheless, in 1942 Sydney was ever more visibly a city at war. Military uniforms were everywhere. The harbour was packed with warships. Newspapers reported the daily progress of the war in anxious detail—while reporting the horseracing news in even greater detail. Increasing numbers of husbands, sons, fathers and boyfriends left home in white, blue and khaki uniforms, while mothers, wives, daughters and girlfriends fretted for their safety. Women joined all three services and donned uniforms, too. Those who didn't were constantly reminded that there was plenty they could do for their country. In a striking phrase, Prime Minister Curtin told the women of Australia: 'The knitting needle is a weapon of war.'

The evidence of war went beyond the profusion of military uniforms. Bondi beach was festooned with barbed wire. Zigzag slit trenches gouged suburban back lawns, ready to provide shelter when the inevitable air raids came. Anthony Hordern's department store in Sydney advertised: 'Now is the time to prepare. Send for your A.R.P. [Air Raid Precautions] equipment.' Among indispensable items for surviving the coming onslaught, Hordern's offered 'new and improved indestructible lampshades, all metal, double purpose, detachable caps for brownouts'. The price was a very reasonable one shilling and a penny ha'penny per lampshade.

Sydney remained a party town. The stuffy Australian Club opened its doors to visiting American officers—though not to Australian officers nor to American other ranks. To the soldiers, sailors and airmen from America, Britain, Holland, India and France, as well as to the Australian troops stationed there or passing through, Sydney was above all a safe city. The lethal jungles of Malaya and the Dutch East Indies were thousands of miles away to the north. So were the howling Zero aircraft and Long Lance torpedoes of the Imperial Japanese Navy, both of which had done so much to give the lie to the name Pacific Ocean. Even when Darwin, Broome and other Australian cities suffered Japanese bombing, it all seemed a long way away. In Sydney, nobody needed to think further afield than Kings Cross, Randwick Racecourse, and the next cold beer.

◆   ◆   ◆

Sydney Harbour was better protected than many. There were shore-based gun batteries facing the sea, anti-aircraft batteries on headlands, searchlight teams to check the skies, armed and unarmed patrol boats scouring the harbour, and a very modest force of fighter aircraft to repel an attack from the air. Outside the harbour entrance, six indicator loops lay on the ocean bed in deep water in a huge arc from the cliffs of Dover Heights in the south to the beach suburb of Dee Why in the north. The loops registered the passage over them of any metal ship. On the night of 31 May 1942, a battleship could have crossed the outer ring without raising the alarm. Two of these six outer loops had failed, so all six were left unmanned.

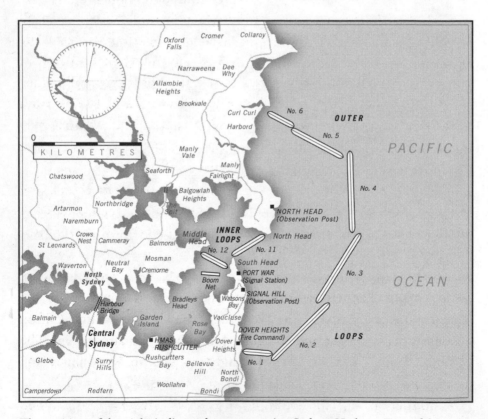

The position of the eight indicator loops protecting Sydney Harbour. Two of the outer loops were not working on the night of 31 May 1942. Of the two inner loops, Inner Loop 12 proved to be the most effective, detecting all three submarines as they entered the harbour.

The next line of defence was a pair of similar indicator loops, this time inside the harbour itself. Inner Loop No. 11 stretched across the entrance of the harbour from North Head to South Head. Further into the harbour lay Inner Loop No. 12, stretching from just inside South Head at Lady Bay (now a celebrated nudist beach), across the inner harbour to Middle Head near Obelisk Bay. The peculiar geography of Sydney Harbour meant that water traffic to the busy and popular harbour suburb of Manly had to cross Inner Loop 12 while still remaining inside the harbour. As well, Inner Loop 12 lay in shallower water than any of its counterparts, at 6 fathoms (11 metres), so smaller and lighter vessels like harbour ferries, tugs and even large launches set off a trace. Inner Loop 12 always had plenty to say for itself.

Watching over all this was the Port War Signal Station on South Head. PWSS checked every vessel approaching the harbour. Any unknown or unexpected vessel would be ordered to halt by Port War until it had been cleared by an examination vessel standing off Sydney Heads. The indicator loops 'tailed' into Port War. As well, PWSS had a secret ASDIC anti-submarine detection system, and a photoelectric beam to detect surface vessels. If Sydney faced a threat from the sea, it was the task of PWSS to raise the alarm and call for help.

The final line of defence was a boom net stretching from the southern shore of the harbour at Laings Point, near Watsons Bay (a short walk today from the famous Doyle's Restaurant), to Georges Head, near the genteel northern harbour suburb of Clifton Gardens. The workings of Sydney Harbour have scarcely altered between 1942 and now: there are two major channels leading from the harbour to the open ocean, the Western and the Eastern. The Western Channel, over on the Clifton Gardens side, is deeper and straighter and is used by larger ships. The Eastern Channel, near Watsons Bay and Camp Cove, is shallower and trickier, and is used by smaller more manoeuvrable ships.

Construction of the boom net began in January 1942. When complete, the net would be 1480 metres long with two gate openings, a 121-metre gate at the western end, and a 91-metre gate at the eastern end. By May 1942 the large centre section of the net and some of the harbour-edge work had been completed, but there were still big gaps facing the channels near each end. Floating boom gates were to be built into these openings, blocking the Eastern and Western channels and completing the defensive line. The gates would be opened and closed by specialist boom vessels. There were no gates, however, and no boom vessels, on the night of 31 May 1942, just two big gaps—275 metres on the eastern side and 293 metres on the western side.

Although the Sydney net was incomplete, in some respects it was superior to nets at other major Allied bases. The central and western section of Sydney's net was strung along 49 clusters of four piles driven into the harbour bed. The eastern end was suspended from floating buoys at the surface. However, the Sydney net was unusual in that it was securely anchored to the harbour bed. Other nets, including the net across Pearl Harbor, simply dangled from the surface to somewhere near the seabed, allowing the possibility that a small submarine might dive under them. Shortly before the bombers struck Pearl Harbor on 7 December 1941, a Japanese midget submarine may have slipped into the harbour past the net defences, possibly taking advantage of the loose net. No submarine could duck under the Sydney net.

◆   ◆   ◆

On that cold and windy night, Jimmy Cargill had one of the loneliest and least enviable jobs in Sydney. He was employed as a nightwatchman by the Maritime Services Board, the civilian authority in charge of all harbours and navigable waterways in the state of New South Wales. His job was to guard two floating crane punts near the western end of the Sydney boom net, part of the net construction effort. Amid the shortages of war, pilfering of building materials, tools, even wood, was a perennial problem, so Jimmy stayed vigilant. He was an ex-merchant seaman, in his mid-50s, with a no-nonsense style. He died in 1986, but he left behind some remarkable audio tapes, recorded in his soft Scottish brogue. He comes across as the kind of man you would want at your side in a crisis.

The southerly wind creates special dangers on Sydney Harbour. Out to sea that night, it was whipping up 2-metre waves and setting the spray flying. Inside the harbour it produced an uncomfortably choppy surface. Spray and rain combined to soak through the most reliable waterproof. Nevertheless, around 7 pm, Jimmy Cargill knew he had no choice but to go out onto the harbour. The guy ropes on one of the crane derricks were swinging dangerously in the wind. They would have to be tightened, even if that meant an uncomfortable and straining journey by rowboat from his shore base. He clambered into his 14-foot skiff and heaved his way across the rough water to the offending punt.

By 7.30 pm the guy ropes were secure. Jimmy Cargill was now out on the harbour, so he rowed across to the floating pile-driver nearby to chat with his fellow nightwatchman Bill Nangle. They were still chatting at 7.55 pm as the Manly ferry crossed Inner Loop 12 on its outbound route to Manly. The ferry, brightly lit and slow moving, could be seen easily by the Royal Australian Navy watchers at the Port War Signal Station. It left a good trace, and the Loop Station watchers could match the trace to its passage.

Four minutes later, at 7.59 pm, an inbound Manly ferry crossed Inner Loop 12 on its way back to the central ferry wharf at Circular Quay. Again, it was brightly lit and again the Loop Station crew had no trouble matching it to the trace.

Two minutes later, at 8.01 pm, there was a smaller blip on the trace paper. Nobody saw anything, and nobody bothered with it.

Some time around 8.15 pm, while Jimmy Cargill and Bill Nangle were still chatting on the floating pile-driver, they noticed what in the darkness looked like a fishing boat near the net. The boat was showing no lights and clearly shouldn't have been there. Cargill decided to row over and investigate.

When he drew closer, he could see that it was no fishing boat. A strange, metallic object stood in the water close to the net. It had two large, protruding tubes, both with capped rounded ends, reminding him of oxyacetylene bottles. With not a little courage he rowed closer, to within a paddle's length of the object. He still didn't know what it was, but by now the likeliest explanation was that it was a mine.

Every night the navy stationed two patrol boats to guard the net, one at each gate. The Channel Patrol boats were converted harbour pleasure launches bought by the Royal Australian Navy and converted to military use. The boats were given limited weaponry, never more than a few depth charges and a World War I machine-gun. It was scarcely suitable armament to stare down the Imperial Japanese Navy.

That night the duty vessels at the net were HMAS *Yarroma* at the western end and HMAS *Lolita* at the eastern end. Cargill thought he should report his findings, and rowed over to the nearest patrol boat, the *Yarroma*. The captain was sceptical: surely it was just a bit of old naval

Trace left by Chuman (I-27's midget) on Inner Loop 12 as he enters the harbour at 8.01 pm.

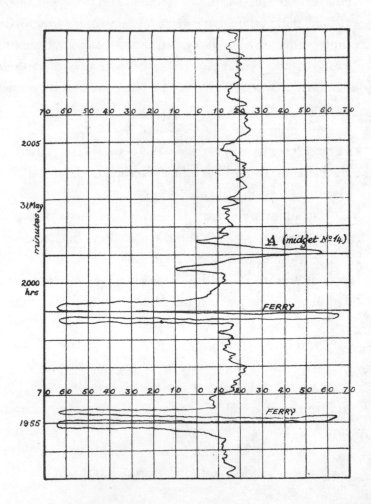

junk that had floated up and got caught in the net. Cargill was adamant. Whatever was stuck there was shiny and brand new, never junk. Cargill asked *Yarroma* to follow him, and rowed off in the direction of the object. *Yarroma* didn't move.

By now angry, Cargill rowed back. *Yarroma*'s skipper explained that he was repairing his searchlight, and invited Cargill aboard. Still reluctant to close in on what was very likely a mine, *Yarroma* instead offered the services of their stoker to row over with Cargill to investigate. Cargill accepted.

The two set off at a leisurely pace to cover the 80 metres or so between *Yarroma* and the mystery object. Again, they closed to within a paddle's length. The stoker shone his torch on the object, which was clearly stuck in the net and thrashing its engines to free itself. By now they could see into the water. In the torchlight were a conning tower, a bow cutting line, and a periscope. The two 'oxyacetylene bottles' were torpedo tubes. The stoker needed no second opinion. 'It's a submarine all right.'

Chapter 2

England expects

Until 1942 Australians lived with a comfortable certainty. Wars took place in that mythic hinterland called 'overseas'. Australia was proud to call itself part of the British Empire, and with that comforting knowledge came an obligation to join with Britain when either homeland or Empire was under threat. Nelson's famous signal at Trafalgar, 'England expects that every man will do his duty', could be heard loud and clear across the oceans to Australia. Before 1942 that invariably meant shipping Australian soldiers and sailors off to some distant land to risk their lives on Britain's behalf. The payoff was obvious enough: if ever Australia came under threat, the invincible British Empire would spring to its defence and crush its enemies with a mighty blow.

Even before 1901, when federation joined the six Australian colonies into a single nation, Australians plunged willingly into Britain's colonial wars. A contingent of 758 soldiers from New South Wales took part in the relief of Khartoum in 1885. A much stronger contingent, totalling 16,175 men, fought in the Boer War from 1899 to 1902. Some 300 Australians, again mostly from New South Wales, fought with British forces putting down the Boxer Rebellion in China in 1900. However, the biggest contribution came in 1914 with the outbreak of World

War I. Some 300,000 Australians enlisted, of whom 60,000 were killed and 156,000 wounded, gassed or taken prisoner. It was a staggering contribution from a nation with a population of less than five million.

Despite the carnage, there was no shortage of volunteers. Each party of Australian troops went off to war in a fanfare of goodwill. They paraded through the cities, watched by cheering crowds. More crowds lined the harbours to wave the troopships off. World War I, and particularly Gallipoli, came to be seen as the birth of the Australian nation. War somehow bound the people of Australia into a single identity. And wars could be relied on to obey three infallible rules: they were fought elsewhere; Britain took the lead; and Britain and her allies won.

Australia, along with Canada, South Africa and New Zealand, enjoyed a high status in the British Empire. The four 'white' countries were dominions, as opposed to British-ruled colonies like India. Each, in theory, was an independent nation owing allegiance to the British crown but self-governing in every other respect, and equal in status to the British motherland.

Reality was far different. Before World War II Australia barely maintained its own diplomatic service. External Affairs consisted of little more than liaison with the Foreign Office in London, there to be kept up to date with the latest British relationships and policies towards the rest of the world. Australian and British interests were identical and inseparable. The dominions had the right to argue and even advise, but ultimately they were expected to fall into line with whatever Britain had in mind.

The way Australia entered World War II graphically illustrates Australian subservience to British foreign policy. The anglophile Australian Prime Minister Robert Menzies, a lawyer, believed Australia was legally at war as a direct consequence of the British declaration of war on Germany. In his speech to the nation announcing Australia's participation, Menzies said: 'Fellow Australians, it is my melancholy duty to inform you officially, that in consequence of a persistence by Germany in her invasion of Poland, Great Britain has declared war upon her and that, *as a result* [author's italics], Australia is also at war.'

Whatever the niceties of dominion status, Australia's independence was immediately thrown out the window. As had happened in World War I, the Royal Australian Navy was simply merged with Britain's Royal Navy into a single force under British command. Australian fighting ships set off for the Mediterranean, the Red Sea and the Atlantic. Australian airmen were shipped to Britain to join the air war against Germany. They fought in Royal Air Force (RAF) squadrons rather than as separate Royal Australian Air Force (RAAF) units. Two entire Australian infantry divisions and part of a third left for the Middle East, where they retained their Australian identity but fought under the overall British command of General Sir Archibald Wavell. When the autocratic Churchill took over as British Prime Minister in May 1940, he made it very clear that conduct of the entire war rested with Britain, and Churchill personally would call the shots. It was business as usual: the war obligingly stayed overseas, and Australians stayed under British control. The only rule which appeared not to be holding was the certainty of British victory.

Poland fell within weeks to an attack first by Germany and two weeks later by the USSR, then Germany's ally. The British and French watched impotently. Seven months of quiet followed—the so-called 'phoney war'—in which little happened beyond the invasion of Finland by the USSR on 30 November 1939. However, during this lull there was one major incident which was to have a curious resonance in Sydney 18 months later.

The Royal Navy used the harbour at Scapa Flow, in the Orkney Islands off Scotland's north coast, as one of their principal bases. The Luftwaffe had flown aerial reconnaissance missions over the harbour, and came back with a good picture of the defences. The commander of the German submarine fleet, Admiral Dönitz, approached one of his best submariners, Günther Prien, with the photographs and a simple question: did Prien think he could sneak into Scapa Flow? Prien said yes.

The German submarine U-47, under Prien's command, arrived off Scapa Flow on the night of 13 October 1939, only six weeks after the declaration of war. Fortunately for the British, the fleet had sailed a few days earlier, leaving only one capital ship, the battleship *Royal Oak*, at anchor in the harbour. If more British ships had been there, the resulting devastation might have had a major impact on the Atlantic war.

The harbour at Scapa Flow is served by four channels between islands. As protection the British had sunk block ships in the channels. Entry to the harbour was via a boom gate. However, the aerial photographs showed that there was sufficient space for a skilful commander to dodge around the block ships, and Prien certainly possessed the skill. He slipped into Scapa Flow via the Kirk Channel shortly after midnight.

Prien fired his first salvo of torpedoes at the *Royal Oak* a few minutes before 1 am on 14 October. One scored a minor hit on the bow of the battleship. The rest missed. The British were so confident that the harbour was impenetrable that they gave no thought to the idea that the blast was caused by an enemy submarine attack. They thought there had been an internal explosion on board the ship, probably in a paint store.

Twenty minutes later Prien fired a second fan of torpedoes. This time there was no escape. All three hit home, tearing huge holes in the hull of the *Royal Oak*. The 29,000-ton battleship rolled over and sank within 10 minutes, killing 833 of the crew in the process. Prien slipped out of the harbour unnoticed and returned safely to Germany and a hero's welcome. Each crew member was awarded an Iron Cross, pinned on personally by Hitler in Berlin. The fanfare of celebration in Germany gave the British the first full explanation of what had happened to the *Royal Oak*.

This was the second-worst naval disaster of World War II for Britain, and the Royal Navy took it very seriously. They set up a Board of Inquiry to investigate how it had happened, and what precautions needed to be taken to prevent a recurrence. Three senior Royal Navy commanders sat on the Board. One was Commander Gerard Muirhead-Gould, an experienced World War I sailor with some knowledge of submarines. Muirhead-Gould was well thought of by the navy, but he suffered from heart problems and was deemed unfit for active service. Shortly after completing the Board of Inquiry, he was appointed Naval

Officer in Command, Sydney, and later promoted to Rear Admiral. He was in control of Sydney Harbour on the night of 31 May 1942. Muirhead–Gould was in a better position than most to know how submarines can sneak into harbours and cause havoc.

◆　◆　◆

The war resumed in earnest in April 1940, and the first fury of *blitzkrieg* sent Europe reeling. On 9 April Germany invaded Denmark and Norway. Holland and Belgium were next to fall. Within six weeks, on 20 May, the Germans reached the English Channel. On 27 May British forces began retreating from the European mainland via Dunkirk. By 4 June the evacuation was complete. Britain and her Empire allies passed it off as a miracle. In fact it was a massive defeat and a humiliation.

The German advance continued. On 22 June France surrendered. Most of Western Europe was now under German control and the simple, brutal truth was that in the space of three violent months Britain and her Empire found themselves alone and losing the war.

Worse was to follow. Britain itself came under attack from the air. Streams of German bombers arrived by day and night, and newspapers around the world carried front-page pictures of British cities in flames. Tens of thousands of tons of explosives rained down on British homes and factories.

Meanwhile, German submarines began attacking shipping convoys in the Atlantic. Vital supplies of food, oil and military equipment from the United States and elsewhere ran a gauntlet of U–boats, with terrible loss of life and tonnage of shipping. Everywhere the news was bad, and no amount of Churchillian rhetoric about finest hours and fighting on the beaches and the hills could disguise the facts.

Australians watched this with a mixture of horror and disbelief. This wasn't how it was meant to happen. Didn't Britain always win? Lines formed outside recruiting offices as young men rushed to enlist, ready to do their bit to turn the tide. The story of my own family was typical. My father was the third of four siblings. The oldest was Molly, then came Jim, my father Fred, and Tom. The brothers discussed what to do. My father was the only one married, so it was agreed that the two unmarried brothers would be sufficient contribution to the war effort from the Grose family. Uncle Tom was first. He joined the army on 20 May 1940, aged 20 years. Uncle Jim enlisted in the army a fortnight later, on 6 June, aged 30 years. Both named my Nan as their next of kin. They were sent off separately in slouch hats and khaki to the Middle East.

Royal Australian Navy ships were soon in action in the Mediterranean and the Atlantic, and Australian airmen fought in the skies over Britain and Europe. However, Australian soldiers had yet to come under serious fire. This respite came to a swift end in September 1940. Mussolini wanted to recapture the glorious Roman Empire for modern Italy. He launched his campaign on 14 September with an attack on Egypt, following this up with an attack on Greece, launched on 28 October. The restoration of the Roman Empire got off to a shaky start. The Greeks took only three weeks to throw the Italians out, and by 7 February 1941, the British, with strong support from Australian troops, had rolled the Italians back to Benghazi in Libya, taking thousands of prisoners in the process. Uncle Jim was there to help. Uncle Tom was busy elsewhere, fighting the Vichy French in Syria. The rout of Mussolini's troops was a rare victory for Britain and Empire, and for a brief few weeks the war looked winnable. Hitler swiftly silenced the optimists.

The German Army commanded by Rommel counterattacked in North Africa on 31 March 1941, and rolled the British and Australians back from Benghazi almost to Cairo, leaving an enclave of mostly Australian soldiers holding Tobruk. The German invasion of Greece and Yugoslavia, launched a week later on 6 April, was equally brutal and swiftly effective. It was followed by the capture of Crete on 2 June. Both Greece and Crete led to heavy British and Australian losses. The war was now 21 months old and going very badly indeed. Australian troops felt they were endlessly let down by poor air support. Only Britain could put this right.

Throughout this period Australia, under the prime ministership of Robert Menzies, played the part of Britain's compliant and uncomplaining supporter. Menzies travelled to London in 1941 and stayed there for months, holding lengthy discussions with Churchill and taking part in some British War Cabinet meetings. On 10 March 1941, he made a statement to the War Cabinet setting out Australia's contribution to the war effort. It is a masterpiece of obsequiousness. In Menzies' own words: 'On the outbreak of war the Royal Australian Navy had been placed at the disposal of the Admiralty.' Australia had one heavy cruiser stationed in the United Kingdom, a second cruiser and four destroyers stationed in the Mediterranean, and two sloops stationed in the Red Sea. 'All, or virtually all these ships', said Menzies, 'have distinguished themselves in action'.

In his War Cabinet statement, Menzies listed the full strength of the RAN: two heavy cruisers, four light cruisers, two armed merchant cruisers, five destroyers, five sloops, one fast auxiliary minesweeping vessel, 19 minesweepers, seven anti-submarine vessels, one depot ship, three boom defence vessels, five patrol and examination vessels and one fleet oiler. By the beginning of 1942 the Australians expected to complete construction of three Tribal class destroyers, one boom vessel, 48 anti-submarine and minesweeping vessels (of which 20 were for the Royal Navy and four for the Royal Indian Navy), plus one oil lighter and one floating dock.

The Australian Army had some 130,000 men in uniform, of which about half were stationed outside Australia. The 6th, 7th and part of the 9th Australian Divisions were in the Middle East. Part of the 8th Division was in Malaya. The rest were in camps in Australia.

The Royal Australian Air Force numbered 8311 men and 223 aircraft, including 96 Hudson bombers and 85 Wirraway fighters. Eight Sunderland flying boats from the RAAF were stationed in the United Kingdom, while 36 RAAF Hudsons and 18 Wirraways were stationed in the Middle East.

The cost of the war to Australians was substantial. In the year before the outbreak of war, Australia's defence budget stood at £14 million. By 1941 annual expenditure had risen to £200 million. Menzies wanted the British War Cabinet to know that Australia was making a major contribution to the war, far beyond what might reasonably be expected of a young country with a population now risen to a mere seven million.

However, Menzies' grandstanding revealed an appalling lack of preparation for the defence of Australia itself. Saloon bar wisdom, which can still be heard today, says that Australia cannot be defended successfully. The long coastline and vast distances make the job impossible. This is far from true. Australia can be defended, but only from the air. Aircraft shrink distances.

Australia's air defence, on Menzies' numbers, was pitiful. The Australian-built Wirraway fighter was slow, under-armed and clumsy. It was no match for a German Me 109 or a Focke Wulfe 190. In any serious dogfight it could expect to be blown out of the sky. The entire fighter force of 85 Wirraways was little more than a day's supply in a serious air war. The Hudson bomber was, if anything, worse. Known to pilots as the Hudswine, it was a converted passenger plane with a formidable record for crashing. It had limited range, limited bomb load, and limited ability to defend itself. In 1941 Australia had none of the best British aircraft—no Spitfires, no Hurricanes, no Wellingtons, no Halifaxes, no Beauforts—and no plans to acquire any.

The RAN might have boasted an impressive number of fighting ships for a small country, but they were geared to supporting a Mediterranean and Atlantic war rather than defending the Australian homeland. Australia had no aircraft carriers, and no submarines. So the RAN lacked the right weapons to harass enemy supply lines, or to meet an invasion force head-on.

There was a further problem: Japan. On 27 September 1940 Japan had signed a Tripartite Pact with Germany and Italy, which effectively placed Japan on side with Hitler and Mussolini. It was a convoluted agreement, but the essence of it was that if any country not already involved in the conflict declared war on Germany or Italy, then Japan would immediately join the war on the German and Italian side. Although the treaty was phrased to apply to any country, the target was obvious. The only way Churchill could hope to turn the tide of war in his favour was to have the United States join the fray. So Japan issued a clear warning to Roosevelt, the US President: join with Britain at your peril. If you do, we will attack.

Back in Australia, the unease was palpable. Newspapers began to publish increasingly sceptical articles about the British direction of the war. The Battle of Britain, fought between July and September 1940, had been a magnificent achievement, holding off the threat of an invasion of Britain itself. But everywhere else the war was being lost. Hitler's ill-judged attack on the USSR, launched on 22 June 1941, had yet to come unstuck. The triumphant German Army swept towards Moscow. Leningrad was surrounded. It looked as though Hitler might succeed where Napoleon had failed. The whole of Europe might soon be in German and Italian hands.

In Australia, Menzies' position was increasingly untenable. His own party saw him as aloof and arrogant. His long absence in London allowed colleagues back home to plot against him. They accused him of spending too much time hobnobbing with Churchill when he should have been back in Australia looking after his own people. He had nailed his colours uncritically to Britain's mast, and this was now beginning to look like a mistake. Australian lives were being lost in badly conducted campaigns in Greece and Crete, as well as the Middle East. Churchill had sacked his Middle East commander, Wavell, and replaced him first with Auchinleck and later with Alexander and the more effective Montgomery. He shifted Wavell to India and the Far East, where he would command British and Australian forces in the event of a Japanese attack. None of this inspired confidence in Australia.

On his return to Australia, Menzies made an attempt to shore up his position by offering a coalition with John Curtin's Labor Party, even offering to stand down as Prime Minister as part of the bargain. Curtin refused. On 28 August 1941 Menzies bowed to the inevitable and resigned, handing over power to his deputy Arthur Fadden.

On his first day in office Fadden pressed Churchill for a stronger voice for Australia in the war. Could Australia have a permanent seat in the British War Cabinet, he asked? Churchill cabled back, on 29 August 1941, on a Prime Minister to Prime Minister basis, saying no. Fadden returned to the attack on 5 September, adopting a rather tetchier tone. 'The views of the Prime Ministers of Canada and South Africa are noted with interest but not with surprise,' Fadden wrote. 'As you are well aware, their attitude is determined by local problems peculiar to each Dominion.' He warmed to his theme:

> We, too, have a special viewpoint based on the closest possible degree of Empire co-operation which, speaking with that frankness permitted within the family circle, is evident by comparison of our all round war effort on land, sea and in the air. The Australian people feel, however, that this effort warrants the right to be heard when vital decisions affecting their interests are being taken.

Churchill said no, again.

The Fadden government lasted five weeks. Two independent members of the House of Representatives held the balance of power and on 1 October 1941 they switched sides and voted against the government's budget. Fadden resigned. On 3 October the Governor-General sent for John Curtin, and Australia had its third Prime Minister in five weeks, a Labor government, and a new outlook on the war.

◆　　◆　　◆

Curtin and Menzies could hardly have been more different. Menzies was an urbane, cosmopolitan lawyer with unshakeable self-belief and an approach to colleagues that was both condescending and high-handed. Curtin had left school at 14. He had never been a minister before he became Prime Minister. His most responsible job had been as secretary of a small trade union and he left that job, so it was said, because he was an alcoholic. (He gave up drink by the time he became Leader of the Opposition, and he stayed teetotal from then on.) He was a tireless political agitator and polemicist, but he was both inexperienced in office and diffident in personal style. Menzies had told the British government Curtin was not up to the job of Prime Minister, and Curtin himself was said to have harboured similar doubts. Nevertheless, he turned himself into a more than adequate wartime leader.

The new cabinet's review of the war situation did not make pretty reading. On the European mainland Hitler's Germany was lord of all it surveyed. Spain, Portugal, Switzerland, Sweden and Ireland were neutral, but every other major European country was now occupied by German and Italian forces, giving them access to the best of Europe's ports and airfields, industry and resources. Russia looked set to fall. In North Africa Rommel was currently on the retreat but regrouping, and far from defeated. German submarines were sinking Atlantic convoys bound for Britain faster than replacement ships could be built or crews trained. The war was at best a stalemate and at worst in danger of being lost. The only way Hitler could be beaten would be for the United States to join forces with Britain. But however close the personal ties between Roosevelt and Churchill, and however much Roosevelt might have wanted to join the war and put a stop to Nazism, the American President was forced by isolationists at home to keep clear. America would not readily join the war.

John Curtin's new government now looked at the disposition of Australian forces. There were three Australian divisions facing the Germans and Italians in the Middle East, and only one division in Malaya to withstand any Japanese attack. Curtin had recognised the importance of air power earlier than others, and knew full well that Australia's lack of any serious air cover was a terrible mistake. But as 1941 drew to a close there was hardly the time, let alone the resources, to put this right.

After only nine weeks in office, as the Australian cabinet retired to their beds on the night of Sunday, 7 December 1941, they must have thought the world looked a dangerous and unpredictable place.

Chapter 3

Running wild

Japan fought alongside Britain and her allies in World War I. The Japanese Navy in particular was pro-Western, and modelled itself on the British Navy. From the beginning of the century, Japanese foreign policy could be reduced to a simple proposition: an Asian nation could and should join the ranks of great powers and, as there were only two Asian nations capable of major power status, Japan and China, Japan should do its utmost to make sure that it and not China prevailed.

Three European powers had colonised East Asia. The French controlled Indo-China (Vietnam, Laos and Cambodia) and a scattering of Pacific islands, the Dutch controlled the East Indies (now Indonesia), and the British controlled Burma, Malaya, Singapore and Hong Kong. The Americans held the Philippines, and the Hawaiian islands, plus a further scattering of smaller islands dotted around the Pacific. The colonies were strategically important in different ways. Malaya had rubber and tin. The Dutch East Indies had oil. Singapore was a major naval base.

The main plank of Japanese foreign policy was the creation of the harmless-sounding if grandiosely named Greater East Asia Co-Prosperity Sphere. This amounted to ending European colonisation of

Asia and replacing it with Asia-for-the-Asians, dominated by Japan. They would be happy to include Australia and New Zealand in this grand scheme, a proposition scorned by both countries. The Japanese plan did not suit the European colonial powers either, nor did it suit the Americans. America's strategic interests would not be best served by the sudden arrival of an Asian superpower as a next-door neighbour. So Japanese ambitions were confronted with hostility all round.

The Japanese were not easily scared off. In 1931 they attacked Manchuria and set up a puppet state there, which they called Manchukuo. In 1933 they withdrew from the League of Nations. Next they withdrew from agreements entered into in Washington in 1922 and London in 1930 which limited their naval strength. They began a furious programme of shipbuilding, while doing their best to conceal its nature and strength.

In July 1937 they attacked China. By December they had taken Nanking, but the war with China remained a scrappy affair. The Chinese government of Chiang Kai-shek offered ill-organised resistance, but the Japanese never seemed able to take advantage of their opponent's feeble performance. By the end of 1938 the Chinese government had withdrawn to Chungking, and Canton and Hankow had fallen, but the war remained in an inconclusive state.

The Japanese fought a couple of battles with the USSR, at Changkufeng in 1938 and Nomonhan in 1939, but these did not add up to a war.

However tentative in its belligerence, the Japanese behaviour could not be ignored. The Americans in particular felt obliged to take action. In 1940 the United States ended its commercial treaty with Japan and imposed sanctions. President Roosevelt stopped the export of scrap iron, aviation fuel, machine tools and other war materials to Japan, and stepped up aid to China.

The Japanese responded by signing their Tripartite Pact with Germany and Italy, and followed it up with a Neutrality Pact with the Soviet Union, signed on 13 April 1941. By getting the USSR safely out of the way, Japan had eliminated the risk of war on two fronts.

They now turned their attention to the European colonies. With France and Holland defeated, and Britain fully occupied with the war against Germany, it must have seemed to the Japanese that it was now or never for the Greater East Asia Co-Prosperity Sphere. Thailand obligingly eased the way by invading French Indo-China, quickly capturing Laos from Vichy French forces. The Japanese mediated the conflict, which amounted to little more than bullying the French into handing over the disputed territories. In July 1941 the Japanese 'stationed' some 120,000 troops in Thailand and northern Indo-China. The difference between this and invasion and occupation by Japanese forces was not readily visible to the naked eye.

This was too much for Britain, America and the Dutch government in exile. They froze all Japanese assets, imposed an oil and steel embargo, and closed the Panama Canal to Japanese shipping. Japan was now cornered. It obtained 80 per cent of its oil from the United States. It had two years of oil reserves in hand, but little more than a year's oil if it had to fight a war. At some point it would have to either capitulate or find a new source. To the south lay Dutch oil and British tin and rubber. Either the Japanese went to war to seize these resources for themselves, or they withdrew and abandoned their dreams of grandeur. War looked inevitable.

Japan's strategic calculation was simple. The French had already demonstrated that they would offer no resistance. The Dutch were relatively powerless. The British, with their Singapore base and their Australian and New Zealand allies, were a more formidable problem. But to fight effectively in Asia would involve diverting resources from a war with Germany which the British were currently losing. The only serious problem was the United States, and in particular the powerful US Navy. Unless the US Pacific Fleet could be taken out of the war quickly, Japan could not hope to win.

The Commander-in-Chief of the combined Japanese fleet, Admiral Isoroku Yamamoto, was a sophisticated and cosmopolitan man. He had studied at Harvard and had a good grasp of America's strengths. He thought Japan could not win a prolonged war with America. The industrial might of the United States would inevitably prevail. He told his political masters: 'If I'm told to fight regardless of consequences, I'll run wild for the first six months or a year. I have no confidence in the second or third years.' Yamamoto therefore proposed to grab everything Japan wanted in the space of a year. After the year, the Japanese could try to reach a peace agreement with the United States which would allow them to hold on to their conquests. But the US Pacific Fleet would need to be knocked out in the first days of the war if any of this was to happen.

The Japanese set a military timetable, dictated by Yamamoto's naval requirements. The campaign would need to start before the north-east monsoon season in the South China Sea, and before the winter gales in the north Pacific. It had to be completed before the end of the Manchurian winter. So early December looked like the ideal starting date. The Japanese estimated they would need 50 days to capture the Philippines, 100 days to conquer Malaya, and 150 days to take the Dutch East Indies. The long Pacific distances would mean doubling the tonnage of shipping needed.

The Washington Naval Treaty of 1922, signed by the United States, Britain,* France, Italy and Japan, limited the build-up of naval power, but was very much confined to World War I priorities. It focused on battleships and cruisers, and to a lesser extent aircraft carriers, while saying nothing about submarines. The 1930 London Naval Treaty added submarines to the restricted list. However, the Japanese pulled out of both treaties in 1936.

The Imperial Japanese Navy was ahead of most strategic thinkers in seeing the importance of air power in future naval warfare. Its leaders set about building up a major carrier-based strike force. As well, the Japanese launched a programme of submarine-building, which included a brand-new weapon, the midget submarine, designed to penetrate

---

* It is a fair measure of Australia's subservience to Britain at this time that the Royal Australian Navy (and the Royal Canadian Navy, for that matter) was simply counted as part of the British Navy. When Britain signed the Washington Treaty and the later London Treaty, she signed on behalf of all the dominions as well as herself.

enemy harbour defences and sink ships while they lay at anchor. The navy went to great pains to keep the existence of the midget submarine force secret.

The decisive knocking-out of the American Pacific Fleet, planned for Pearl Harbor, would involve two attack forces. Carrier-based planes would strike from the air, and a small group of midget submarines would swarm around the harbour and attack from below the surface.

◆   ◆   ◆

The Japanese midget submarine force at Pearl Harbor has an almost forgotten distinction in World War II history: the first shots fired by Americans at Japanese forces on 7 December 1941 were directed at a midget submarine, and they were fired with deadly effect. Just after six in the morning on the fateful day, the target-towing ship *Antares* spotted a Japanese midget sub on its way into Pearl Harbor. The sighting was picked up by a Catalina seaplane on coastal patrol, which dropped a smoke marker, then confirmed by the destroyer USS *Ward*. At 6.45 am the destroyer opened fire with its no. 1 gun. The first shot missed. A few seconds later the *Ward* fired again with its no. 3 gun from a range of 500 metres, hitting the base of the sub's conning tower and sending it reeling. The shot sliced through the conning tower at precisely the spot where the commander, Ensign Akira Hiro-o, would have been standing. He is almost certainly the first Japanese casualty of World War II.

Ward followed up with a pattern of four depth charges, but the sub was already doomed and on its way to the bottom. The first encounter between the US Navy and the Imperial Japanese Navy at Pearl Harbor was a clear win for the Americans.

The *Ward* made frantic efforts to report the encounter to the higher command and raise a general alert. But a combination of poor communications and ill-judged scepticism meant *Ward*'s messages were not taken seriously. It is doubtful if the message would have made a difference to subsequent events. However, it provided history with a nice chance to repeat itself in Sydney six months later.

Forty minutes after the *Ward*'s opening shot, the planes arrived.

The devastation was terrible. Four American battleships were sunk and another four damaged. Three cruisers were damaged, and two destroyers sunk along with two other ships. A total of 188 aircraft were destroyed, mostly on the ground, and another 155 damaged. Military deaths stood at 2335, while civilian deaths totalled 68. Injuries were 1143 military and 35 civilian. Japanese losses were light: 29 planes shot down, and 55 airmen killed. No Japanese surface ships were attacked, let alone sunk.

Appalling though these losses were, Pearl Harbor was not the knockout blow Yamamoto needed. The American aircraft carrier force escaped entirely. Two were at sea on delivery runs to Midway and Wake islands, while the third had just completed a refit and was still tied up at San Diego on the American mainland. As well, an astonishing number of US ships survived unscathed in Pearl Harbor itself—five cruisers, 26 destroyers, nine submarines and 48 other ships were left undamaged, as were 47 aircraft. Not only ships and aircraft survived: the vital oil tank farms remained largely intact, as did the submarine pens, the machine shops and the port and dock facilities. The US Pacific Fleet might be in trouble, but it still had plenty of fight left in it.

The midget submarine element of the raid was a total failure. Five midgets took part, and all were lost. There was so much confusion and false alarm in the harbour that it is hard to work out, even after all this time, exactly what happened to all of them. One was certainly sunk by gunfire from USS *Ward*. One, commanded by Kazuo Sakamaki and with Kiyoshi Inagaki as crew, never made it to the battle at all. Just before their launch from the mother submarine they found their midget had an unserviceable gyro compass, essential for navigation while submerged. The crew decided to set off anyway, planning to navigate visually either on the surface or at periscope depth. This failed, and the two men repeatedly became disoriented, sometimes heading in hopelessly wrong directions. They finally made it to the entrance channel to Pearl Harbor.

By the time Sakamaki and Inagaki arrived at the harbour entrance, the Japanese air attack was in full swing, and ships in the harbour were alert and had begun to respond. The baby sub was repeatedly shot at and depth-charged, to the point where it was almost totally out of control. Sakamaki ran aground on a reef, damaging one of his two torpedoes. Pinned on the reef, he was shot at by the destroyer USS *Helm*. It may be that the *Helm's* shells actually helped Sakamaki to break free, because he backed off the reef and submerged.

The sub now began to fill with poisonous fumes. The two men repeatedly passed out. They battled all morning, long after the bombers had departed, to bring the submarine under control. They struck another reef, and damaged their second and final torpedo. All this time they slipped in and out of consciousness. The sub drifted off the reef, still out of control. Near dawn on 8 December and over 24 hours after they launched, the tiny sub struck its final reef. With its batteries near exhaustion, there was no escape. The two crew set their demolition charge fuse burning and leapt into the sea. The fuse failed and the submarine remained intact, stranded on the reef. Inagaki drowned. His body was recovered several days later. Sakamaki made it to shore, where he found himself staring into the muzzle of a pistol held by the Japanese-American corporal David Akui, one of a five-man patrol from the nearby Bellows Field Army Air Base. Sakamaki became America's first prisoner of war in World War II.

At 8.35 am on 7 December, with the air attack 40 minutes under way, the destroyer USS *Monaghan* was on its way out of Pearl Harbor via the North Channel when it saw the seaplane tender USS *Curtiss* firing at close range at something in the water. *Monaghan* quickly identified it as a submarine. The destroyer joined the attack, firing at the sub with its no. 2 gun from a range of 1200 yards (about 1000 metres). The shot missed and instead started a fire on a derrick barge. *Monaghan* now decided a ramming attack might be less threatening to the surrounding scenery and set off at flank speed to run down the midget.

At this point the submarine counterattacked, firing a torpedo. It is not clear whether the torpedo was aimed at *Monaghan* or *Curtiss*, but it passed between them both, missing *Monaghan* by an uncomfortably narrow margin. It then exploded against Ford Island, doing no significant damage. The destroyer continued undeterred on its ramming course while the Executive Officer, Lieutenant H.J. Verhoye ordered: 'Stand by depth charges, set on 30 feet.'

Monaghan finally closed the gap and caught the sub a glancing blow. As the midget slid along *Monaghan's* starboard side Chief Torpedoman G. Hardon, without waiting for orders, dropped a depth charge. Now under orders, he dropped a second charge and prepared a third. As he was about to drop the third charge, *Monaghan's* flank speed charge took a disastrous turn and she ran aground on a mudbank. Thinking quickly, Hardon abandoned the release of the third charge, knowing it would very likely destroy his own stranded ship. Seconds later there were two tremendous explosions off *Monaghan's* stern, followed by a massive oil slick. The US Navy had sunk its second submarine. *Monaghan* gingerly eased herself off the mudbank and continued towards the open sea.

The exact fate of the remaining submarines is still a mystery. Shortly after the USS *Ward's* first shots, the destroyer USS *Chew* dropped no fewer than 28 depth charges on submarine contacts, and claimed to have sunk two. A navy plane claimed to have sunk another at 7 am. At 9.50 am the destroyer USS *Blue* made three separate attacks on submarine contacts, dropping eight depth charges, and believed it had sunk at least one submarine. The light cruiser USS *St Louis* saw two torpedoes racing towards it, took evading action, and saw the two torpedoes explode on a nearby shoal, again doing no damage. The cruiser fired at what it thought was a conning tower but recorded no hits. Nevertheless, there were four or five claimed sinkings of two submarines.

The submarine sunk by *Monaghan* was recovered from the harbour bottom a few days after the attack. In 1960 US Navy divers found the remains of a small submarine in shallow water at Keehi Lagoon, near Pearl Harbor. It had been holed, apparently by a depth charge. The find was mysterious in that there was no trace of the crew, who appeared to have escaped. In 2002 the hulk of a midget was found outside the harbour in 400 metres of water. It had a shell hole passing through the conning tower, but was otherwise undamaged. It was almost certainly *Ward's* submarine. The fifth submarine has never been found.

The submarine element of the Pearl Harbor raid was a catastrophe for the Japanese. All five submarines were lost, and none of their crew found their way back to the mother submarines. Worse, Japan's most secret weapon, the midget submarine, had fallen intact into American hands on the first day of the war. Sakamaki's wrecked submarine, together with the recovered submarine sunk by *Monaghan*, was an invaluable source of intelligence on this new weapon. However the Americans chose not to share this intelligence fully with their Allies, to Sydney's cost six months later.

What followed in Japan was bizarre, even by the usual standards of truth as the first casualty of war. On the evening of the raid, the Japanese mother submarine I-69 sat outside the entrance to Pearl Harbor hoping to pick off any American ships on the way out. At 9.01 pm, the captain reported that he had seen a huge fire inside the harbour, followed by heavy anti-aircraft fire. In fact what he witnessed was the shooting down of some American planes by over-zealous anti-aircraft gunners from their own side. The submarine captain interpreted it differently: he believed he had witnessed an American battleship being sunk by a midget submarine.

Meanwhile, one of the midgets, probably from the mother ship I-16, sent a message at 10.41 pm on the night of the raid using the phrase: 'Tora, tora, tora [Tiger, tiger, tiger].' This was the agreed code to notify the Japanese fleet that the raid had succeeded. The midget's message was sent almost 15 hours after the planes had first struck, and was probably intended to do no more than confirm that the air attack had indeed gone well. However it was taken as confirmation of I-69's surmise: the midget must have sunk a battleship. The midget stayed in radio contact for a further hour before lapsing into silence. Just after midnight the crew sent a final message: 'We are unable to navigate.' They were never heard from again.

The Japanese propaganda machine seized on these two garbled reports, and spun them into a gigantic myth. It began with the official Japanese communiqué describing the raid, which declared: 'Our special attacking force consisting of special submarines broke through the well-guarded entrance of Pearl Harbor. Together with our air forces they attacked the main enemy forces. The special submarines sank at least one of the *Arizona*-class battleships besides inflicting a severe blow on the enemy fleet.'*

This was the first the Japanese public knew of the Special Attack Force of midget submarines. The propaganda machine now set about converting the midget submariners into superheroes. Captain Hideo Hiraide, chief of the Imperial Japanese Navy's information department, broadcast to the whole Japanese nation: 'The unprecedented, peerless, sacrificial spirit of the attack thoroughly demonstrated the tradition of the Imperial Navy, and should be recognised as one of the greatest achievements of the outbreak of this war.' Hiraide then abandoned fact and switched to pure fiction, imagining scenes inside the submarines as the ice-cool crews lay in wait on the bottom of the harbour. The men spent the waiting hours with jigsaw puzzles, said Hiraide. They had packed lunchboxes with chocolates and soft drinks. 'It was just like going on a picnic,' he reported one as saying. Another submariner recited a poem as he lay in wait, including the line: 'I heard Roosevelt whimpering before the King of Hell.' This was all nonsense, and the Japanese navy well knew it, but it worked.

The nine sailors who had died were deified as war gods, the highest level of acclaim available to Japanese warriors. They became the subjects of endless newspaper articles; professors of literature called for books to

---

* In 1998 the US Naval Institute's magazine *Naval History* published an elaborate article arguing that one of the submarines had successfully fired torpedoes at the USS *Oklahoma* and the USS *West Virginia*. The evidence for this came from a digitally enhanced photograph taken by one of the crew of a Japanese Kate bomber flying over the harbour. However, the case for this is thin: the image itself was built from a newspaper print, with all the dubious quality this implies. The 'conning tower' in the photograph might just as easily be a piece of lint, or an ink smudge. There were hundreds of eyewitnesses to the original attack, and none reported seeing this submarine. The photograph purports to show evidence that the sub's propellers had broached the surface, but the 'rooster tail' effect could just as easily come from the propellers of air-launched torpedoes. The highest probability is that no torpedoes were fired successfully by the midget submarines taking part in the Pearl Harbor attack.

be written honouring their deeds, and had their prayers answered with a novel turned into a film; they were likened to cherry blossoms, the spirit of Japan. The myth-making got so out of hand that newspapers began to imply that the midget submarines and not the planes had been the spearhead of the attack. The sinking of the *Arizona* by the submarines became an unchallengeable fact, to the point where one Japanese newspaper felt able to write: 'The Navy Eagles [i.e. the pilots of the raiding aircraft] saw the *Arizona* go down and knew at once that the daring underwater attack by the death-defying corps had borne fruit. They held death at bay until they fulfilled the task that went a long way towards changing the map of the Pacific.'

This particular nonsense was too much for the pilots. They knew exactly what had happened to the *Arizona*. It had been sunk by high-flying 'horizontal'—in other words, not dive—bombers, and there were plenty of witnesses to this fact. More woundingly, the nine dead submariners had been posthumously promoted two ranks and raised to the status of war gods. The 55 airmen who died had been promoted only one rank, and none was considered a war god. Lieutenant-Commander Mitsuo Fuchida, who led the first wave of planes over Pearl Harbor, complained bitterly about this injustice and issued an ultimatum: 'The air force cannot co-operate in future operations under this one-sided treatment.' Fuchida got his way. The 55 were belatedly promoted two ranks instead of one. However, they were never elevated to war gods.

The midget submarine raid on Pearl Harbor also led to one of the oddest stories of the war. Kazuo Sakamaki, the submariner who swam to shore after his submarine was wrecked, felt abjectly ashamed of his surrender. While a prisoner of war he repeatedly asked to be allowed to commit suicide, the proper destiny for a Japanese warrior. He was, of course, refused. When he was repatriated to Japan in 1946, he was vilified. He received hate mail, including the repeated suggestion that it was not too late for him now to take the honourable course and end his life. Instead he married and moved to Sao Paulo in Brazil, where he lived for 42 years. He became president of the Brazilian branch of the Toyota motor company. In 1983 he returned to Japan and a more sympathetic reception.

◆   ◆   ◆

The Pearl Harbor attack was the start of Australia's worst nightmare. For the first time in 160 years of European settlement, Australia was directly threatened. The fury of the Japanese follow-up was devastating. Australia's entire defensive strategy depended on the merged British and Australian navies retaining control of the seas around Australia. Even before Pearl Harbor, Churchill had agreed to meet the Japanese threat by reinforcing Singapore with two of Britain's most up-to-date battle cruisers, the *Prince of Wales* and the *Repulse*. Japanese planes sank them both on 10 December 1941, two days after Pearl Harbor. (The International Dateline's position in mid-Pacific meant that the Pearl Harbor raid took place on 8 December, Singapore time, not 7 December.)

On 8 December, Japan attacked the Philippines, Hong Kong and Malaya. By 10 December they had captured Guam. On 11 December they attacked Burma. Hong Kong surrendered on 18 December. Wake Island fell on 23 December.

The new Australian government watched this with horror and incredulity. Their attitudes and Churchill's could not have been further apart. Churchill made no secret of his delight with Pearl Harbor. Now America had joined the war and would tip the balance. Roosevelt and Churchill had already agreed on a policy, should Japan enter the war, which was popularly rendered as 'beat Hitler first'. Churchill later wrote of the American entry into the war: 'Hitler's fate was sealed. Mussolini's fate was sealed. As for the Japanese, they would be ground to powder.' But later, of course.

From Australia's point of view, a beat-Hitler-first policy amounted to a half-hearted holding operation in the Pacific while the two great powers focused their attention on the Atlantic. Australia welcomed America's entry into the war, but for entirely different reasons. It was increasingly apparent that Britain could not, never mind would not, defend Australia against the Japanese. Only America could. On 27 December Curtin published an historic article in the Melbourne *Herald*. The article was mostly directed at telling Australians that beating Japan would require immense effort and sacrifice from every Australian. However, it contained some historic declarations, and it is worth quoting from it more fully than usual. Curtin wrote:

> We refuse to accept the dictum that the Pacific struggle must be treated as a subordinate segment of the general conflict. By that it is not meant that any one of the other theatres of war is of less importance than the Pacific, but that Australia asks for a concerted plan evoking the greatest strength at the Democracies' disposal, determined upon hurling Japan back.
>
> The Australian Government regards the Pacific struggle as primarily one in which the United States and Australia must have the fullest say in the direction of the democracies' fighting plan.
>
> Without any inhibitions of any kind, I make it quite clear that Australia looks to America, free of any pangs as to our traditional links or kinship with the United Kingdom.
>
> We know the problems that the United Kingdom faces. We know the constant threat of invasion. We know the dangers of dispersal of strength, but we know too, that Australia can go and Britain can still hold on.
>
> Summed up, Australian external policy will be shaped toward obtaining Russian aid, and working out, with the United States, as the major factor, a plan of Pacific strategy, along with British, Chinese and Dutch forces.

This brought something akin to an audible gasp from the entire Australian population. The *Sydney Morning Herald* called the article 'deplorable' (while republishing it in full). Curtin's assertion that Australia looks to America is the most quoted line. But the whole thrust of the article was remarkably radical. Japan was not merely to be contained but to be hurled back. Australia and America, not Britain and

America, would direct the Pacific war. The British, the Chinese and the Dutch could tag along if they liked, but Australia and America would be the major players.

The implications were enormous. No longer would the Australian Navy, in Menzies' phrase, be placed at the disposal of the British Admiralty. Australian ships would fight where the American and Australian governments wanted them, and if that meant in Pacific seas rather than the Mediterranean, so be it. Australian soldiers would be deployed in defence of the homeland if their government required it. Australian and American airmen, equipped with modern aircraft, would take the air war to Japan.

It was a bold strategy, but if the intention was to send a warning to the Japanese that life would be different from now on, the Japanese showed no signs of taking notice. Their relentless advance continued unchecked. On 11 January 1942 they attacked the Dutch East Indies. They swarmed through Malaya, rolling back the Australian 8th Division as well as the Indian and British armies. Nothing and nobody seemed able to stop them. The military situation in Asia went from tranquil to desperate in the space of five weeks.

The Allies had always underestimated Japanese capabilities. The briefings given to Allied troops on the Japanese threat were a mixture of infantile racism and groundless optimism. They were told the Japanese were puny, myopic, afraid of the dark and badly armed. All of this was not only wrong, but dangerously wrong. The Japanese understood the use of air power better than their enemies, and capped this with better equipment. The Zero fighter made mincemeat of the outdated aircraft trying to block its path.

The Japanese on the ground employed superior tactics. They improvised, using small tanks and even bicycles. The statistics of the campaign were simply horrific. The normal military calculation is that, to be confident of success, an invading force needs to outnumber the defence by about three to one. In Malaya and Singapore, 60,000 Japanese defeated 130,000 British, Indian and Australian troops. Not just defeated: routed. Far from being afraid of the dark, the Japanese used darkness to encircle the Allied defence positions, racing confidently through the jungle. The writer and journalist Russell Braddon, then a 21-year-old gunner with the Australians in Malaya, noted bitterly after the war: 'We would have done much better had we been armed as the Japanese were armed, supported in the air as they were supported, led as they were led, and motivated as they were motivated.'

Not only that, the local Asian populations did not exactly rush to take the side of their colonial masters. The Japanese promised a Greater East Asia Co-Prosperity Sphere, with a bonus of Asia-for-the-Asians. Well, why not? Large sections of the local populations watched the war with impartial interest, in the spirit of the polite stranger beside you in the bar who offers to hold your coat while you join in the bar brawl.

By 24 January the Australian government saw the situation as out of control. Worse, they had been told by Earl Page, their representative in London, that the British were considering abandoning Singapore. This went beyond heresy. Singapore was the most potent symbol of British power and presence in the Far East. Curtin cabled Churchill: 'After all the reassurances we have been given, the evacuation of Singapore would be regarded here and elsewhere as an inexcusable betrayal.'

Curtin asked for immediate transfer to the RAAF of '250 aircraft of the Tomahawk, Hurricane II or similar type'. His exasperated tone was plain. 'It is impossible to expect us to give effective resistance with the inadequate aircraft at our disposal,' he cabled.

Within Australia, invasion fever mounted, stoked by the government. They produced a propaganda poster showing an ugly and terrifying Japanese soldier, bayonet at the ready, trampling the world underfoot. Above him was the caption: 'HE'S COMING SOUTH.' Advertisements appeared in Australian newspapers with a mass of black arrows thrusting down a map of Asia, and a headline 'The spearhead reaches SOUTH, ALWAYS SOUTH.' The advertisement urged Australians to end strikes and lockouts, avoid wasting money, food or precious petrol, and generally to give their all to the war.

Men who had hesitated to volunteer while the war was being fought in the Middle East now rushed to join up. Again, the story of my own family is typical. My father's two unmarried brothers had urged him, as a married man with family responsibilities, to stay home. In January 1942 he decided that Sydney was too close to the invading Japanese for my mother and five-months-old me. The three of us travelled by train to my Nan's house in Adelaide, where my mother and I were told to stay put until the war ended. My father enlisted in the army on 3 February 1942 at Collinswood in South Australia, naming my mother as next of kin. He was then 30 years old, and I had a long wait ahead of me for my first birthday.

◆　　◆　　◆

The author James Leasor's excellent book on the fall of Singapore is sub-titled: *The Battle that Changed the World*. It was no exaggeration. The fall of Singapore marked the end of white supremacy in Asia, the end of British naval power in the Far East, and the end of British superpower status south of the Equator. The *Sydney Morning Herald* editorial, headed 'Singapore and Australia' was graphic: 'Singapore has been to this country what the Maginot Line was in France—and in the hour of crisis it has no less tragically failed us.'

For a battle with such far-reaching consequences, it has attracted its fair share of myths, of which the most enduring is that Singapore fell because the guns were facing the wrong way. The truth is simpler. The guns that mattered were not the south-facing shore batteries but those mounted on British ships. And the British ships that mattered were at the bottom of the ocean, sunk by Japanese aircraft on the second day of the Pacific war. Singapore was never intended to be defended from land attack: the plan was to have the all-powerful Royal Navy prevent any landing. With the navy shattered, Singapore became indefensible. Churchill knew this, hence his weighing up of the possibility of withdrawing from Singapore with minimum losses.

With hindsight, Curtin would have been better advised to accept Churchill's proposal. To the Australian government, however, this would have been a grotesque betrayal of a solemn British promise made only weeks earlier. On 7 December 1941, the day before Pearl Harbor, the

British Minister in the Far East, Duff Cooper, had told the Australian War Cabinet: 'It has always been the intention of the United Kingdom government to reinforce the Far East, and they are prepared to abandon the Mediterranean altogether if this is necessary to hold Singapore.' The Australians insisted that the British keep their promise and defend Singapore to the end, and Churchill reluctantly agreed.

Singapore fell on 15 February 1942. For Australia this was the worst news yet in a war which brought no shortage of bad news. Apart from the 1789 Australian dead and 1306 wounded in the defence of Singapore, some 15,395 troops from Australia's 8th Division were taken prisoner. The Japanese had a well-deserved reputation for treating prisoners harshly. What fate awaited these men? They were the main land force intended to block Japan's southward thrust, and now they were gone. It seemed as though nobody and nothing stood between the Japanese and invasion of Australia.

Three days later, the Japanese confirmed these worst fears. They bombed Darwin twice. This was the first time since European colonisation that Australia itself had been attacked. Wars, it seemed, were no longer fought overseas. Contemporary newsreels did their best to conceal the extent of the carnage and the inadequacy of the defences. The commentary talked of Japanese planes being handed no end of a lesson by the anti-aircraft batteries. But the footage which accompanied this travesty showed burning docks, airfields and buildings, and no burning or crashing Japanese aircraft. The public were not fooled. The newspapers were heavily censored, so Australians were unable to read the full story of the numbers of dead and wounded, nor were they told of looting, desertion and near anarchy immediately after the attack. It was a shameful episode in Australia's history. The lurid rumours which spread south did nothing to boost the already sagging morale of the civilian population.

How was Australia to be defended now? The answer from the grand strategists in London and Washington was that two divisions of US combat troops were on their way to Australia, and that should be sufficient. This did not satisfy Curtin. As far back as 15 December

Churchill had put it to his chiefs of staff that one of the two and a half Australian divisions in the Middle East should be switched to the defence of Singapore. On 3 January the British formally requested the Australian government to allow two Australian divisions to be transferred from the Middle East to the new Far East command ABDA (standing for American, British, Dutch and Australian forces). The Australians quickly agreed. Both divisions would go to Java in the Dutch East Indies. In all 64,000 Australian troops would be moved, between January and April 1942.

The first eight ships had already sailed when the Australian cabinet began to have second thoughts. Australia's generals advised that, without control of either air or sea, the Dutch territory could not be held. Better to bring the boys home.

What followed is now the stuff of legend. On 15 February, the day Singapore fell, Curtin cabled Churchill requesting that the troops be diverted to Australia. Churchill replied with a request that they be diverted to Rangoon. He did not tell Curtin that he had already ordered some of the ships to Rangoon. Simultaneously, Churchill cabled Roosevelt asking him to put pressure on Curtin to switch the troops to the defence of Burma. To the fury of both Churchill and Roosevelt, Curtin stood his ground. For five days blistering cables flew backwards and forwards between Churchill, Roosevelt and Curtin. In the end, Curtin had his way. The ships turned back from Rangoon. The boys could come home.*

◆　　◆　　◆

The rampaging Japanese continued their drive south and east. They attacked the Dutch East Indies. The newly formed ABDA determined to

---

* In fact they largely stayed overseas. Some went to Java, as originally planned, where they were promptly captured by the Japanese. Others remained in Ceylon, ready to defend India if the need arose. The 9th Division, including my Uncle Jim, remained in Syria until 1943. By the end of June 1942, half of Australia's land forces were still deployed west of Singapore. Nevertheless, Curtin had made his point.

stop them before they seized Java, the last remaining Allied stronghold. A large naval force, under Dutch command and incorporating Dutch, British, American and Australian ships, set off to intercept the Japanese troopships. On 27 February the two navies clashed in the Java Sea. It was a catastrophe for ABDA. They lost five cruisers and five destroyers sunk, with 2300 sailors killed. The Japanese lost four troop transports, but their fighting ships emerged almost totally unscathed. It was the biggest naval engagement since the Battle of Jutland in World War I, and the Allies had lost it badly. With its defeat at the Battle of the Java Sea, ABDA lost all credibility. However, the Americans had lost only three ships, the cruiser USS *Houston* and two destroyers. It was a dreadful loss, but it was not the decisive defeat of the US Pacific Fleet which Yamamoto needed.

On the home front in Australia, invasion fever was now endemic. The Japanese kept it well stoked by continuing their air assault on northern Australian towns. They bombed Broome and Wyndham on 3 March, and Katherine on 22 March. In the major cities there were air-raid drills. Blackouts were enforced. Brown paper covered windows. Festoons of barbed wire appeared on beaches. Gun emplacements sprang up on headlands and hills. Sirens were tested. Searchlights roamed the night sky. Newspapers carried 'Know Your Japanese Planes' features.

The reality of war began to hit home. At school assemblies, head-masters read out the names of past pupils killed in action. Shocked schoolboys listened numbly while the cricket captain of only two years ago, someone they had idolised, joined the ranks of the dead or missing. They itched to join the war and wreak revenge. Meanwhile, potatoes were scarce. Petrol was rationed. So was tea.

Jim Macken was a 14-year-old schoolboy at Sydney's St Ignatius College, popularly known as Riverview. He remembers:

All of us were in the cadets. We had a full armoury underneath the school. We had live ammunition and all the rifles. Everybody lived for the cadets. School holidays were spent in army camps. Nobody expected anything other than that the Japanese would sooner or later arrive.

Old boys who were already in the army would come back to the school and on cadet parade they'd give us some idea of military training. They were looked on as local heroes. They were in the real thing.

The relentless Japanese advance continued unabated. Batavia fell on 2 March. The Japanese penetrated the Indian Ocean, bombing Ceylon on 4 April. On 9 April the Americans surrendered in Bataan. Mandalay fell on 1 May. Corregidor followed on 6 May, with 12,000 Americans taken prisoner.

American troops poured into Australia. Their guns, planes and ships were welcome. So were their bulging pay packets and gifts of nylon stockings. Australian women found them polite, even gallant, a sharp contrast with rough Australian male manners. With touching enthusiasm though little regard for political correctness, the Americans returned the warm feelings. Private George Huffman from the US Army told the Sydney *Daily Telegraph:* 'I come from God's own country and I arrived in this burg expecting to find niggers and kangaroos. I found a bunch of fine people instead.'

Churchill and Roosevelt agreed that Britain would control the European war, while America controlled the Pacific war. This suited Curtin. In March 1942 he asked that the politically well-connected General Douglas MacArthur, recently escaped from the Philippines, be appointed Supreme Commander of Allied Forces in the South-West Pacific, and based in Australia. Roosevelt agreed. Australian troops would be placed under MacArthur's command. Australia now unambiguously 'looked to America'.

MacArthur arrived in Darwin on 17 March and travelled by train to a hero's welcome at Flinders Street station in Melbourne. Australia's war role was now taking shape. It would be a barracks, a farm, a harbour and an airfield. Essentially it would be a secure base from which the Americans could mount a counterattack on Japanese positions.

This did not suit the Japanese. In truth the Japanese had no plans to invade Australia. In MacArthur's less than flattering appraisal, 'spoils here are not sufficient to warrant the risk'. However, Yamamoto still needed to finish off the American Pacific Fleet. He could not allow it a secure base in Australia, within striking distance of Japan's fresh conquests. Japan continued to have naval and air superiority, and he was spoiling for a fight.

Yamamoto agreed that the next Japanese move would be an invasion of Port Moresby. With New Guinea secured, Australia would be isolated. The Japanese could use the New Guinea base to block American supply routes, in effect forcing them back from their safe base in the south. Australia would be forced out of the war. Yamamoto assembled his invasion fleet. If this lured the American Pacific Fleet into battle, so much the better.

That part of Yamamoto's plan succeeded. Armed with intelligence warnings of the Japanese fleet movements, a combined fleet of American, Australian and British ships raced north to block the invaders. Between 6 and 8 May, the two fleets clashed in the Coral Sea. It was a battle unique in all naval history: neither fleet saw the other. It was fought entirely by carrier-based aircraft. For two days carrier planes flew strike and counterstrike. At the end, the Japanese withdrew, abandoning their invasion of Port Moresby.

Both sides thought they had won. Captain Hiraide, of Pearl Harbor and midget submarine fame, took to the airwaves again in Japan. He told the populace that America and her allies had suffered a crushing defeat. Such were the losses that the United States was now a third-rate power. General MacArthur was a nervous wreck. The *Japan Times and Advertiser* added: 'The effect of the terrible setback in the Coral Sea is indeed beyond description. A state of mania is prevalent in the American munitions fields.' General Tojo, the Prime Minister, weighed in by telling the Japanese parliament that Australia was now 'the orphan of the Pacific'.

The Americans were equally vocal in claiming victory. The *New York Times* headlined its report: 'Japanese Repulsed in Great Pacific Battle'. In Sydney, the *Sunday Sun* crowed on 10 May: 'Jap Fleet Beaten Off— Invasion Armada Smashed in Coral Sea Battle'. The *Sunday Sun's* war correspondent Norman Stockton began his story: 'A full-scale attempt to invade Australia has been turned aside.' This was nonsense, of course, since the Japanese target was Port Moresby, not Australia. However Stockton's report fitted in with the anxieties of the times. On page 2, the *Sun* continued its crowing under the headline: 'America Throbs with Excitement Over Naval Victory'.

The truth was, as usual, different. The Battle of the Coral Sea ended, to use a sporting metaphor, as a score draw. The Americans lost the aircraft carrier USS *Lexington*, a destroyer and an oiler, as well as taking some damage to their second aircraft carrier USS *Yorktown*. The Japanese lost a light carrier, a destroyer and some smaller ships. The aircraft carrier *Shokaku* received serious bomb damage and her sister carrier *Zuikaku's* air group was badly depleted. The Japanese sank a greater tonnage of American ships than they lost themselves. However, the Japanese lost more aircraft and took more casualties. Strategically, they lost the battle: Port Moresby was not invaded, the American Pacific Fleet had been brought to battle and not crushed. For the first time since the Pacific war began five months earlier, the Imperial Japanese Navy did not run wild.

The battle-scarred ships of America and Australia steamed back to port. The American cruiser USS *Chicago* and its destroyer escort USS *Perkins* headed for Sydney, along with the Australian cruiser HMAS *Canberra*. They returned to a heroes' welcome. Both ships and their crews would rest up and refit, before returning to the fray. They could reassure themselves with the knowledge that there was no safer place in the Pacific to rest up than Sydney Harbour.

Chapter 4

Rather peculiar instruction

Reg Andrew came from a long line of sea captains—eight generations, in fact. But he had chosen not to follow the family tradition: at the time he enlisted in the Royal Australian Navy he was the shore-based manager of a Woolworths store in the Sydney suburb of Mosman.

He might easily have chosen the Royal Australian Air Force ahead of the navy. He was an experienced and talented pilot, and had worked as a flying instructor in the aviation business set up by the legendary Charles Kingsford-Smith. The call of the sea proved too strong, however, and on 23 March 1942 he volunteered for the navy.

Despite the flying and the shore job, he had not cut himself off entirely from the sea. With his two brothers he had formed the Manly Sailing Club, which specialised in 16-foot skiffs. At one stage Reg had been state secretary of the 16-foot Skiff Association of New South Wales. Like all keen sailors, he got to know Sydney Harbour well. However, he had no naval experience, and no experience with motor launches, on the day he volunteered. He was 32 years old, and he intended to apply for torpedo patrol boats, which operated in the North Sea, Atlantic and Mediterranean. This would involve a training course at Flinders Naval College in Victoria, then further training in England.

In long taped interviews, recorded in 1977 and 1978, he described the initial training at Flinders as 'rather peculiar instruction'. The entire course lasted only six weeks. Great slabs of precious time were taken up with the navy's biggest 6-inch guns—how to lay them, how to fire them, and how to call the numbers. By the end of six weeks Reg could have pulled a 6-inch gun apart and put it back together again like a seasoned professional. This might have been useful to an officer on a 30,000-ton battleship, but it had no relevance for anyone on a 42-day crash course leading to command of an armed motor launch.

Signal training was a particularly sore point. 'We were supposed to spend a week in signal class at Flinders,' he recalled. 'On the Monday morning the Chief Petty Officer got up in front of the class and he said: "I can't teach you anything. A rating has to be here for 18 months before we allow him to go on the bridge of a warship. You've only got a week. Don't make a noise. I'll be in the next room if you want me. Knock on the wall." The whole week was spent doing our own thing. We signalled to ourselves, and we carried on our own class.'

They were taught about torpedoes. By the end of the course they could recite the number of links on a chain to drop a mine. They learned about all the pistols in the navy since Nelson's day. None of it was remotely relevant. Reg Andrew could expect his first command to be a patrol boat armed with a .303 Vickers machine-gun and anti-submarine depth charges.

The Vickers was not exactly a state-of-the-art weapon. It first went into service with the British Army in 1912. It so happens that I trained on a Vickers in the school cadet corps back in the 1950s. I remember it as a bad-tempered beast, with 13 different ways to jam. We beginners had to learn to strip the complicated lock and reassemble it quickly, as well as learning to work out how and why it jammed. At our annual training camps we were each allowed to fire a 250-round belt of live ammunition, which was great fun though it can't have contributed much to Australia's future defence. Reg Andrew's training consisted of walking past a stand with a Vickers mounted on it and being told: that's a Vickers machine-gun. At the end of his six weeks at Flinders he had no instruction on handling depth charges. He had never even seen a depth charge fired, except in the movies. For someone about to take command of a fighting ship in a shooting war, he could have had better weapon training with me in the Barker College cadets.

◆   ◆   ◆

The defences of Sydney Harbour concentrated, perfectly sensibly, on keeping an enemy out. Nevertheless, the navy had not entirely overlooked the possibility of an enemy getting into the harbour itself. Large warships would be unsuitable to counter this threat—they need plenty of room to manoeuvre. So the navy relied on a fleet of 12 converted luxury launches, mostly built by the Halvorsen yard in Sydney. The conversion involved mounting a Vickers on the deck, and strapping depth charges to the stern. Some of the boats were fitted with ASDIC anti-submarine detection gear. These were known as Channel Patrol boats. They were crewed by full-time Royal Australian Navy sailors, often men who had seen action overseas and were sent back to Australia for rest and recuperation. Some, like the motor mechanics, were newly trained and did a spell on the Channel Patrol boats before moving on to larger fighting ships. The commanding officer was often fresh out of Flinders Naval College. The navy viewed the Channel Patrol boats as a safe enough place for a newly graduated officer to build up experience.

The navy had a second group of converted motor launches at its command inside Sydney Harbour. These were not requisitioned: they were offered up freely by their owners for navy use. The owner usually continued as skipper, and the crew were volunteers. *Lauriana* was typical. It was owned and skippered by Harold Arnott of Arnott's Biscuits fame.

This second group was known collectively as the Naval Auxiliary Patrol, contemptuously dismissed as 'Nap-Naps' or 'Nappies'. As their official name implied, they were patrol vessels rather than fighting ships. In May 1942 they were all unarmed. The whole collection of small boats, with their crisp-uniformed crews and vaguely effete luxury launch aura, were known derisively as the 'Hollywood Fleet'. The regular navy regarded them all as weekend sailors, not to be taken seriously.

The formation of the Hollywood Fleet led to endless rows over money. The story of *Sea Mist* is typical. She was one of the larger boats, 60 feet (18 metres) long and weighing 35 tons, built in 1939 by Lars Halvorsen and Sons in Sydney. *Sea Mist* was requisitioned by the navy on 17 June 1941. She was owned by the racing-car driver Hope Bartlett, who valued her at £5500. Lloyds valued her at £4000. The navy would not budge from £4000. After months of wrangling Bartlett and the legal owner of the boat, a hire-purchase company called Automobile and General Finance, had to back down. Bartlett claimed for the cost of petrol bringing *Sea Mist* from Huskisson, on the New South Wales South Coast, to Garden Island in Sydney—166 gallons at two shillings and seven pence a gallon, a total of £21.8.10. The navy painstakingly calculated that the boat would have used 48 gallons at 8 knots or roughly 80 gallons at 10 knots. In the laborious, handwritten Register of Requisitioned Motor Patrol Boats and Miscellaneous Examination Vessels and Harbour Craft, an anonymous Royal Australian Naval hand opined: '80 gallons appears to be a fairly generous allowance for the trip.' That particular row rumbled on for 10 months. The navy eventually paid £10.6.8—the cost of 80 gallons of petrol at 1941 prices.

Money raised different issues at the Naval Auxiliary Patrol. They were crewed by volunteers, who actually paid for the privilege of serving. They handed over ten shillings to enrol in the NAP, and paid a subscription of a shilling a week. The navy paid for any alterations to the boats when converting them to military use, and paid for fuel and oil while on duty, but no more. The volunteer crews were expected to dip into their own pockets for the rest. Crews were required to pay for their own uniforms, for instance. Service in the Naval Auxiliary Patrol was open to men who met three conditions: they should not be of military age; they should know something of the ways of the sea; and they should be prepared to give up their spare time to patrol activities. They were a Dad's Navy, but they would be right in the front line if the war ever found its way into Sydney Harbour.

When Reg Andrew graduated from Flinders Naval College as a fully fledged Lieutenant in the Royal Australian Navy, he returned to Sydney to await a posting. After a few weeks of nothing to do, he was told his first command would be the Channel Patrol boat *Sea Mist*.

◆　　◆　　◆

Even before Pearl Harbor, Yamamoto had ordered his Special Attack Force of midget submariners to study charts of Singapore, Sydney and Suva harbours. At the time of Pearl Harbor, the crews were told Singapore would be next. However, the speed of the Japanese advance dictated a change of plan. By early February 1942, it was clear Singapore would fall soon. The Imperial Japanese Navy looked around for new places to strike.

The Japanese had beaten the world with the creation of a remarkable weapon: a reconnaissance aircraft which could be launched from a submarine. The British, French and Italian navies had all dabbled with the idea. The Japanese made it work. The two-seater, single-engined Yokosuka E14Y Glen seaplane and its launching system were major technical achievements. The Japanese adapted some of their large 'I' class submarines by extending the conning tower forward, to create a watertight hangar space for a folded Glen. They then built an aircraft catapult which could be mounted on the foredeck of the submarine. A Glen could be dragged out of its hangar and assembled in as little as 10 minutes. It could be ready for launch in under an hour.

Take off was every pilot's worst nightmare, particularly at night. Unlike an aircraft carrier, even a large submarine's deck is only 2 or 3 metres above sea level. So every launch began with the aircraft perilously close to the water, giving the pilot little or no time to get himself out of trouble if anything went wrong. Worse, there was a delay between the pilot's order to fire the catapult and the moment when the aircraft actually took to the air. An aircraft fired from a catapult cannot be pointed up at too steep an angle or gravity will eat into the airspeed, and the plane will stall and crash. On the other hand, if the angle is too shallow then the aircraft will fire straight into the water at full catapult speed, with disastrous results. So the pilots had to time the order to launch to perfection: sit on the catapult with the engine roaring at full throttle, wait until the bow was plunging down towards its lowest point, then call; in the second or so delay before they were airborne, hope that the next wave would swing the bow up from the water but not too far. Then go. Get it right and bingo, they were flying. Get it wrong and they were in the water with 2500 tons of submarine charging down on them from behind.

The search for profitable new targets for midget submarine attack began in early February 1942. The Japanese mother submarine I-25 with a Glen stowed aboard arrived off Sydney on Saturday, 14 February, the day before Singapore fell. The captain, Lieutenant Commander Tagami, brought his sub close enough to Sydney to see the searchlights in the distance. But seas were too rough to launch the Glen, so he retreated 160 kilometres east and waited for better weather.

By Monday night the seas had calmed down, and Tagami agreed to a reconnaissance flight. Just after sunset on 16 February he brought the I-25 back closer to Sydney, and checked by periscope that all was clear. The submarine surfaced in darkness, recharged its batteries and refreshed its air supply. The Glen was assembled after midnight and at about 4.30 am on 17 February, with Warrant Flying Officer Nobuo Fujita at the controls and Petty Officer Second Class Shoji Okuda as observer, it took off. They timed the flight to bring them back to the submarine just after sunrise.

The Glen was not an ideal observation plane. Its wings were low rather than high, blocking large areas of view from the cockpit. Allied reconnaissance seaplanes like the Catalina had high wings, giving the pilot and observer a better look down. The Glen cruised at 90 knots— about the same speed as the slower training aircraft used at flying clubs today. So it was a sitting duck for any anti-aircraft battery. It carried a light machine-gun, operated from the rear cockpit by the observer, but this would have been close to useless against even a Wirraway fighter.

Neither anti-aircraft fire nor enemy fighters presented Fujita with any problems that morning. The two airmen crossed the Australian coast at

La Perouse on the southern outskirts of Sydney, flying comparatively high at 8000 feet. They dropped down to 3000 feet to avoid some cloud, heading west across Botany Bay past Sydney's main airport at Mascot. After crossing the bay they turned north-west in the direction of Parramatta, still with no response from the Sydney defences. Fujita's track must have taken him close to Bankstown, which at this stage was a military airfield. For the last two days this had been the home of the Kittyhawk fighters of the US Army Air Forces' 7th Pursuit Squadron, the 'Screamin' Demons'. Nobody screamed. Nobody even stirred.*

Fujita now turned north towards the Sydney suburb of Ryde then tracked back east over Artarmon and Northbridge, with a clear view of the harbour on his right. Okuda, the observer, counted 23 ships in the harbour, including a large three-funnel warship, two destroyers and five submarines. Sydney was clearly a worthy target. Fujita continued east, still unmolested, and crossed the coast at North Head. He had some trouble finding the mother submarine, but eventually succeeded. The Glen landed safely on the water and was hoisted onto the I-25 and stowed.

Tagami now took the I-25 south. He cruised down the east coast of Tasmania and back up the west coast, fighting bad weather most of the way. He prowled around in Bass Strait, waiting for the right moment for a Glen flight over Melbourne. On 26 February conditions were right and Fujita and Okuda took off again. They followed the coastline to the Point Lonsdale lighthouse at the entrance to Port Phillip Bay and then at 5000 feet turned north-east towards Melbourne. Thick cloud now blocked Okuda's view, so Fujita dropped down through the murk, unsure of his position. He broke cloud at 1000 feet, plumb above Laverton air base, home to Melbourne's fighter defences. This time he

---

* As a footnote to history, the 7th Pursuit Squadron is still active today. It went through a succession of name changes, and is now known as the 7th Combat Training Squadron. It specialises in training pilots for the F-117A 'Stealth' fighter programme. It could fairly claim to have been one of the earliest USAF squadrons to see stealth tactics up close.

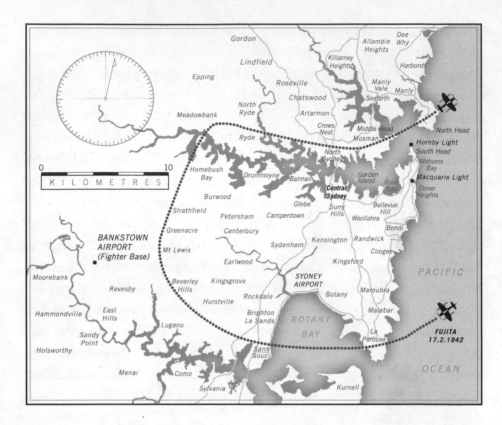

Fujita's track reconnoitring Sydney is fairly well established. He crossed the Australian coast at La Perouse, flying at about 8000 feet, then descended to 3000 feet with Sydney Airport on his right. He crossed the Botany Bay coast near Brighton le Sands, and shortly afterwards turned north-west in the direction of Parramatta. He may or may not have known that this track took him close to Bankstown fighter air base. He then turned right, towards Ryde, before turning back towards the main area of interest— Sydney Harbour. He flew along the north shore of the harbour, passing over Artarmon and Middle Head while getting a good sight of 23 ships in the harbour, before crossing the Australian coast again at North Head.

was spotted. Two fighter aircraft scrambled, but Fujita climbed into the cloud and disappeared.

Fujita now kept popping down into clear air to take a look around, then climbing back into the cloud to hide. One of his sorties below cloud took him into the open over the Williamstown anti-aircraft battery. Again, he was spotted. Instead of opening fire, the Lieutenant in charge responded by telephoning headquarters for permission. By the time he had an answer, Fujita had disappeared back into the cloud again. The Glen flew over the suburbs of St Kilda, Brighton and Frankston, with a clear view of Melbourne's port. Okuda counted 19 ships. More significantly, he counted six warships in single file heading in to Port Melbourne. So Melbourne had possibilities, too. Fujita and Okuda landed safely at the rendezvous point near Cape Wickham lighthouse, hoisted their aircraft back aboard the submarine, and I-25 headed south again.

On 1 March Fujita and Okuda flew over Hobart. They saw five merchant ships but no warships. This time the Glen damaged a wingtip while being hoisted back onto the submarine, but the crew managed to repair it, if roughly. I-25 crossed the Tasman Sea to New Zealand. On 8 March Fujita and Okuda flew over Wellington Harbour. On 13 March they flew over Auckland Harbour. I-25 now turned its attention to Fiji. On 18 March the Glen reconnoitered Suva Harbour. Throughout the entire odyssey not a single shot was fired at it. His mission complete, Tagami turned the I-25 north for home and to report.

◆　◆　◆

In April 1942, with the disaster at Pearl Harbor five months behind them, crews from the Special Attack Force of midget submariners intensified their training at home in Japan, readying themselves for the next operation. Submariners always believe they are the elite in any navy, and these were the elite of the elite. They were what we would now call special forces in the tradition of the SAS, Special Boat Squadron, Delta Force, Spetznaz. In Japanese they were known as *Tokubetsu Ko-geki-tai*, reduced to *Toku-tai*. All were graduates of the three-year course at the Imperial Naval Academy, on the island of Eta Jima in the Inland Sea. They were selected for the midget submarine programme on the basis of courage, discipline and skill. They needed to be lightly built yet supremely fit, with plenty of stamina. They were unlikely to be chosen if they were married, or the eldest son: their chances of returning from a mission were slight. They were sworn to secrecy. Not even their immediate family could be told of the special weapon.

Midget submarine training began in April 1941 at the Kure Naval Arsenal. First the crews were taught weapon handling and tactics. In May they moved to the seaplane tender *Chiyoda*, where they trained in the release of submarines from a mother ship. In June they switched to Mitsukue Bay, still in Japan, where they learned to handle torpedoes.

At this stage the men paired off into crews, and each crew stayed together for the rest of the training period, and into battle. The two-man crew consisted of a senior officer, who gave helm and firing orders, operated the periscope and decided course, speed and depth, and a petty officer who operated the helm, the valves for diving and surfacing, the sliding weights for balancing and trimming the submarine, and the torpedo firing trigger.

The men were now introduced to their submarines. It was a shock. The crews found them cramped and uncomfortable, and smaller than they expected. Worse, they were difficult to manage in the water. The midgets were given to sudden and unpredictable rushes to the surface, followed by equally unpredictable plummets to the bottom. If this happened, the crew had to work frantically with a clumsy system of moveable weights to bring the submarine back under control. The controls themselves needed constant attention. A slight lapse of concentration and the sub would roll through a sideways somersault.

Nevertheless, the midgets were potent weapons. They were powered by a single 600-horsepower electric motor fuelled by 224 two-volt batteries, giving them a top speed of 23 knots on the surface and 19 knots submerged. This was faster than most conventional submarines. The batteries had an endurance of 25 hours at low speed, but not much more than an hour at top speed. Their effective range was about 200 kilometres, provided they travelled slowly. The two torpedoes each packed 350 kilos of high explosive, more than most other torpedoes then in use. The torpedoes travelled through the water at 44 knots, and could outrun any ship in any navy. They were driven by a revolutionary internal combustion engine fuelled by a mixture of kerosene, oxygen and sea water, instead of the compressed air and alcohol used in other nations' torpedoes. This gave them a range of 5500 metres, up to three times the range of their Allied counterparts. The fuel system also reduced their wake, making the torpedoes harder to see and avoid.

Given the limited range of the midget submarines themselves, they had to be delivered to the target zone by a mother ship. At first the Japanese experimented with surface ships, often converted seaplane carriers. But these were too easily spotted by the enemy. So even before Pearl Harbor they switched to an ingenious 'piggyback' arrangement, whereby the midget was transported to the target zone strapped on the afterdeck of a large 'I' class mother submarine. The mother submarine and its midget passenger could submerge during the day and surface at night to charge batteries and refresh air supplies, maximising the chances of surprise.

The midgets were emphatically not suicide vessels. Indeed, Yamamoto had made it a condition of approving the midget submarine programme that the crew should be recovered afterwards. However, the midgets were one-mission vehicles. Each sub carried scuttling charges. After each mission the midget crew were to rendezvous with the mother sub and be taken aboard. Then they would scuttle their midget and send it to the bottom, returning to base aboard the mother submarine.

American press reports on the salvage and inspection of the midget submarines from Pearl Harbor gave the Japanese valuable intelligence on the problems the submarine crews faced. They were particularly interested in the reported damage to Sakamaki's submarine. They also had reports from the commanders of the mother submarines on the problems the midgets faced in a real war situation. They began a number of much-needed improvements to the design. Before Pearl Harbor, the crew could enter their midget only while the mother submarine was on the surface. This meant that any servicing of the midget, or launching it for a mission, involved exposing both midget and mother sub to the attentions of enemy ships and planes.

After Pearl Harbor, a special hatch was cut in the bottom of the midget's hull. This formed a seal with a matching hatch on the deck of the mother submarine. The crew could now move between the mother sub and the midget even when both were submerged. The ties holding the two submarines together could be released from inside the submarines. With the crew on board and the hatches re-sealed, the baby sub could be detached from the mother sub while both submarines were below the surface, making both subs much less vulnerable to attack during launch.

The designers responded to complaints from the crews about comfort. Seats were added, and the conning tower rearranged to give the crews a bit more room. The designers added a 'sled' cage to the bow of the midget, so that it would slide over obstacles underwater. They built another cage around the propeller to prevent fouling. A saw-toothed net-cutting line now ran from the bow to the top of the conning tower, giving the submarine a reasonable chance of hacking its way through harbour net defences. Four small saw-toothed blades were fitted to the noses of the torpedoes. With their ferocious speed and jagged blades, the torpedoes would pass unchecked through most nets.

When the five midgets set off for Pearl Harbor in December 1941, the crews had the benefit of three or four years of intensive training at the Imperial Naval College, plus seven months of specialist midget training at other locations around Japan. After Pearl Harbor, the crews for the next mission could add a further four months of intensive midget submarine training, this time on their improved subs. They were a formidable fighting unit, armed with a formidable fighting machine. All that remained was the choice of target.

Chapter 5

Date of attack will be notified

At home in Australia, the government fretted over the population's refusal to take the war seriously. Newspapers carried pages of war news every day. However, they continued to carry even more pages of horseracing results, tips and forecasts. On 1 January the *Sydney Morning Herald*, in a sombre leading article, warned: 'Never before has a year dawned on us with the menace of direct attack.' Next day's regular 'On The Land' feature could find nothing more menacing than the warning: 'Blowflies may be bad.'

There were endless strikes, particularly in the coal mines and on the wharves. The wharfies, the Australian nickname for America's stevedores or Britain's dockers, were particularly militant. They frequently refused to load ships even when they were due to depart next day with troops aboard. The troops were regularly forced to do their own loading and unloading. The wharfies preferred not to work in the rain. The Americans in particular were appalled. John Curtin's Labor government pleaded repeatedly with the trade unions to cooperate with the war effort and keep Australia working. The strikes continued.

In early May 1942 there was a major fiasco over clothing supplies. John Dedman, the Australian Minister for War Organisation, announced that clothing rationing would be introduced in mid-June. People downed tools, deserted their workplaces and headed for the shops, determined to buy all the clothing they could before rationing took over. The shops simply emptied. Within days there was no clothing left to sell. Big stores like David Jones in Sydney and Myer in Melbourne witnessed fights over their fast-disappearing stocks. For two weeks the clothing wars took up almost as much space in the newspapers as the war with Japan. The *Sunday Sun*'s 10 May headline on page 2, 'America Throbs with Excitement Over Naval Victory' (over a report on American reaction to the Battle of the Coral Sea), was matched by an even larger headline on page 3: 'Panic Rush to Purchase Clothes—Many City Stores Are Stripped Bare'. An embarrassed government blamed it all on Mother's Day.

Brown paper covered windows—the so-called 'brown out'. People who lit cigarettes in the open at night were booed. Air-raid drills were stepped up. People were showered with bizarre advice. The best place to shelter inside a house is under the kitchen table after covering the table with a mattress. Shove the table into a corner for even better protection. In the event of an air raid, fill the bathtub with water. Make sure you turn off the gas at the mains. Schoolkids, bite on a ruler during an air raid. Or bite a clothes peg. This will save biting your tongue, and will keep the passages to the ears open and reduce the risk of blast-ruptured ear drums. Wear a name tag on a string around your neck. Carry a drinking cup on another string. It was surreal.

Throughout this period, the government, the military and the civilian population all agreed on two major dreads: air raids, and a land invasion. They braced themselves for both.

◆　　◆　　◆

As early as March 1942, Yamamoto agreed to give the midget submarines a second and final chance to prove themselves after the fiasco at Pearl Harbor. By late April the targets were known. There would be simultaneous strikes by two attack forces: a Western Attack Group, under the command of Rear Admiral Noboru Ishizaki, would sail from Penang and head for the Indian Ocean in search of British warships; the Eastern Attack Group, commanded by Captain Hanku Sasaki, would sail from Truk Lagoon in the Caroline Islands, north of New Guinea, and head south-east. Its final target would be one of the ports nominated as the most promising by the I-25's Glen in February: Suva, Auckland and Sydney.

Sasaki had commanded the submarine force at Pearl Harbor. This time he was determined to get it right. His Eastern Attack Group would consist of six mother submarines, four carrying midgets and two carrying Glen floatplanes. The four midgets and their crews were ferried to Truk, to await collection by their mother subs.

We know from Japanese postwar records that the purpose of the attack was threefold. It would send a signal that nowhere was safe from the attentions of the all-conquering Imperial Japanese Navy. The Eastern Attack Group would make the Americans think twice about Australia as a secure base from which to counterattack in the Pacific, while the Western Attack Group would threaten the Indian Ocean sea route, blocking the flow of supplies and men between Britain and Australia. Finally, the sinking of American capital ships by the Eastern Attack Group would be another nail in the coffin of the US Pacific Fleet. In its postwar review, the Japanese Navy Ministry summed it up in the following words: 'Our offensive operations proceeded smoothly and our strategic situation had been strengthened and expanded. Nevertheless the enemy fleet still survived. Surprise attacks with midget submarines were planned to wipe it out.'

The Eastern Attack Group consisted of six 2500-ton I-class mother submarines: I-21, I-22, I-24, I-27, I-28 and I-29. Two of the mother subs—I-21 and I-29—were designed to carry Glen floatplanes. The remaining four would carry midget submarines. The two Glen-carrying subs left first. Captain Sasaki slipped out of Truk on 27 April 1942 on the I-21, with its floatplane stowed aboard. He arrived off Noumea on 4 May, and prowled around for ten days looking fruitlessly for Allied warships. However the I-21's journey was not entirely wasted: on 5 May it sank a 7000-ton American 'Liberty' ship, *John Adams*, with its precious cargo of 2000 tons of gasoline. On 7 May it sank a smaller Greek freighter, *Chloe*. After this last sinking, the Japanese gallantly handed out biscuits and tinned food to the survivors in the lifeboats, and pointed them in the direction of Noumea.

Sasaki left Noumean waters for Fiji on 14 May, arriving off Fiji some time around 18 May. Now the Glen could be assembled. On 19 May it took off with Warrant Flying Officer Susumo Ito at the controls and Ordinary Seaman Iwasaki as observer. Their unmarked plane flew over Suva Harbour, where they counted one light cruiser and seven submarine chasers. They flew close enough to the ships to see individual sailors on the decks. Some sailors on the cruiser spotted the Glen. Iwasaki asked Ito if he should open fire with the machine-gun. Ito had a better idea. He ordered Iwasaki to wave. The sailors waved back. The flight continued unchallenged, and Ito landed safely beside the I-21. Suva looked none too promising, he told Captain Sasaki, who reported this by radio to Japanese Sixth Fleet Headquarters at Kwajalein atoll in the Marshall Islands.

Meanwhile, the second seaplane-carrying mother submarine from the Eastern Attack Group left Truk Lagoon on 30 April. The commander, Captain Juichi Izu, headed the I-29 south for Sydney, arriving off Sydney on 13 May. On 14 May there was a flurry of excitement. Izu saw two warships heading for Sydney Harbour—a destroyer, and a large warship which he wrongly identified as the British battleship HMS *Warspite*. The I-29 set off in hot pursuit of this highly prized target. However, Izu never managed to get into the right firing position with his torpedoes, and in the end gave up the chase. Never mind, he might have reassured himself. *Warspite* would make a perfect target for the midgets when they got into Sydney Harbour.

On 16 May off the New South Wales coast near Newcastle, Izu fired two torpedoes at the Russian merchant ship *Wellen*. Both missed. He then surfaced and attacked the *Wellen* from close range with his deck gun. The *Wellen* turned out to be armed, and fired back. Izu chose to retreat. This attack was a serious mistake on Izu's part: the

Russian merchant ship was not worth the trouble, and he had now alerted the Australian defences to the presence of a hostile submarine off the New South Wales coast. Sydney had its first serious warning.

◆　◆　◆

The four midget-carrying I-class Japanese submarines, fresh from escorting the ill-fated invasion fleet for Port Moresby, were ordered on 11 May to return to the submarine base at Truk Lagoon to collect their midgets. Three came from escort work during the Battle of the Coral Sea, the fourth from patrol further north.

The Eastern Attack Group suffered two major setbacks before it could get fully under way. On 17 May the American submarine USS *Tautog* spotted the I-28 on the surface and on its way to Truk. The *Tautog* made no mistake. Three torpedoes later the I-28 was on its way to the bottom, taking its entire crew of 88 with it. Only three midgets could now be ferried south. The Japanese had lost a quarter of their attacking force even before setting out for the target zone. The fourth midget, scheduled to be carried south on the I-28, would have to stay behind at Truk instead. After the war, Sub-Lieutenant Teiji Yamaki, the commander of the midget due to sail on the I-24, remembered the crew of the fourth midget, Sub-Lieutenant Ban and Petty Officer Ashibe, making no secret of their bitter disappointment.

The next victim was Yamaki's own midget. On their first day out of Truk, the crew were servicing their submarine while the mother sub, the I-24, ran on the surface. Gas leaked inside the midget and exploded, with both crew on board. The explosion blasted Petty Officer Matsumoto, who had been working in the conning tower, out through the hatch and into the ocean where he was never found. The explosion also seriously injured Yamaki, who had been working inside. The midget was unusable, and was abandoned. The mother sub turned back quickly to Truk, unloaded the wounded Yamaki, and collected a jubilant Ban and Ashibe together with their intact submarine. The I-24 then raced south to catch up with the rest of the fleet.

Meanwhile, the skirmish with the *Wellen* stirred the Australian defences into action. Rear Admiral Muirhead-Gould, Naval Officer in Command, Sydney, ordered all merchant ships to remain in Sydney and Newcastle harbours. He then mounted an air and sea search for the aggressive submarine. After 24 hours, with no trace of the sub, he reopened the harbours. The search continued for several days. The Allied ships and planes found nothing.

It was now time for both Glens to come out from their covers. On 23 May Izu took the I-29 from wherever he had been hiding after the *Wellen* attack and moved to within range of Sydney. There he launched his Glen. Very little has been written about this flight. Many accounts of the midget submarine raid leave it out altogether or confuse it with Ito's subsequent flight over Sydney on 29 May. Yet this was arguably the most important flight of all: it settled Sydney's fate.

The crew of the Glen were not new to the task: Warrant Flying Officer Nobuo Fujita and Petty Officer Second Class Shoji Okuda had already reconnoitred Sydney Harbour once in the early hours of 17 February from the I-25. This time they were even more audacious: the flight took place in broad daylight. The risks involved in a daylight flight were massive. The mother submarine had to sit on the surface for an hour or more, exposed and vulnerable, while the Glen was assembled and launched. Then the mother ship had to return to the surface at the agreed rendezvous place and time to recover the aircraft and crew. This would mean another 30 to 45 minutes on the surface. If the flight was detected and the defences followed the spy plane back to the rendezvous point, then both plane and mother submarine would almost certainly be lost. However the quality of information from a daylight flight would be so much better than that gleaned from a night flight. Izu must have judged it worth the risk.

There is no record of this flight in any of the official Australian accounts of the Sydney midget submarine raid. But we have two remarkable eyewitnesses. Signalman Arthur ('Darby') Munro was on duty at the Port War Signal Station on South Head as Fujita flew down the harbour. And army Gunner Don Caldwell Smith was manning a mobile radar station parked at Iron Cove, 5 kilometres south-west of the Harbour Bridge.

Darby Munro was the first to see Fujita. He had just come on watch, which sets the time as just after midday. Darby was a visual signaller, and worked on the top floor of the Port War Signal Station. The top floor had a 360-degree view both out to sea and up the harbour. Darby first saw a 'white' floatplane approaching the entrance to Sydney Harbour from the north, flying at about 500 feet.* He followed the plane's progress up the harbour as far as the Harbour Bridge. At this point he reported the sighting to Naval Headquarters at Garden Island. Darby recalls Garden Island's response: 'He didn't know what to do. He told me to put it on to Richmond.' Richmond was then the base for the Wirraway fighters of the RAAF. Richmond proved even less helpful. The voice on the end of the telephone told Darby: 'It's no use telling us. By the time we sent someone, he'd be gone.'

Don Caldwell Smith, at the mobile radar station at Iron Cove, now takes over the story. The existence of a radar unit in Sydney was still highly secret, and the brand-new operators had spent their training time attempting to track a Tiger Moth which the RAAF sent up to fly around Sydney as a practice target. The wood-and-fabric biplane was hopeless. Its flimsy frame barely returned an echo on their radar screen. Now, to the delight of the radar crew, they had an unexpected and strong return. The all-metal Glen was a much better quarry. They tracked it enthusiastically down the harbour, with no thought that it might be an enemy aircraft, only that at last they could get in a bit of genuine practice with their secret weapon. The radar unit was linked to a nearby anti-aircraft gun, so the radar crew gave the gunners instructions on the range and bearing of the convenient intruder. Everyone was pleased.

At this point the regulations called for the radar unit to report the intruder to Combined Defence Headquarters near Circular Quay. Don's unit grabbed the telephone. 'The next thing, headquarters came back

---

* A Glen was usually painted grey underneath and green above. As Darby was looking at the underside of the aircraft, white is a fair description.

and they said: Stop! We've just been in touch with the Air Force and they have no aircraft in the air at the moment. So you'd better get that machine of yours tested by an artificer [radar technician] tomorrow.' Combined Defence Headquarters had clearly weighed up the possibilities. If there was a plane over Sydney it had to be one of theirs. So if none of their planes were over Sydney that left only one explanation: the radar must be on the blink again.

Fujita's flight continued undisturbed. At the Harbour Bridge he turned left, still watched by Darby Munro, and headed south-east across the heart of Sydney towards Bondi. He re-crossed the Sydney coast a little south of Bondi, over Waverley cemetery, and turned left along the famous surfing beaches of Bronte, Tamarama and Bondi. He continued north along the coast towards South Head before turning right to head east for the open ocean and a rendezvous with the mother submarine.

We know nothing more of this flight beyond the fact that the Glen must have crashed on landing. It was not available to Sasaki and the Eastern Attack Group when it was badly needed nine days later. However, Fujita and Okuda survived, to bring their precious sketches and reports of promising targets back to the I-29 for transmission to the whole attack group. The spy flight was Sydney's second serious warning in the space of seven days. Not a single alarm bell rang.

◆　◆　◆

While Izu's I-29 checked out Sydney, Sasaki's floatplane-carrying I-21 had sailed from Fiji to New Zealand and arrived off Auckland. On the morning of 24 May the regular team of Ito and Iwasaki launched their Glen. Fog blanketed Auckland Harbour, and they could not see anything. However, their reception in New Zealand was nothing if not courteous. As they groped their way in the skies over Auckland, they must have sounded to experienced ears in the control tower at Auckland airport like a lost aircraft trying to find the airfield in the fog. The controllers obligingly turned on the runway lights. Ito declined this well-intentioned offer. He returned to the I-21 to report that he had not been able to see which ships, if any, lay in the harbour.

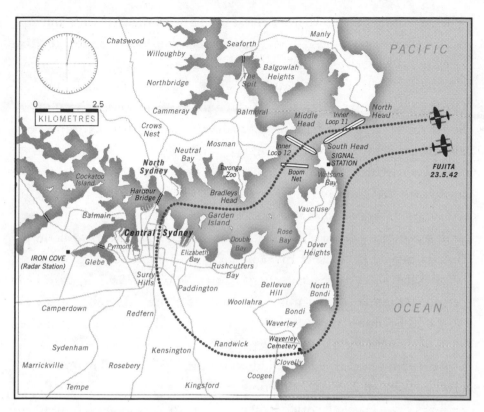

Fujita's second flight over Sydney is not as well documented as his 17 February flight. However, based on eyewitness accounts, he arrived from the north-east, tracked down the centre of the harbour as far as the Harbour Bridge, giving him a good view of fighting ships in the harbour. He then turned south, with a view of Sydney Airport, before crossing the coast a little south of Bondi. He then followed the coast back as far as South Head before heading out to sea for a rendezvous with the mother submarine.

Nevertheless, the brass at the Japanese Sixth Fleet Headquarters at Kwajalein now felt they had enough information to make a decision. Noumea and Suva were out. Auckland was an unknown quantity. But from Fujita's and Okuda's report Sydney appeared to be full of ships, including the possible major prize of the battleship HMS *Warspite*. On 24 May Vice-Admiral the Marquis Teruhisa Komatsu radioed the necessary orders to Sasaki. Sydney was to be the target. The mother subs headed for Sydney.

◆   ◆   ◆

The airwaves now began to crackle with traffic. On the evening of 26 May, from somewhere in the Tasman Sea, Sasaki sent out his order to the Eastern Attack Group.

> Telegraphic order No 3
> 1.   Date of attack will be notified.
> 2.   Order of dispatching the sheaths [the Japanese term for the midget submarines] will be I-27, I-22 then I-24. The order for the sheaths entering Sydney Harbour will be: I-27, 20 minutes after moonrise, then I-22 and I-24 following at 20 minute intervals.
> 3.   Targets for the attack will be at the discretion of sheath commanders, who should concentrate on the following:
>   (a)   If there is a battleship or large cruiser beyond the Harbour Bridge then I-22 is to attack the battleship and I-24 the cruiser. If there are two cruisers then I-22 and I-24 will attack them and I-27 will attack the battleship.
>   (b)   If there is a battleship or aircraft carrier before the Harbour Bridge then attack it.
>   (c)   If there are no suitable targets before the Harbour Bridge then try as much as possible to attack the battleship and large cruiser beyond the Harbour Bridge.
> 4.   After completion of the attack, the recovery position will be: Day 1—No 4 recovery rendezvous off Broken Bay; Day 2— No 2 recovery rendezvous off Port Hacking.

There is no evidence that this message was ever decoded by either the Australians or the Americans. However, it did not pass unnoticed. Naval Intelligence officers in New Zealand locked onto it with direction-finding equipment. They placed the Japanese unit which had sent it, probably a submarine, some 700 nautical miles east of Sydney. This wasn't a bad fix.

Appendix II deals in some detail with the activities of the American and Australian code-breakers. At this point it is sufficient to say that by May 1942 the Allies had made substantial progress in breaking the Japanese Navy's JN-25 code. The code-breaking process was still slow and far from complete. We can gain a pretty good insight into just how slow from a declassified US Navy intelligence report, available in the Australian War Memorial in Canberra. The report is signed A.H. McCollum. Arthur McCollum worked on the Far East Desk of the Office of Naval Intelligence in Washington and prepared daily intelligence summaries for the White House. The first page ends with this melodramatic instruction: 'It is requested that this document be burned as soon as it has served its purpose and that in the mean-time it not be placed in any general file.' Only seven copies were made, of which the War Memorial's is number three, marked for 'NAVAL AIDE'. The naval aide in this case was Captain John R. Beardall, who reported directly to Roosevelt. Beardall clearly didn't do as he was told and burn the document, for which we must all be grateful. The surviving copy is headed 'Summary of Japanese Naval Activities of June 2, 1942'.

Item 4 on the first page deals with Japanese submarine activities. It begins:

> At various times in the past it has been reported that the principal source from which the Japanese gain intelligence of the movements of Allied forces in the South Pacific appears to be submarines reconnoitring close inshore. At least one such submarine spent several days reconnoitring the vicinity of Sydney around the middle of May, and reported details of naval ship movements which in general appeared to exaggerate the actual facts. This particular boat is the one which unsuccessfully attacked the SS *Wellen*.

Another boat, or possibly the same one, spent the period May 19–23 in the vicinity of Suva, Fiji, and reported a number of ship movements.

This intelligence summary reveals a great deal. First, it is clear that messages from the I-29 off Sydney and the I-21 off Suva had been intercepted *and decrypted,* because McCollum appears to know the contents of each message in some detail. His amused reference to the fact that the I-29's report 'appeared to exaggerate the actual facts' is a response to Izu's rather wild estimate of the size and number of warships in Sydney Harbour at the time. McCollum's uncertainty over whether the Sydney report and the Suva report came from the same submarine or from two different submarines suggests that the decrypt was only partially successful. That was correct, as we shall now see.

The Australian government has not released the contents of intelligence reports gathered by FRUMEL (Fleet Radio Unit Melbourne), the joint Australian–American code-breaking unit which was one of a chain of stations around the Pacific at the forefront of the attack on JN-25. However, the American government is not nearly so secretive. Any Australian who wants to read the original documents should get in touch with the Naval Historical Foundation in Washington, which will be happy to oblige. The digest of 30 May decrypts is dated 31 May and the first page, second paragraph, reads as follows. The long dashes indicate undecipherable passages.

0 SB 8 (Jaluit radio (conceals for Comsubfor))—25 May—partly readable 'Reconnaissance report of Sydney Harbour.' 'On the 15th saw one destroyer, and on the 19th one patrol boat patrolling off Port Kembla. On the 16th at 1800 fired 2 torpedoes at 5000 ton merchantman off Newcastle but both missed. Following that fired several rounds of gunfire but she evaded any hits —— (COIC report No 246 indicates USSR vessel 'Wellen' received this attack).' The report then indicates that at 25 miles north of Shark Island saw one BB [US Naval code for battleship] or CA [heavy

cruiser]. In —— of Garden Island were two medium class destroyers (or second class cruisers) and three CA. On patrol to the south of Clark Island were 3 CA. There was a great deal of merchant shipping in the —— (specified anchorages at Harbour Bridge). —— 3 airport hangars at Mascot ——.

This is obviously Izu's report. It is pretty wild stuff. Shark Island is just off Rose Bay in the heart of Sydney Harbour, so 25 miles north would put Izu's battleship or heavy cruiser in the hills to the west of Gosford, where it would certainly have stood out but might have been hard to attack by submarine. The three heavy cruisers patrolling to the south of Clark Island would have found manoeuvring a little tight in the less than 350 metres of harbour which separate this tiny island from the Sydney suburb of Darling Point. Either Izu's geography was weak, or the FRUMEL code-breakers still had a way to go.

The decrypted version of Izu's report hugely exaggerates the size and number of warships in the harbour at the time. This is not wholly surprising. It is not the first time, nor will it be the last, that an intelligence report overstates the enemy's strength (think of Iraq). Whether Izu, or Fujita and Okuda, stretched the facts or whether the FRUMEL code-breakers simply got it wrong, is simply unknown.

Nevertheless, the circumstances of this decrypt provide a gold mine of information. The original message was intercepted on 25 May. It was decrypted on 30 May. So we know that messages were taking up to five days to decrypt. The digest itself was distributed on 31 May, the day of the attack, and does not require years of training in intelligence to interpret. Clearly the Japanese were weighing up targets in Sydney Harbour. The wide geographic spread of nominated targets as well as the reference to airport hangars at Mascot suggests that the report was based on aerial reconnaissance. On the basis of this decrypt, Sydney could expect anything from an isolated submarine attack on ships leaving the harbour to a full-on Pearl Harbor-style mass air assault on the city itself.

◆　　◆　　◆

There was a peculiar protocol for passing on FRUMEL decrypts. The commanding officer at FRUMEL, Lieutenant Rudolph Fabian of the US Navy, passed the decrypts to Vice-Admiral H.F. Leary USN, Commander of Allied Naval Forces, South-West Pacific Area, also based in Melbourne. Leary passed them on to Washington and, at his discretion, to anyone else he felt might benefit from them and was cleared to see them. Leary was notoriously tight with this distribution. Not even General Douglas MacArthur, the Supreme Commander of Allied Forces in the South-West Pacific, received them automatically. This failure led a frustrated MacArthur shortly afterwards to set up his own independent signals intelligence operation.

It beggars belief that this message was not highlighted by whoever decrypted it on 30 May and passed it on to Leary. In the FRUMEL digest it is not even the first item—pride of place is given to the news that 15 Zero fighters had arrived in Rabaul from Truk on 25 May. However Leary appears to have missed its significance, too. He did nothing to alert the Sydney defences to what might have been very serious danger indeed. Given that three US Navy ships were at risk along with dozens of ships from five other Allied navies, Leary's failure might have cost his own navy dear along with those of his allies. Leary was later to complain about the state of Sydney Harbour's defences. He can certainly be credited with one of the major failures in the Battle of Sydney Harbour. Sydney had its third serious warning, in plenty of time to put the defences on notice that one or more enemy submarines were poised off Sydney. Nobody passed it on. Nobody did anything. After all, it was the weekend.

Chapter 6

Day of attack shall be May 31

Susumo Ito is one of the most engaging characters in this entire story. He is still alive at the time of writing, probably the only living Japanese survivor of the raid on Sydney. He has given endless interviews over the years to newspapers and magazines, to television documentary makers and to authors. He invariably comes across as modest, humorous, brave and skilful.

Born in Hyogo province on the largest Japanese island of Honshu, Ito went straight from junior high school to naval flying school at the age of 16. In one of his television interviews he recalls how friends warned him against it—in those days planes were particularly prone to crashing. However, he turned out to be a born flier, and was quickly singled out as one of the Imperial Japanese Navy's outstanding pilots. He flew reconnaissance and attack-directing missions during the war with China. Then he was transferred, like so many skilled pilots, to flying instructing. He returned to active service in September 1941, assigned to the I-21's Glen. He was 27 years old and a seasoned veteran when he strapped himself in to his cockpit in the early-morning darkness of 29 May 1942. The plane had had its Rising Sun red insignia painted out so it could not be readily recognised as Japanese.

Pilots have an expression to describe a bad flying day: 'Even the birds are walking.' May 29 was certainly a day for perambulating birds, especially seagulls. Visibility was fair below a cloud base of about 2000 feet. But there was a strong wind whipping up the sea and making—for reasons already discussed—any catapult launch from a submarine deck a particularly hazardous affair. Ito was equal to the task and, with his regular observer Iwasaki, he clawed his way into the air some time around 3.45 am. The launch point was 35 nautical miles north-east of Sydney, roughly off the New South Wales coast at Terrigal.

Flying time from the launch point to the entrance to Sydney Harbour was about 25 minutes. A little after 4 am Ito crossed the Australian coast at 1500 feet. There are huge discrepancies between the various published accounts of Ito's flight. For instance most accounts, including Muirhead-Gould's official report, describe him circling *Chicago*. However Ito's own sketches show him doing no such thing, but instead circling Cockatoo Island on the other side of the Harbour Bridge and well down the harbour. It seems safest to trust Ito's own version of the flight. It is also a reasonable guess that he used South Head's Hornby Light and Macquarie Light, both of which had been thoughtfully left burning, to guide him in. His sketched track takes him about halfway between them, directly over the Port War Signal Station on South Head, then on to the easterly end of the boom net. He appears to have decided to leave close inspection of the net for later, and instead dropped down to 1000 feet and continued into the harbour.

The boom net stretched from Laings Point on the eastern side of the inner harbour to Georges Head on the western side. Georges Heights, above Georges Head, commanded a good, clear view of the harbour from the entrance right around to the Harbour Bridge and beyond. The Sydney defences knew what they were doing when they placed an army artillery battery there.

In a television interview, Phil Dulhunty, then an 18-year-old serving with the battery, described what happened next:

This particular night I was on guard duty and I caught the 4 till 6 morning period … the graveyard shift, which was pretty nasty. I was there half asleep and playing around with a couple of possums in a tree. Then suddenly I heard this big truck coming up the hill from down in the artillery battery.

I thought: he's getting an early start. As the noise got closer and closer I saw it was an aeroplane going by, a seaplane. I just thought: it's off the *Chicago* or one of the American warships. You didn't worry about it, nobody worried about it. Everybody thought it was American.

To be fair to the Georges Heights battery, this was not an unreasonable conclusion. When the *Chicago* arrived in Sydney from the Coral Sea a couple of weeks earlier, her spotter planes had flown down the harbour with her. So American cruiser-launched seaplanes were a familiar sight in Sydney. And, as Dulhunty said later, how could a Japanese plane come all this way? It was impossible.

Nevertheless, this was a serious miss, even on a dark night. All servicemen had to study aircraft recognition, and know the difference between Allied and Japanese types. The men at the battery believed the plane to be an American Falcon. Apart from the non-existent American markings—Ito's plane had all its markings painted out—anyone wanting to distinguish a Falcon from a Glen could make a good start by counting the wings: the Falcon was a biplane; the Glen was a monoplane. Furthermore, the Falcon was a land plane. The floatplane version of the Falcon used by US Navy cruisers was the Curtiss Seagull.

The battery crew felt they couldn't simply ignore the aircraft, however harmless. The commander telephoned Garden Island naval base to report it. The duty officer, Lieutenant Percy Wilson, took the call. Wilson was both an able and alert intelligence officer. The report he now received, far from reassuring him, made him very nervous indeed. The battery commander told Wilson the plane was an American Curtiss Falcon float-plane, and that the crew had seen its American markings. On the face of it, the battery commander's report meant there was no problem. Wilson knew differently. He had received an intelligence report that the Japanese had captured a Curtiss Seagull observation plane and therefore might use it for clandestine operations. This particular aircraft type was used only on American cruisers, and Wilson knew from his intelligence plot that, apart from the *Chicago* moored a few hundred metres away, there was no American cruiser anywhere near Sydney Harbour. He asked the security officer at Garden Island, Commander C.F. Mills, if he could go over to the *Chicago* and ask if they knew anything about it.

Meanwhile, Ito's track took him past Rose Bay and Shark Island on his left, and over a fully lit Garden Island and the main concentration of Allied warships. Again he appears to have decided to leave the detailed inspection for later. He continued across Sydney's Central Business District, across Darling Harbour and Birchgrove, to the naval dockyard at Cockatoo Island and the second possible concentration of Allied warships. He made a couple of circuits around Cockatoo Island, noting flashes from the welders' torches, and headed back towards the main harbour.

His flight could not pass unnoticed forever. The searchlights now began to stir. Three times Ito was caught in their beams. Each time he simply climbed into the cloud and disappeared. Nobody fired a shot. A Japanese plane over Sydney Harbour? Impossible.

Ito's track next took him across North Sydney, over the northern harbour suburbs of Neutral Bay, Cremorne and Mosman, behind the battery at Georges Head, across the Royal Australian Navy shore base at HMAS *Penguin* (in Mosman, near the harbour beach of Balmoral) and on to Middle Head. His sketch map shows him at 2300 feet for most of this part of the flight. Clearly he chose to stay close to the cloud base so he could climb for cover if the need arose. He appears to have climbed as high as 3300 feet by the time he reached Middle Head.

At Middle Head Ito turned back towards the inner harbour and began a sharp descent, giving Iwasaki a second chance to sketch the layout of the boom net. He levelled off at a seriously dangerous 160 feet. Harbours, particularly in wartime, are prone to have cables strung across them and to be strewn with various towers and other high obstructions, none of them lit. However at 160 feet Ito could give his observer Iwasaki a chance to identify as well as locate the target ships. So there was no choice. The Glen skimmed towards Point Piper, below the mast height of some big ships, taking a look at the military flying boat base at Rose Bay on its way.

Ito now turned right towards Garden Island. At this low altitude, the low wing design of the Glen was a serious handicap. It blanked out a lot of the view from the cockpit. Ito was forced to bank the plane continually to let Iwasaki see what was below them. They crossed Garden Island at low level, noting a large warship at anchor (the *Chicago*), which Ito doubted was HMS *Warspite*, the battleship he had been told to expect. However here was a cruiser at the very least, with another cruiser (HMAS *Canberra*) further down the harbour. The entire anchorage was littered with juicy targets—destroyers, armed merchant ships, even a submarine.

Ito's mission should have ended now, as he flew past *Chicago*. The cruiser's gunnery officer, William Floyd, had issued instructions that the anti-aircraft guns stay manned even when the ship was at anchor. He recalled later: 'All of the time, day and night, while in the dockyard and later in Sydney Harbour, two anti-aircraft guns, one anti-aircraft director and the associated control party and lookouts were manned.'

However the anti-aircraft crew completely missed the Glen. 'In the *Chicago* not one of the anti-aircraft personnel noted it,' Floyd remembered. 'The Officer of the Deck was the only person who saw it. He was an aviator and identified it as an enemy plane. But it was then too late to take action and it escaped. Obviously during the approximately two weeks in port the watch standing on the anti-aircraft battery had become slack and lackadaisical.'

It is truly incredible that an anti-aircraft crew could fail to notice an unidentified aircraft flying within 200 feet of them. Yet they did. When he heard what had happened, Floyd was furious. He ordered the gun crews to go to a high state of alert. From now on, all hands on watch on the battery would be standing, except the pointers, trainers and rangefinder operators, whose battle duties required them to stay seated. If any more Japanese aircraft appeared, *Chicago* would be ready for them. None did.

Some 20 to 30 minutes had now passed between the Georges Heights sighting of the Glen and the *Chicago* sighting. It is not clear whether Lieutenant Wilson made contact with the officer of the deck on *Chicago,* but it seems unlikely. He returned to Garden Island from *Chicago,* having confirmed that the cruiser's Seagulls were still firmly tied down on the deck. The mystery plane was not *Chicago*'s. Wilson telephoned Fighter Sector Headquarters, then based in a tunnel near Circular Quay in the centre of Sydney. His report relied entirely on the Georges Heights sighting. An unidentified aircraft had been sighted flying in the prohibited area over Sydney Harbour, but Wilson did not specify that it was an enemy aircraft. At 5.07 am fighter headquarters issued an alert and scrambled two Wirraway fighters from Richmond air base, 15 minutes flying time away on the far north-west fringes of Sydney.

None of this troubled Ito and Iwasaki. As they passed over the *Chicago* at Garden Island, Ito's next problem would be the Harbour Bridge, now towering over them. He set the engine roaring at full power and put the Glen into a climbing right turn, giving Iwasaki a lingering chance to look back at Garden Island and the proliferation of targets. The Glen climbed over Kirribilli and followed the northern harbour shore over Cremorne Point and Bradleys Head. The crew had a third and final look at the boom net, then headed out to sea at 3300 feet. The Wirraways never even came close.

This was Sydney's fourth and most serious warning of all. A Japanese reconnaissance plane had flown over the city and been recognised. Yet the *Chicago*'s positive identification of the Glen as a Japanese aircraft does not seem to have been passed on to Rear Admiral Muirhead-Gould or to anyone else in the defence setup. No extra state of readiness was ordered. No defences were stepped up. Instead, Sydney did what it usually did on a Friday: thought about the weekend, perhaps with a lingering look at the racing pages in the papers to see if there was a horse out there somewhere that could make the bookies squirm.

◆　◆　◆

The final moments of Ito's flight posed a serious problem—landing the Glen. Strong winds blowing over the sea create large waves, and the

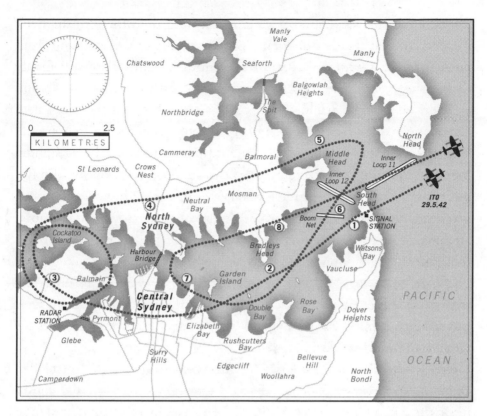

This diagram is based on Ito's own sketch of his track over Sydney. The sequence is: (1) crosses South Head at about 1600 feet, with a good view of the Boom Net; (2) descends to 1000 feet for his first pass over Garden Island and USS *Chicago*, anchored 400 metres east of Garden Island; (3) continues at 1000 feet over central Sydney to Cockatoo Island, where he circles; (4) climbs to 2300 feet as searchlights pick him up; (5) climbs to 3300 feet, probably entering cloud; (6) descends to 160 feet, below the mast level of some ships in the harbour, for a close look at Rose Bay flying boat base and a second intimate inspection of USS *Chicago*; (7) climbs to 500 feet and turns right to avoid Harbour Bridge; (8) continues to climb to 3300 feet while passing over warships anchored in Athol Bay, north-west of Bradleys Head, before crossing the Australian coast at North Head.

waves move in the same direction as the wind. So a seaplane pilot faces an impossible choice in a high wind. If he tries to land into wind, and thereby touch down at the lowest speed, he will inevitably be facing the oncoming waves. The most likely outcome will be for his dangling floats to dig into the crest of an approaching wave and force the plane in a forward somersault onto its back. On the other hand, if he tries to land parallel to the waves, he faces a tricky night crosswind splashdown at higher speed, with the combined wind and waves trying to lift a wing and flip his aircraft sideways onto its back. Either way, he loses. The general rule is: *never* land on water in a strong wind. Ito had no choice.

He appears to have opted to land into wind, and accept the inevitable. His float structure collapsed as the float pontoons bit into an oncoming wave, and the plane flipped onto its back. The two crew were now upside down in cold water, and weighed down with heavy equipment like binoculars. Both kicked their way free and found themselves barely supported by their lifejackets. Ito began swallowing water. In the rough seas, he lost contact with Iwasaki. The next few minutes were taken up with confusion and struggle. Then the mother sub appeared. A line was thrown. Ito hauled himself aboard where, to his relief, he found Iwasaki.

Ito later recalled his emotions as he was being hauled aboard. He thought: 'I must look a mess. What a disgrace!' When he was safely on deck, there was a further, vital duty to be carried out. 'I had to apologise to the commander', he recalled, 'for wrecking the Emperor's aeroplane.'

After the drama of Ito's rescue, the submarine's crew faced an unexpected and comic problem. The Glen refused to sink. They tried firing at the floats with pistols and rifles, but the little aeroplane stubbornly refused to give in. They could not use the sub's big deck gun: the noise and flash would have brought the defences racing to the scene. With sunrise already upon them and the near certainty of patrolling ships and aircraft arriving imminently, the problem became desperate. Eventually the crew attacked the floats with sledgehammers, and the Glen had to admit defeat. It slid under the water, shortly to be followed by a grateful and much relieved submarine and crew.

This story has one final and rather touching episode. Phil Dulhunty, the young soldier who first heard the Glen from his Georges Point guard post, later became a qualified seaplane pilot. He rose to become president of the Seaplane Pilots Association of Australia. He devoted a lot of time and trouble to tracking down Susumo Ito in Japan. He then invited him to become an honorary member of the Australian Seaplane Pilots Association. Ito was delighted to accept.

◆ ◆ ◆

On the evening of 29 May and armed with Ito's detailed report, Sasaki sent his final orders to the Eastern Attack Group:

Telegraph order No 4

1. Day of attack shall be May 31.
2. The enemy situation in Sydney Harbour is:
   (a) One US battleship 400 metres east of Garden Island. One large US transport ship 900 metres north of Garden Island. Several destroyers tied up on the west side of Garden Island. These have anchor lights on. Cockatoo Island has no enemy vessels around it. However there are two light cruisers and a destroyer inside the dockyard.
   (b) No special harbour defences other than a boom net, which must be opened frequently to allow the passage of enemy vessels. There are no enemy patrol boats at the entrances.
   (c) There are no control lights inside the harbour. The lights are on at Barrenjoey lighthouse.
   (d) Merchant ships move in and out of the harbour frequently, with lights on. However some vessels may show anchor lights as a decoy.
3. The following alterations are made to telegraphic order No 3:
   (e) Day 1—No 2 recovery rendezvous off Port Hacking. Pickup point will be 180° 20 nautical miles from Sydney harbour entrance, bearing 100° and 4 nautical miles from Hacking Point, four vessels: I-29, I-27, I-22 and I-24 four kilometres apart. One vessel I-21 to stand 6 kilometres 190° from centre point.

(f)   During daytime standby and night withdrawal, set
       submerged course of 190° and 10°.

(g)   Depending on the situation, some submarines may be
       ordered to search the foreshores on Day 2.

4. For your information: I-21 reconnaissance aircraft
    overturned on landing, no casualties.

Again the New Zealanders intercepted the message. This time their
direction-finding unit placed the sender as a single submarine
40 nautical miles east-south-east of Sydney. Again, it wasn't a bad fix.
And again, there is no evidence that the message was ever decrypted.
Nor is there any evidence that Sydney stepped up its defences, despite
the New Zealanders' warning that there was an enemy sub close off the
heads. Sydney had missed its fifth chance.

◆   ◆   ◆

There was one more chance to come. On the evening of 30 May,
the day after Ito's flight and with almost 24 hours still to go before the
Sydney attack, the midget submarines of the Western Attack Group
struck in the Indian Ocean. In early May the British had successfully
invaded the island of Madagascar, off the east coast of Africa, capturing
it from the Vichy French. This did not suit the Japanese, who almost
certainly wanted it for themselves, particularly the port facilities at Diégo
Suarez on the northern tip of the island. This would have given them a
good command of the Indian Ocean and a chance to disrupt supply
routes between Britain and Australia.

The usual Glen reconnaissance flight was spotted by the British over
Diégo Suarez harbour at 10.30 pm on 29 May. The Royal Navy was
quick to act. The largest ship in the harbour, the elderly battleship HMS
Ramillies, darkened its lights, upped anchor and began moving around
the harbour before anchoring at a new site. All next day it steamed in
circles in the harbour, with its crew on full alert.

Around dusk on 30 May the Western Attack Group launched two
midgets, at least one of which made it into Diégo Suarez harbour.

At 8.15 pm the baby sub fired its first torpedo, which blasted a massive 9-metre square hole in *Ramillies'* plates. The battleship began taking on water and threatened to sink. However, the crew managed to seal off the damaged area and save their ship. An hour later a second torpedo might have finished the job. But the motor tanker *British Loyalty* manoeuvred itself inadvertently into the torpedo's path and paid the price: it sank with the loss of six crew.

The British did not immediately alert their allies around the world. For a start, they were unsure whether the raiders were Japanese or Vichy French. Secondly, they thought it might help the enemy if they were too forthcoming about the success of the raid. So, for the next couple of days, nobody told Sydney that Japanese midget submarines were currently on the prowl, and sneaking into Allied harbours.

Chapter 7

Somehow come back alive

The very new Lieutenant Reg Andrew RAN was due to take command of the Channel Patrol boat HMAS *Sea Mist* at midnight on 31 May. He decided, however, to take his first look at his new ship in daylight, and arrived at Farm Cove around 4 pm on the Sunday afternoon. The handover was about as thorough as the training he had received at Flinders Naval Depot.

'The officer I took over from took the *Sea Mist* away from the moorings in Farm Cove,' Andrew recalled. 'He did a circle around Farm Cove and he brought her back ready to go alongside one of the other ships there. He said to me: "You take over the controls and bring her in alongside." All I had to do was slow reverse and put the line on board, and that was it. He said: "You're okay. You're the commanding officer from now on."'

Sea Mist was not due to go out on patrol that night, so Reg Andrew simply stowed his gear on board and set about getting to know his crew. Each Channel Patrol boat had a crew of around eight. They usually worked a four-on, four-off shift system so that the entire crew seldom sailed together. The rule was simple: each boat should carry a minimum crew of three at all times. The rest was up to the skipper and the roster.

On the night of 31 May, *Sea Mist* had on board a coxswain, Potter; a signalman, Hunter; a stoker, Williams; and a motor mechanic, Winstanley.

Reg Andrew approved of his crew. Coxswain Potter he described as 'a short man with a balding head who was very proud of his ship. I was informed he nearly cried when I managed to put green seas over his beloved fo'c'sle.' Potter was an experienced seaman. Unlike the skipper, he knew how to set depth charges.

Signalman Hunter 'was dark in complexion and used to stutter. He was a good, all-round able seaman.' Stoker Williams was 'a wiry man in his forties, older than Hunter but like a teenager with his practical jokes'. Mechanic Winstanley was 'fair, tall and young and gave the impression of being a GPS graduate. He was a good motor mechanic and did an excellent job.' In Sydney, GPS stands for Greater Public School and refers to the city's eight most prestigious fee-paying schools. Branding Winstanley as being like a GPS graduate but a good mechanic was Reg Andrew's way of saying that, despite his polished accent and manners, Winstanley was a good bloke.

As the weather was foul and *Sea Mist* was not on duty that night, there was no incentive to hang around on the deck. Around nine o'clock, while one man kept watch, the new skipper and crew opted to go below and get a good night's sleep.

◆　　◆　　◆

Roy Cooté was one of the Australian Navy's most skilled and experienced divers. In 1942 the scuba (self-contained underwater breathing apparatus) diving system had yet to be invented. Divers instead dressed in heavy and clumsy watertight suits weighed down with lead-lined boots and topped with a brass helmet. Underwater they could see out through three small glass windows built into the helmet. A tender on the surface pumped air at high pressure down to the diver below. As well as the airline, the diver was connected to the surface by a telephone line and a lifeline, so he was able to communicate and perhaps be rescued if something went wrong. The work was difficult and dangerous. On top of the regular diving hazard of the 'bends', the diver's vital airlines and lifelines to the surface were vulnerable to jagged edges underwater, particularly on the hulls of damaged or wrecked ships. The suit was also vulnerable to puncture, and to leaks.

In wartime, the work was particularly demanding and Roy Cooté often worked weekends. However, he had one piece of good fortune: he lived in Mosman, a northern harbourside suburb of Sydney which was home to HMAS *Penguin*, the shore base for navy divers. He was able to go home to his family when not on duty.

His son Kevin remembers the weekend of 30 and 31 May as like any other. The two Cooté boys, Kevin and Jeff, regularly spent their weekends with the Sea Scouts. They would go to the clubhouse in Mosman Bay on Friday evening and sleep there on Friday and Saturday night, spending the daytime on Saturday and Sunday sailing on the harbour. While they were safely with the scouts, their parents invariably set off on a trip somewhere, perhaps to Newcastle or to the Blue Mountains. The family reassembled at home on Sunday evening about six or seven o'clock.

That weekend Roy Cooté finished work at 1 pm on Saturday, so he still had most of the weekend to himself. The previous week had been busy, ending with a particularly tough Friday. His dive log for the fourth week of May 1942 records:

Monday 25: Dived HMIS Madras, had cable round screws and rudder.
Thursday 28: Dived on boom net.
Friday 29: Dived telephone cable No 1 Buoy and for stores at Garden Island. Dived for damage to Battle Practice Target.

Given the problem of absorption of nitrogen into the blood during prolonged dives—the cause of the 'bends'—three dives in a single Friday was a lot to undertake. As the Cooté family went to bed in Mosman on Sunday night, Roy Cooté probably hoped Monday wouldn't be quite so demanding.

◆   ◆   ◆

An overweight English admiral with a hyphenated name and a reputation for pomposity is about as soft a target as exists. Yet to portray Gerard Charles Muirhead-Gould as some kind of Gilbert and Sullivan caricature would be both unjust and untrue.

He was the son of a British Army officer, and joined the Royal Navy as a cadet in January 1904. He served with distinction in World War I, being awarded a DSC. He was also made a Chevalier of the Legion of Honour by France and a Chevalier of the Order of the Redeemer by Greece. He spoke five languages.

Having spent some time in Naval Intelligence, between 1933 and 1936 he was sent to serve in the British Embassy in Berlin as naval attaché. Here he showed both courage and a clear head. Hitler's massive military build-up was well under way, and Muirhead-Gould set out to raise the alarm. Winston Churchill was in the middle of his 'wilderness years', cast out from mainstream British politics and a lone voice warning against the Nazi threat. Muirhead-Gould agreed with Churchill. He crossed the border from Berlin into Poland to post personal letters to Churchill setting out both his knowledge and his fears. The correspondence can be found in the Churchill archive.

In a letter dated 28 October 1935 Muirhead-Gould wrote to Churchill praising Churchill's speech in the House of Commons on German rearmament. He added that he had to leave Germany before sending the letter as the Germans were so annoyed with Churchill for telling the truth that no letters addressed to him would have got out of the country. Churchill's enemies had to concede that he always appeared remarkably well informed about German affairs: Muirhead-Gould was one of his sources. Given that the British government was in the midst of its appeasement phase, Muirhead-Gould was acting against government policy while still a serving British diplomat. If he had been caught it might have cost him his job. If the Germans had found out what he was up to, they might have taken even more drastic steps.

Despite a reputation for pomposity, Muirhead-Gould was capable of a light touch. In 1944 he wrote an article 'Berlin Memories' for the

Australian War Memorial journal *HMAS Mk III*. In it he recalled how he had met Hitler only once, at a state banquet in Berlin. He was introduced to the *Führer* by Goebbels, who briefly left the two men alone together. Hitler talked about films. He particularly admired a Hollywood film *The Lives of a Bengal Lancer*, a 1935 black-and-white British Raj blood-in-the-dust epic starring the unlikely figure of Gary Cooper in the title role.

'I liked it very much,' said Hitler. 'I have seen it six times. It is a remarkable film, and I have given orders that it is to be shown to every school in Germany. It will show my young men how the pure Aryan races handle the barbarians.' This astonishing piece of social history, with a little film criticism thrown in, certainly falls into the category of little-known facts about Adolf Hitler.

In February 1940 Muirhead-Gould was posted to Australia as Naval Officer in Command, Sydney. It was a prestigious appointment, though usually reserved for an officer headed for retirement. Muirhead-Gould might have gone on to greater things. When he became Prime Minister in May 1940, Churchill was said to have considered recalling him from Sydney to become head of Britain's Secret Intelligence Service, MI6— the role of 'M' in the James Bond books and films. However, Churchill's musings came to nothing, and Muirhead-Gould stayed in Sydney until September 1944.

His was not a popular appointment. Muirhead-Gould came from the more class-ridden traditions of the British Navy, where officers are gentlemen and other ranks know their place. It was a world of servants, fine claret and good silverware, and remote from the more egalitarian Australian Navy, where pomposity could cost an officer a bloody nose as well as loss of his authority. Muirhead-Gould was variously known as 'Manurehead-Gould' and 'Boofhead' (a popular comic strip of the time.)

One of the perks of Muirhead-Gould's appointment was 'Tresco', a magnificent sandstone house on the western shore of the fashionable inner Sydney harbour suburb of Elizabeth Bay. A long set of steps led from the rear of the house down to the water, where the Admiral's barge took less than five minutes to deliver him to his headquarters on Garden

Island, 500 metres away. It offered Sydney Harbour's commander and his wife a gracious life, as befitted a senior naval officer in his final appointment before retirement.

Muirhead-Gould turned 53 on 29 May 1942—the day of Ito's flight over Sydney Harbour. There is no record of how he marked the day. However, we do know how he planned his Sunday evening on 31 May. He had invited Captain Howard Bode (pronounced 'Bow-de'), commander of the USS *Chicago*, and a group of *Chicago*'s senior officers to dinner at 'Tresco'. This would have been an all-male affair, with officers turning up in black tie and full-dress naval uniform. As well as the normal courtesy extended to the captain and officers of an important visiting Allied warship, the dinner would be something of a celebration. *Chicago* had just returned scarred but triumphant from the Battle of the Coral Sea.

If things ran according to the usual British invitation-to-dinner pattern, the evening would begin around 7 pm with pre-dinner drinks, followed by a dinner with wine served some time after eight, all of it prepared and brought to the table by Muirhead-Gould's personal stewards. The food and wine we can only guess at. But we do know that Muirhead-Gould regularly offered visiting officers a glass or three of pink gin. For the uninitiated, this is a traditional tipple of British naval officers: swirl a few drops of Angostura bitters in the bottom of a glass, then stir in neat gin, quantity at the discretion of the pourer. No ice. No water. No lemon. No tonic. It is not a drink for the faint-hearted.

◆　　◆　　◆

On the Japanese mother submarines of the Eastern Attack Group, now assembled off Sydney Heads on 31 May, the mood was sombre. The crews were painfully aware that five midget submarines had set off for Pearl Harbor on 7 December, and none had returned. Nine of the 10 Pearl Harbor crews were presumed dead. The Sydney mission would be perilous in the extreme, and there was little chance those remaining behind on the mother submarines would see any of the midget crews again.

The naming and numbering of the midget submarines is endlessly confusing. The Japanese often treated the midgets and their mother submarines as each having the same number. For instance, in Sasaki's third telegraphic order recounted in Chapter 5 he refers to the midgets themselves as I-22, I-24 and I-27, although this was in fact the number of their mother submarines. The most common convention is to number the midgets after their mother subs, but using an 'M' instead of an 'I'. Under this numbering system, the original four midget-carrying 'I' class mother subs I-22, I-24, I-27 and I-28 carried midgets designated M-22, M-24, M-27 and M-28 respectively. I-28 had been sunk by the American submarine *Tautog* before reaching Truk, leaving only I-22, I-24 and I-27 to carry their midgets south. The midget M-24 had been damaged on its first day out of Truk lagoon, so I-24 returned to Truk and collected M-28. Under the conventional numbering system, the final attack group consisted of M-22 aboard I-22, M-27 aboard I-27, and M-28 aboard I-24.

However, the Japanese Navy used a different numbering system, giving each midget a unique designator beginning 'Ha', and this system has been followed in a number of accounts, most importantly in Muirhead-Gould's two reports on the raid. Under this system M-27 is more correctly designated Ha-14, while M-22 becomes Ha-21. To compound the confusion Muirhead-Gould refers to Ha-14 as M-14, and to Ha-21 as M-21. He then adds into his account a Midget 'A' (Ban's midget) and a Midget 'B' (which didn't exist, being Matsuo's midget mistakenly counted twice). To spare the reader (and the author) a lot of unnecessary head-scratching, from now on in this narrative the midgets will be identified by the names of their commanders: Chuman's midget (M-27 or Ha-14 or M-14 or I-27); Matsuo's midget (M-22 or Ha-21 or M-21 or I-22 or Midget 'B'); and Ban's midget (M-28 or Ha-24 or I-24 or Midget 'A'). Whew!

Although the midget commanders had all attended the same naval college and passed through the same training programme, they were very different personalities. The most senior was Lieutenant Keiu Matsuo. His life is also the best documented.

Matsuo was born on 21 July 1917 in Yamaga in the Kumamoto province, the son of an elementary schoolmaster. He had an older brother Jikyo and a younger sister Fujie. He came from a long line of warriors—he could trace his *bushido* ancestry back to the 14th century. He was a black belt judo champion. Matsuo was unusually tall for the midget programme, fair-skinned and softly spoken. He is remembered as gentle, but he could be roused to volcanic anger when things went wrong. He took risks. His fellow students' strongest memory was of his determination: once he had decided on a course of action, he never gave up.

Matsuo's role went well beyond manning the midget which entered Sydney Harbour. He had been one of the principal strategists of the midget submarine programme. In the early days of the midgets, the intention had been to launch the tiny subs from warships in the midst of a battle, and have them wreak havoc on the enemy. Matsuo argued differently: naval warfare would in future not be waged in a series of tumultuous clashes between powerful opposing fleets. So this role for the midgets would be unproductive; war at sea would be decided by air power. The better role for the midgets would be to penetrate enemy harbours and sink warships at anchor.

In October 1941, two months before Japan entered the war, Matsuo was sent to Honolulu aboard the Japanese freighter *Tatsuta Maru* to reconnoitre Pearl Harbor. Quite simply, he was a spy: he travelled under an assumed name, with false papers. During the raid on Pearl Harbor he acted as Captain Sasaki's assistant, briefing the midget crews on the basis of knowledge he had gathered on the spot six weeks earlier.

Much has been made over the years of whether these midget submarine raids were suicide missions. They were not. In the early 21st century the suicide attack is, sadly, a more familiar weapon than it was in 1942. But a suicide bomber boarding a bus in Tel Aviv or a Tube train in London knows that his or her own death is an integral part of the mission. For the attack to work, the bomber must die too. This was never true of the midgets. The crews carried food and water for a week, and were under strict orders to do their utmost to return. It has been said that there was a pact among the midget crews not to meet up with the mother subs, because the rendezvous would expose both mother sub and midget crews to attack. Better for two men to die on the midget than risk 101 lives on the mother sub. But this makes no sense either: the mother subs were all committed to wait at the rendezvous point for three or four days after an attack, and the midget crews knew they would do this. The rendezvous point was necessarily close to the scene of the attack, because the midgets had limited range. So if the midget crew returned as agreed, the mother sub could make a quick getaway. If the midget crew did not return, the mother sub would be condemned to spend three or four days loitering under the noses of an angry and vengeful defence. The mother subs were exposed to much greater risk from the non-return of the crews than they ever would be from a successful rendezvous and a quick departure.

That having been said, everybody involved in the midget programme knew that the chances that a midget crew would survive a raid were close to nil. Nine of the 10 submariners at Pearl Harbor were thought to have perished. And, although they were in no position to know this at the time in Sydney, the crews of the midget submarines which had attacked Diégo Suarez less than 24 hours earlier had also been killed. So there was every reason to be downcast, however glorious the prospects of the attack might be.

Keiu Matsuo certainly seems to have been reconciled to his death. At the end of March, two months before the raid, he had asked his parents and brother and sister to meet him at Kure naval base for dinner. His mother thought he looked pale and stressed. He told his family he would shortly be embarking on a secret mission, of which he could tell them nothing. At the end of dinner he asked his family to tell his fiancée, Toshiko Knoshita, that their engagement must be broken.

After dinner his father presented him with a short, ceremonial sword wrapped in red brocade from his mother's wedding-day *obi* (kimono sash). His sister Fujie presented him with a 1000-stitch *senninbari* (stomach protector). This was a traditional gift to a warrior about to go into battle. As ceremony required, the first stitch was applied by someone close to him, in this case, Fujie. The remaining stitches each came from 999 other women. A lucky five-sen coin had also been sewn into the *senninbari* by Fujie. It would protect Matsuo.

On 27 May, while still on board the mother submarine, he wrote a last letter to his parents. He told them of his love for Toshiko. 'I find it unbearable that I shall not see her again. She knows my feelings for her but I ask you to take care of her.'

Matsuo's crewman aboard the midget was Petty Officer First Class Masao Tsuzuku. He was a farm boy who had left school early, never reaching secondary school. However, he studied hard to enter the navy. He failed his first entrance exam on health grounds, but passed his second with flying colours, overtaking others with full secondary school education. In his final letter to his brother Ichiza he wrote: 'When you receive this letter you will know that I was killed in the Australian area on May 31. I have nothing to regret. Today I will enter —— harbour in order to strike an enemy battleship. Take care of my parents and sisters.' He left 50 yen to his village elementary school.

We know less of the other two crews. The next most senior was Lieutenant Kenshi Chuman. He is remembered as the most conventional and the most unassuming of the three midget commanders. He wrote a last letter to his parents just before the attack, assuring them that he would succeed in his mission. The letter was to be delivered after his death. He gave 500 yen to crewmen on his mother submarine I-27, to be given to relatives of his navigator, Petty Officer First Class Takeshi Omori, in the event of their death in the attack. On the mission, Chuman took with him his short, ceremonial sword. He tucked it into a leather scabbard and tied it up with a brown tasselled cord in a long bag of soft, purple silk. The lining of the bag had Chuman's name inscribed inside it.

Sub-Lieutenant Katsuhisa Ban was the most junior of the three commanders. He was the son of a highly decorated soldier, and could have chosen a career in either the navy or the army—he had passed the entrance exams for both the Naval and Military acadamies. Ban joined the Sydney attack at the last minute, after the explosion aboard I-24's midget. He is remembered as the most dashing, the daredevil of the three midget commanders. His handsome young face stares clear-eyed from his photographs, his jaw firm and his back straight. Ban was the most outspoken in his dismissal of the fear of death. 'Nations that fear death will surely be destroyed,' he wrote just before the attack. 'It is necessary for the youth of Japan to take notice of this. "Sure to die" is the guiding spirit that will bring about the final victory.'

His crewman, Petty Officer First Class Mamoru Ashibe, was the third sibling in a family of eight brothers and sisters. Although Ashibe did not expect to survive the mission, he expected to die gloriously. The midget submarine programme was top secret, and Ashibe said nothing about it to his parents or neighbours. However, he confided to his younger brother Itsuo: 'If the war starts, I will be in a special two-man submarine. It will attack at close range. If war breaks out, I'll be first to perform a feat. Look forward to hearing about me.' Aboard the I-24 mother submarine he wrote a final letter to his mother, asking her not to weep when she heard he had been killed.

As they waited off Sydney Heads, the three crews had practical duties to perform. Based on the briefing from Ito's flight over Sydney, they had to ensure that their torpedoes were correctly set for the task ahead. One of the weaknesses of the Japanese midget design was the sheer difficulty of altering torpedo settings from inside the midget. The torpedoes were 'muzzle loading', which meant they were loaded into their tubes from outside the submarine. They had to be pre-set and fitted into their launching tubes well before an attack (for the Sydney raid, they were probably set and loaded at Truk Lagoon, but they may have been set as far away as Japan). Each torpedo tube then had a bow cap clamped over it, which could be cleared away remotely from inside the midget before firing. In theory the crew could change a torpedo's settings whenever they liked from inside the midget, but in practice this process was slow and complicated, not something to be attempted in the heat of battle. The commander was largely stuck with whatever setting had been programmed into the torpedo before the mission began. As they waited with the mother submarines off the heads on 31 May, the crews had a last chance to choose their torpedo settings.

Torpedoes can generally be set for speed, depth of running, and deflection. There was no need for the midget commanders to worry about speed. Their torpedoes had only one setting: flat-out at 44 knots.

Depth of running would determine which ships could be attacked and which could not. A torpedo set to run deep would pass harmlessly under a small warship but do maximum damage to a battleship or an aircraft carrier. Matsuo and Chuman set their torpedoes to run at 6 metres below the surface—a fairly deep setting even for a battleship or heavy cruiser—while Ban chose the slightly more conservative 5 metres.

The next question was deflection. The Type 97 Special torpedo carried by the Japanese midgets could be set to turn after firing by up to 60 degrees to the left or right, with the deflection angle marked in 5-degree intervals. A submarine commander might choose his deflection with one of two plans in mind. If he thought he would be attacking a moving ship, then deflection could take into account the movement of his target. It is a complicated calculation, though no more complicated than the instinctive judgement of a clay pigeon marksman: aim ahead of the target's movement, so that the target glides into the line of the shot. A commander might line his submarine up pointing directly at a target moving right to left, and fire his torpedo with 30 degrees left deflection. The target would then—he hoped—keep moving left into the torpedo's path.

However, there was a second reason for choosing a deflected shot: it made the whereabouts of an attacking submarine less easy to trace. Torpedoes leave a highly visible wake in the water: follow back along the line of the wake and there's the submarine. If the torpedo is set at 60-degree deflection and the submarine moves off quickly after firing, then the wide angle between the torpedo's wake and the submarine's course makes the sub harder to find and attack. Matsuo and Chuman set their torpedoes at zero deflection. The dashing Ban set his torpedoes at 60 degrees left deflection.*

---

* It is worth noting that Matsuo's and Chuman's midgets were loaded aboard their mother submarines on a different day from Ban's submarine. Matsuo's and Chuman's midgets were loaded onto their mother submarines first. Ban's midget joined the attack a day later, after the explosion at sea aboard I-24's midget. This difference in timing of loading may be a factor in the variation in settings. However, it is more likely that each commander knew what he was doing, and chose the setting which suited him best for the task ahead.

The torpedoes had to be checked to confirm that they would 'arm' correctly. Torpedoes have an abundance of anti-social habits, but two in particular trouble a submarine commander. The sudden jerk when launching can cause an 'armed' torpedo to explode in its tube, destroying its submarine. And a runaway torpedo is capable of turning in a full circle after launch and attacking its own submarine instead of the target. This is particularly true of torpedoes set with a large deflection. To guard against these dangers, each torpedo has to be set to 'arm' well after launch. A small propeller on the outside of the torpedo is made to spin by its movement through the water. After the propeller completes a chosen number of revolutions, it 'arms' the torpedo. Only then is the torpedo capable of exploding. The torpedoes carried on the midgets needed to run some distance underwater before they armed. The actual trigger which then detonates the armed torpedo is an 'inertia pistol'. This is a simple device which sets off the torpedo when it stops suddenly—as it does when it hits the side of a ship, or anything else solid. All three midget commanders carried torpedoes set to arm only when well clear of their submarines.

Finally, the submarines needed to be stocked with provisions for seven days. Each sub took aboard mineral water, wine, whisky and concentrated foods. A typical meal might be 100 grams of soda biscuits, 25 grams of dried bonito, 10 pickled plums, 10 peas, 25 grams of soft chocolate and six caramels. The submarines also carried what were delicately referred to as sanitary utensils.

◆   ◆   ◆

On the afternoon of 31 May, the midget crews began the traditional Japanese warrior's eve-of-battle purification. Each crewman cleansed himself with sake wine, and put on clean clothing, including clean underwear. Their clean uniforms had previously been impregnated with perfumed oil. Some shaved their heads. Each man prayed to his god-emperor at a candlelit Shinto shrine. They drank a little warm sake with the crew of the mother subs, to bring them all health and long life. They ate a farewell meal.

At the end of his meal, Keiu Matsuo asked one of the crew of his mother sub I-22 to cut his hair. While the cutting proceeded, Matsuo was heard to say, almost to himself: 'I wonder what my mother is thinking now?' Sub-Lieutenant Muneaki Fujisawa, the stand-in barber, concluded that Matsuo knew he would not return from his mission. 'Unconsciously, my hand holding the clippers stopped,' Fujisawa recalled. 'I can feel a man's determination hidden in his mind. Lieutenant Matsuo had resolved to die—I felt that intuitively.'

Susumo Ito, whose last-minute flight in the Glen had confirmed the value of Sydney as a target, remembers the mood on board the mother submarines. 'It was heart-rending for those of us who sent them off,' he recalled. 'We knew it was for the sake of our country, but it would cost the lives of six young men. It was so painful to see them go to an almost certain death. We wished they would somehow manage to come back alive.'

Part II

ATTACK

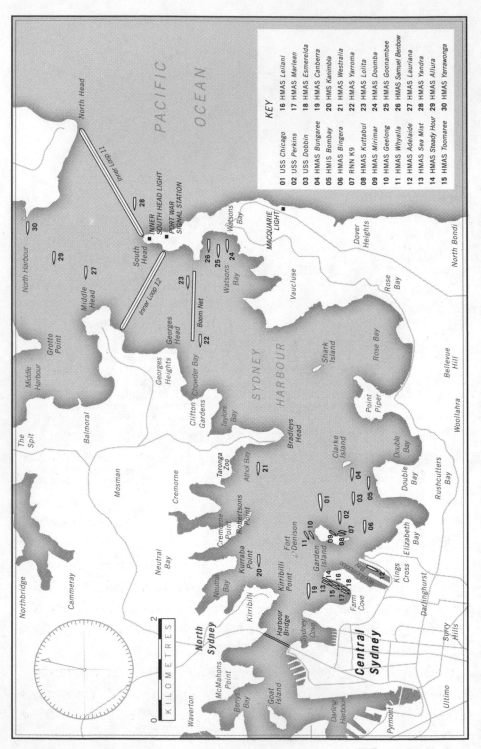

KEY

01 USS Chicago	16 HMAS Leilani
02 USS Perkins	17 HMAS Marlean
03 USS Dobbin	18 HMAS Esmerelda
04 HMAS Bungaree	19 HMS Canberra
05 HMIS Bombay	20 HMS Kanimbla
06 HMIS Bingera	21 HMAS Westralia
07 RNN K9	22 HMAS Yarroma
08 HMAS Kuttabul	23 HMAS Lolita
09 HMAS Mirimar	24 HMAS Doomba
10 HMAS Geelong	25 HMAS Goonambee
11 HMAS Whyalla	26 HMAS Samuel Benbow
12 HMAS Adelaide	27 HMAS Lauriana
13 HMAS Sea Mist	28 HMAS Yandra
14 HMAS Steady Hour	29 HMAS Allura
15 HMAS Toomaree	30 HMAS Yarrawonga

Allied fighting ships in Sydney Harbour on the night of 31 May 1942. These are their positions at 8 pm.

Chapter 8

The net

There was no shortage of fighting ships inside Sydney Harbour on the night of 31 May 1942. There were three US Navy ships: the heavy cruiser USS *Chicago*, the destroyer *Perkins* and the destroyer tender *Dobbin*. The Australian Navy had the heavy cruiser HMAS *Canberra*, the light cruiser *Adelaide*, the armed merchant cruiser *Westralia*, two corvettes *Geelong* and *Whyalla*, two anti-submarine vessels *Bingera* and *Yandra*, three minesweepers *Goonambee*, *Samuel Benbow* and *Doomba*, a minelayer *Bungaree*, 10 Channel Patrol boats *Yarroma*, *Silver Cloud*, *Steady Hour*, *Sea Mist*, *Lolita*, *Toomaree*, *Marlean*, *Miramar*, *Leilani* and *Esmerelda*, three Naval Auxiliary Patrol boats *Lauriana*, *Allura* and *Yarrawonga*, and the converted ferry, now a depot ship, *Kuttabul*. The British Navy had an armed merchant cruiser HMS *Kanimbla*. The Indian Navy had a corvette HMIS *Bombay*. The Dutch Navy had a submarine RNN *K9*. The Free French had a destroyer *Le Triomphant*. It was a fair-sized force to face six men in three midget submarines.

However, most of these ships were off duty and on various levels of notice, from four hours to 12 hours, before they could move. Many of their crews were on shore leave. Inside Sydney Harbour, the final line of defence rested with six duty ships. They were the anti-submarine vessel HMAS *Yandra*, patrolling the area between the boom net and the open ocean, two unarmed Naval Auxiliary Patrol boats *Lauriana* and *Allura* covering the area between North Head, Manly and Middle Head, and the third unarmed NAP launch *Yarrawonga* standing off inner North Head outside the Quarantine Station. Further inside the harbour two Channel Patrol boats HMAS *Yarroma* and *Lolita* with their Vickers machine-guns and depth charges, guarded the boom net and its entrance channels. The Western Channel had been closed to shipping for a fortnight, so ferries and other traffic passed down the Eastern Channel and through the gap at the eastern end of the boom net. *Lolita* covered the busy eastern gate; *Yarroma* could look forward to a quiet night at the western gate.

HMAS *Yandra* was neither new nor particularly well armed or equipped. She was built in Copenhagen in 1928, and had been working for the Coast Steam Ship Company of Adelaide before being requisitioned for the Royal Australian Navy on 27 June 1940. She was commissioned on 22 September 1940, having been converted to anti-submarine warfare by the addition of some detection gear plus a 4-inch gun, a .303 Maxim machine-gun, a .303 Vickers, a two-pounder and two depth charge throwers. She could scarcely be said to be bristling. She was also slow and comparatively heavy at 990 tons.

The *Lauriana* was the most senior duty NAP on the night of 31 May, and put to sea with a crew of nine including her owner and regular skipper Harold Arnott, the biscuit baron. That night she carried the NAP flotilla leader L.H. Winkworth on board, so Winkworth and not Arnott was the most senior officer.

The *Lauriana*'s log for 31 May opens with the usual trivia of a dull night on patrol.

> 1810: Left moorings. Duty officer requested us place a man on 'Yarrawonga' as crew. Spoke 'Yarrawonga' gave written instructions. Handed 'Allura' instructions. Proceeding. Contacted Channel Boat 1845 E. end of boom. Got very sketchy instructions L.F.B. [Licensed Fishing Boat] list and note that Air Force launch

Vera with Air Force men possibly American returning to port. Put D. Howell aboard Yarrawonga. Proceeding with Patrol. All lights out.

1900: Proceeding O.K. S.E. roll. No moon. Channel Boat on boom. Allura off for tea.

1950: 'Allura' back on patrol. We going to Q'tine for tea.

2008: Moored for Tea, Q'tine.

2050: Proceeding with patrol. Moon up but cloudy, contacted Y'wonga.

◆   ◆   ◆

The five mother submarines of the Eastern Attack Group moved to their initial positions off Sydney Heads some time around the middle of the day on 31 May. They first took up station on a huge arc with a 20-nautical-mile radius from the harbour entrance. The I-27 carrying Chuman's midget waited on the north-east rim of the arc, the I-22 carrying Matsuo's midget stood off to the east, and the I-24 carrying Ban's midget positioned itself to the south-east. A little further outside the arc, the floatplane carrier I-29 waited between the I-27 and the I-22, while the other floatplane carrier I-21 waited between the I-22 and the I-24. The I-21 carried the attack group's commander Hanku Sasaki.

As the afternoon progressed, the three midget-carrying mother ships crept fully submerged in to positions about 7 nautical miles off the heads. It is possible that they had intelligence that the harbour was protected by indicator loops, because they chose their new stations at a point well beyond the six outer loops. Not that it mattered. Two of the six loops were unserviceable, so the whole lot had been left unmanned. The three mother subs were all at their launch points around 4 pm, giving the midget crews an hour to squeeze into their subs and carry out final checks before launching. The sun set at 4.54 pm. The crews waited a little longer for total darkness.

Matsuo launched first. Captain Kiyoi Ageta, who had carried a midget to Pearl Harbor on the same I-22 six months earlier, gave the fateful order, 'Cut the line. Remove the second band. Take off,' some time around 5.20. Ageta heard the midget's propellers begin turning at 5.21. The raid had begun.

Chuman launched next, at 5.28 pm. Ban was last to launch, at 5.40 pm. The full moon would rise at 6.15 pm. The plan called for Chuman to enter the harbour ahead of the others, some time around 6.35 pm, when the moon would give a little light. Matsuo and Ban would follow at 20-minute intervals.

Each submarine carried copies of three British Admiralty charts: Admiralty no. 1021 covering Port Jackson (Sydney Harbour) to Port Stephens north of Sydney; Admiralty no. 1020 covering Jervis Bay south of Sydney to Port Jackson; and Admiralty no. 1069 showing Port Jackson in detail. On Admiralty no. 1020 the crews had pencilled in the rendezvous point off Port Hacking, to the south of Sydney, to which they would return after the raid. The old rendezvous point off Broken Bay had been pencilled in on 1021.

On Admiralty no. 1069 Matsuo had carefully drawn his intended track into Sydney Harbour: the midget would enter the harbour from a position 200 metres south of North Head, then track north-west parallel to the North Head coast; from a position south of the Quarantine Station on North Head he would then turn south-west towards Middle Head; at 150 metres from Middle Head he would turn further south, following the Western Channel through the gap in the boom net and on to a point 1500 metres south of Bradleys Head; then he would turn towards Garden Island and the USS *Chicago*.

The heavy swell outside the harbour made navigation difficult. As well, the strong currents gave the crews some awkward decisions. The prevailing sea current outside Sydney Heads flows from north to south, at 1 to 2 knots. The subs' most economical cruising speed was 3 knots. To fight their way across the current, the commanders would have to set a higher speed. But that would place a strain on their battery reserves. All three subs found the going difficult. They all ran very late.

Navigation as far as the harbour entrance was simplified by the thoughtfulness of the port authorities. The Hornby Light on the tip of

South Head burned brightly, as did its companion Macquarie Light 1500 metres further south on Outer South Head. The Sydney port command, civilian and naval, didn't want any ships to miss their harbour entrance. At 5.25 pm, four minutes after launch, Matsuo fixed his position as 7.2 nautical miles from the Macquarie Light, on a bearing of 260 degrees, putting him directly outside the harbour entrance. He made three more fixes on his way towards the heads: 4.1 nautical miles from the Macquarie Light, on a bearing of 253 degrees; 3.6 miles on 247 degrees; and 1.7 miles on 260 degrees.

Each commander knew that navigation inside the harbour would be fiendishly difficult. The subs would need to travel submerged, or at best at periscope depth. Although the two lighthouses on South Head burned brightly, the lead (navigation) lights inside the harbour had been blacked out. The commanders would be in a strange harbour at night, with strong tides and unpredictable currents, and a boom net to negotiate, all by the weak light of a moon blocked by cloud. It says a great deal for their skill and seamanship that all three made it.

◆   ◆   ◆

Chuman arrived first, as planned. During training the sub crews had devised a simple tactic for entering harbours—follow somebody else. This had everything going for it. Submarines are detected by hydrophones, listening devices which pick up engine and propeller noise, and by sound echoes from anti-submarine detection devices like ASDIC. But if the submarine is close to another ship then there is every chance that any indications given off by the sub will be misread as coming from the other ship. A further and equally important advantage is that the navigation problem is solved: the fully lit ship being followed can be presumed to know what it is doing when it comes to dodging rocks and reefs, not to mention boom nets.

Manly ferries normally use the Western Channel in Sydney Harbour. However, the Western Channel was closed to shipping on 31 May, so the 7.30 pm ferry from Manly to Circular Quay was forced to head across the harbour for the Eastern Channel. Chuman tucked in behind it. The ferry was already running late, and the extended journey across the harbour made it run even later. At 7.59 the ferry crossed Inner Loop 12. At 8.01 so did Chuman. Both, as we have seen, left a good trace. Nobody stirred.

What happened next is a matter for conjecture. We know that Chuman's fellow submariner Matsuo intended to enter the harbour via the Western Channel, and it may be that all three submarine commanders planned to use this wider and simpler way in. We also know that *Lolita* was stationed on the net close to the entrance to the Eastern Channel while *Yarroma* was a fair distance from the Western Channel gap. It may be that Chuman sized this up and decided he stood a better chance of passing through the western gate undetected. For whatever reason, instead of following the ferry through the eastern gate, Chuman headed across the harbour, past the Sow and Pigs reef, to the western end of the boom net and its easier entrance. He slipped gratefully through the gap into the inner harbour and target zone.

At this point it is worth noting that so far Chuman had cleared the ring of six outer indicator loops (not in service), crossed Inner Loop 11 without leaving a trace, evaded the specialist anti-submarine patrol of HMAS *Yandra* guarding the harbour entrance, evaded the three NAP boats *Lauriana, Allura* and *Yarrawonga* watching the area immediately inside the heads, crossed Inner Loop 12 which picked him up but whose human monitors ignored him, then slipped through a 293-metre gap in a net built for the specific purpose of keeping submarines out. All this while evading detection by the Channel Patrol boat *Yarroma* charged with the task of keeping an eye on the very gap he had just used. He deserved a better fate than that which now befell him.

Almost every published account, from G. Hermon Gill's official history of the Royal Australian Navy to the various books, magazine articles and television documentaries about the raid, describes Chuman charging head first into the ocean side of the boom net while trying to find his way into the harbour, and getting stuck in the process. Some accounts go into elaborate detail, describing the sub backing and shoving, trying to use its bow cutters to hack its way in. This is not what happened.

The only account which fits all the known facts comes from Jimmy Cargill, the nightwatchman who first saw the sub. In his own words, and in his delightful Scottish brogue, this is how events unfolded.

> The first Jap that came in, he must have seen me and he dived to get through the gate, like so I wouldn't see him. The gate was open . . . it wasn't finished then. He came through the gate and about 80 feet [around 24 metres] inside the gate he went off his course a little bit and hit the Pile Light. Of course, he was submerged on the bottom then. Well he went astern and he got one of the big rings [of the net] around his propeller.

This account makes total sense. We can ignore the suggestion that Chuman dived after seeing Cargill: he was probably already well submerged when he attempted to pass through the gate. Having found the gap, Chuman would need to turn left, towards the centre of the harbour. Contemporary photographs show the Pile Light as just inside the net opposite the third pile. The midgets were about 24 metres long. If the Pile Light was a bit over 24 metres from the net, and Chuman bumped into it while submerged and in the dark, his first instinct would be to put the sub into reverse and back off the obstruction. He would not need to back far to jam his propellers into the net, and that is certainly what he did—as Roy Cooté's photograph in the photo section illustrates. Chuman was trapped between the second and third piles of the net—directly opposite the Pile Light.* Jimmy Cargill's version matches the facts. No other account could make the same claim.

We can now imagine the state of panic aboard the sub. Continuing to rev the propellers made matters worse. Chuman probably considered

---

* The two Pile Lights, popularly known as the 'Wedding Cakes', marked the entrances to the Western and Eastern channels out of Sydney Harbour. The Western Pile Light survived Chuman's collision and other rigours of war until it was rebuilt in 1947. However it proved to be less than immortal, and at 4.30 pm on 12 December 2006 it comprehensively disintegrated, leaving nothing behind but a swirl of water and some wooden wreckage.

that his best bet was to try to twist the sub free. He had snagged himself about 1.5 metres from the bottom of the net, in around 13½ fathoms (81 feet or 24.7 metres) of water. So whether by accident or design, Chuman swung the bow of the sub sideways and upwards until it was almost vertical, with its hull parallel to the net. The torpedo tubes on the bow protruded from the water, but the rest of the submarine was still below the surface. When he revved his engines the net vibrated, but nothing moved. The sub stayed firmly stuck, tangling itself more deeply in the coils. This commotion is what first attracted the attention of Jimmy Cargill and Bill Nangle, chatting on the deck of the nearby floating crane. Jimmy Cargill rowed over for a closer look at the frantic mystery object.

◆　　◆　　◆

Accounts differ widely on what happened next. This is hardly a surprise because for the next couple of hours, with the honourable exception of Jimmy Cargill, nobody defending Sydney Harbour exactly covered themselves with glory. Instead they dithered.

Jimmy Cargill saw the sub at around 8.15 pm. He had to row first to the sub, about 50 metres. Then he rowed another 80 metres to *Yarroma* to report his findings. On a blustery night on the harbour this will not have been quick. However, the struggle with the oars turned out to be the least of his problems: *Yarroma*'s skipper, Sub-Lieutenant Harold Eyers, wanted nothing to do with Cargill's mystery object. If, as the nightwatchman suggested, it might be a mine then Eyers thought it would be risky to approach it. Among his many concerns, he was carrying the still highly secret ASDIC anti-submarine detection equipment. He did not want to place it at risk at the hands of a mine or submarine. Anyway, he doubted that the object was anything so interesting—more likely it was a piece of naval junk which had got stuck in the net.

It is all too easy to be critical of Eyers. In his 22 June report on the raid, Rear Admiral Muirhead-Gould described his behaviour as 'deplorable and inexplicable'. Muirhead-Gould, who had every personal reason to look for scapegoats, wanted Eyers court-martialled for failing to engage the enemy. He was dissuaded from this by Sir Guy Royle, the Chief of Naval Staff. 'I feel his chief fault was foolishness', Royle wrote to Muirhead-Gould on 16 June 1942, 'and that an admonition by you would meet the case'. The most important thing to say about Eyers is that, although he was a commissioned officer in full and sole command of a Royal Australian Navy ship, he was only 21 years old on the night of the raid. He had enlisted in Melbourne on 4 September 1939, the first day of World War II and a few days short of his 19th birthday. He does not sound like a coward. Before enlisting he worked as a shipping clerk.

Cargill's first proposal to Eyers was that *Yarroma* should follow him while he rowed over to the object. Eyers asked him to describe it. Cargill recalled:

Well, I said, the nearest I could tell there was two great big oxy bottles with bumper bars or guards over them. But, I said, follow me and I'll put you onto it. I went back to it and he didn't follow me. So I went back to him again and told him that it was still there. I said: If it's a mine you'd better hurry up, or you'll have no bloody Navy left.

He then told me to come on board, as something was wrong with the searchlight. Well, I went aboard and I told him to go back to the Pile Light. We were halfway there when he stopped and said: 'It looks like naval wreckage.' I said: Gee, I've been alongside it and I could touch it with my paddle. Everything is shining brand new. Give us one of your men and I'll take him over to it.

So I went down the ladder with this bloke. He was halfway down the ladder when he was pulled up and another man went down to join me. We went over to it, nearly a paddle's distance away from it. It had stopped struggling and we could see the conning tower and the ridge rope and the whole outline of the submarine. The bloke said to me: 'It's a submarine all right. Put me back on board and we'll see what we have to do.'

This whole process seems to have taken an incredible amount of time. Taking Jimmy Cargill's narrative at face value, he spotted the sub at 8.15 pm. First he had to row from the floating crane to the sub. He then rowed over to *Yarroma* and spoke to Eyers. He then rowed back to the sub. When *Yarroma* did not follow him, he rowed back to the patrol boat again. He then waited while Eyers repaired his searchlight. After this Eyers moved *Yarroma* a little closer to the sub before stopping again. More talk. Then the offer to row a crew member over to the object. Then a change of crew member. Then another rowboat journey to the sub, and another rowboat journey back. By the time the process was complete, over an hour and a half had passed. In the course of the 97 minutes, *Yarroma* made increasingly frantic efforts with its signal lamp to alert the Port War Signal Station on South Head that there was a problem. No one responded.

◆   ◆   ◆

It is worth breaking off the narrative at this point to look at communications on Sydney Harbour that night. In the 21st century, when hordes of schoolchildren communicate with each other remotely by phone or text message from a radio telephone in their pocket or schoolbag, the primitive military communications of May 1942 are hard to imagine. Yet as we shall shortly see, they were a key element in the chaos about to engulf Sydney Harbour.

The navy's main communication centre in Sydney was on Garden Island. Here powerful radio sets could send signals around the world, even as far as the Admiralty in London. In 1942 radio communications came in two forms. The simplest was R/T or radio telephone. This allowed signals by voice. People spoke to each other in the familiar 'over and out' style of World War II movies. However R/T had comparatively limited range. Without going into the arcane issues of skip distances and the reflective properties of the ionosphere, it is sufficient to say that R/T voice signals were 'line of sight'. If hills or headlands or the curvature of the earth blocked the way, the signal would not get through.

The more usual form of radio communication was W/T or wireless telegraphy. This involved a skilled operator sending audible signals by radio in Morse code. W/T signals had longer range than R/T. They could be received and understood 'over the horizon'. W/T was used for long-range communication with ships at sea. R/T was used for short-range ship-to-ship and ship-to-shore messages. Although R/T would be the simplest and best way to communicate with fighting ships inside the harbour, the main communications centre on Garden Island did not have a radio telephone set installed on the night of 31 May 1942.

For short-range traffic around the harbour entrance, the navy's key communications centre was the Port War Signal Station on South Head. PWSS was essentially a lookout and relay station. It occupied a three-storey building with an open platform above. On the ground floor of PWSS the indicator loops guarding the harbour 'tailed' in. There was also an ASDIC submarine-detection device, and a photo-electric beam skimming the water above Inner Loop 12 to detect surface vessels entering the inner harbour. The ground floor staff watched the traces given off by the indicator loops, kept an eye on the ASDIC screen, and waited for any interruption to the photo-electric beam. It was their job to raise the alarm if they came across any strange blips or echoes.

Above them were the radio signallers. Unlike Garden Island, Port War did have R/T as well as W/T. However, the correct R/T set had yet to be fitted, and the improvised set available on the night of the raid failed comprehensively. Not that it mattered. Only the larger and newer warships on the harbour that night were fitted with R/T.

On the top floor and platform were the visual signallers. Their messages could be sent out by something as simple as a string of flags hoisted up a pole. (Nelson's famous signal 'England expects that every man will do his duty' was passed to the rest of his Trafalgar fleet by signal flag.) The lost art of semaphore was also important. A signalman with a flag in each hand could spell out a message by holding the flags in different positions, each position signifying a letter of the alphabet. However, flags and semaphore were largely useless at night.

The most common form of visual signalling involved flashing light beams. The signalman sent his message in Morse code with a series of long and short flashes. This system worked in darkness as well as in daylight. At night the signal light had to be covered by a red or green filter—white light would destroy the night vision of the signaller and the receiver, as well as those around them. To state the totally obvious, all visual signals were also 'line of sight'. Light signals functioned best with two men at each end: at the receiving end, one man 'read' the signal while the other wrote down what he said. A lone signalman could read and transmit, but the system worked much better with two men.

The visual signallers on the top floor or Port War had a 360-degree view of both the harbour and the ocean beyond, so they acted as both lookout and signaller. If someone on the ground floor picked up an ASDIC echo or an unexpected blip from the indicator loop or the photo-electric beam, they would telephone upstairs and ask the top floor to check it out visually.

The signallers at Port War also had telephones to communicate with shore defence centres, including naval headquarters on Garden Island. In 1942, however, telephone capacity was limited by the number of 'lines' available. The system would go into overload very quickly if there was any kind of crisis, and the plaintive cry would go up: 'I can't get a line.' The signallers preferred their trusty signal lights to the unpredictable telephone system, even for messages between Port War and Naval Headquarters 5 kilometres away on Garden Island.

While the Port War Signal Station housed Sydney's most com-prehensive set of naval communication equipment, it had no authority to issue orders. These had to come from Naval Headquarters on Garden Island. PWSS simply acted as a relay station. Ships signalled to Port War, who passed the message on to Garden Island, who replied to Port War, who passed the order back to the ship. Generally Port War sent its messages to Garden Island by light signal. Garden Island replied either by telephone or light. It all took time.

Garden Island did not have to send all its signals via Port War. It had its own visual signals section. The signallers operated from a specially constructed tower on high ground overlooking the headquarters buildings below. Despite the tower's height, parts of the harbour were masked from it by surrounding headlands. Garden Island had no way of sending visual messages to significant numbers of the warships under its command. They had a clear 'line of sight' to Port War, but no way of communicating visually with either the Channel Patrol boats on the boom net or with ships further up the harbour and beyond the Harbour Bridge. Finally, because signal lamps are directional, they had to be aimed at a particular ship for it to receive a message. So if a signal needed to pass to all ships, it would in practice have to be sent out a ship at a time. With 30 warships in the harbour, getting even a short message through to all of them by visual signal was a daunting undertaking.

All ships large and small carried visual signalling equipment. All of the larger warships on the harbour carried W/T, and some also carried R/T. However, the Naval Auxiliary Patrol boats and most of the Channel Patrol boats had neither W/T nor R/T on the night of 31 May 1942. They had to rely on light signals to communicate with each other and with Port War and Garden Island. They also had to contend with far from ideal equipment. Their signal lamps were heavy, but were nevertheless hand-held and designed to be operated with one hand. The operating hand had to pull two triggers simultaneously—one trigger turned on the light; the second trigger tilted an internal mirror to make the light 'flash'. The light was directional, and had to be sighted accurately at the recipient for the signal to get through. From a swaying deck on a choppy harbour, it was no mean feat to keep the light pointing at the precise spot occupied by the intended recipient.

On the night of 31 May 1942 only one duty Channel Patrol boat on the harbour carried radio. *Yarroma* was equipped with an FS6, a clunky and primitive piece of kit which nevertheless cost around £1000— $52,000 at today's prices—so the navy felt it could not afford to install them in the whole Channel Patrol boat fleet. An FS6 would simply astonish a 21st-century schoolchild. It weighed a bit over 71 kilos, and needed two men to carry it. (My current mobile phone, which carries about 1000 times the communicating power of an FS6 set, weighs in at

0.1 kilo.) With the flip of a toggling switch, an FS6 could be used either as an R/T voice communications set, or as a Morse code W/T set. However, it was subject to interference from any electrical equipment operating nearby, particularly from spark plugs in an engine. A shipboard FS6 set was next to useless if the ship's motor was running.

There was one other means of communication from ship to ship: audio signals. Each ship carried a loud-hailer and a horn or siren. Messages could be passed by shouting through the loud-hailer, or just by shouting. The horn or siren could be used to raise the alarm.

◆   ◆   ◆

There is no record of the manning level at the Port War Signal Station that night. When ships were expected, a normal Port War watch consisted of a Lieutenant-Commander in overall charge, with a Yeoman or Leading Signalman plus three signalmen on the top floor, a Petty Officer or Leading Seaman Wireless Operator plus three wireless operators on their floor, and a Petty Officer or Leading Seaman ASDIC operator plus three ASDIC operators on the ground floor. The raid took place on a Sunday night, however, and nobody expected anybody of importance to enter Sydney Harbour that night—certainly nobody was expecting a working visit from the Imperial Japanese Navy. 'Darby' Munro, the PWSS signalman who had seen the Glen flight eight days earlier, is of the opinion that when Chuman entered the harbour there might have been only one man on duty on the ground-floor Loop Station and ASDIC centre of PWSS, and one man on the R/T and W/T floor. If Darby is correct, it would go a long way towards explaining why the indicator loop traces from the submarines passed unnoticed.

It also follows that around 9.30 pm there may have been only a single team of two men on the top floor to receive *Yarroma*'s light signals, and a lone R/T watch keeper below to answer the radio. Each would then need to pass the signals on to Garden Island and await instructions. As pressure built up, the signallers no doubt called for help from their sleeping mates in the nearby huts, but it will have taken some time to get the system up to working strength.

Accounts vary on how the message eventually got through. The most likely scenario is that Port War received at least some of *Yarroma*'s light signals but the overstretched light signals crew could not acknowledge them and raise the alarm at Garden Island at the same time. *Yarroma* probably also tried to get through to Port War on the R/T, but this appears to have failed totally, and their radio messages simply vanished into the ether. Finally, somebody on *Yarroma* had the bright idea of toggling the FS6 radio from R/T mode to W/T mode, and sending a Morse signal direct to Garden Island. All that is known with any certainty is that the message finally got through to Naval Headquarters by W/T rather than light signal. At 9.52 pm, 97 minutes after Jimmy Cargill's first sighting, Garden Island received *Yarroma*'s message: 'Suspicious object in net.' Naval Headquarters responded by ordering Eyers: 'Close and investigate.'

◆　　◆　　◆

By now Chuman's midget was not the only Japanese submarine in the harbour. All three midgets had to battle the currents outside the Heads and all arrived late. Next to arrive was Ban. He was due at 7.15 pm. He reached the harbour entrance some time around 9.30, over two hours late. At 9.48 pm, four minutes before *Yarroma*'s first message to Garden Island, Inner Loop 12 recorded an isolated, sharp blip. A second pair of Japanese torpedoes was now in the harbour, past the boom net, and looking for trouble. Again, nobody stirred.

◆　　◆　　◆

At about 10.10 pm Eyers responded to the request from Garden Island to 'close and investigate' with a second message reporting that the mystery object was metal, with a serrated edge on top, and that it was moving with the swell. Although he now had good reason to believe it was a submarine, he chose not to pass on this last fact. Garden Island responded to this latest message by ordering him to give a fuller description. If there is to be criticism of Eyers, then it would be for his next action. He had been ordered to investigate further. He responded by signalling with his Aldis lamp to his fellow Channel Patrol boat HMAS *Lolita* to please come over from her station at the other end of the boom net. Although *Lolita*'s skipper Warrant Officer Herbert 'Tubby' Anderson was almost twice Eyers' age at 38, he was the more junior officer. At around 10.20 pm Eyers ordered Anderson and *Lolita* to do the investigating. If anyone was going to tangle with an enemy mine or submarine, it was not going to be Eyers and his top-secret ASDIC.

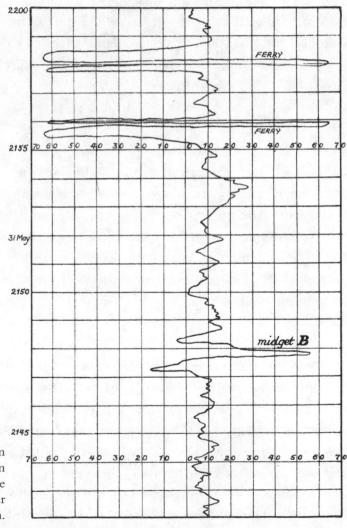

Trace left by Ban (I-24's midget) on Inner Loop 12 as he enters the harbour at 9.48 pm.

Lolita was on the seaward side of the net. Anderson raced the remaining length of the net and swung *Lolita* through the western boom gate and prepared to take a look. His handwritten draft report takes up the narrative:

> Stood off about 20 feet with stern towards object and machine gun covering same. Inspected object by flashing Aldis Lamp on it, which proved to be a submarine. The bow was pointed approximately south east. She was inside the net, her bow being approximately two feet above water, periscope showing about a foot, and stern entirely submerged. She appeared to be struggling to extricate herself. I realized at once the necessity for immediate action and gave the order to stand by depth charges.

Jim Nelson, *Lolita*'s signalman, recalls flashing a message by light to the Port War Signal Station: 'Have sighted enemy midget submarine and proceeding to attack. Lolita.' The signal was acknowledged.

Lolita dropped its first depth charge and roared off at full throttle to get out of the way of the blast. There was none. Depth charges explode once they reach a pre-set depth. Those aboard the Channel Patrol boats were regularly set to explode at 100 feet (about 30 metres). Without a change of setting, in 81 feet (24 metres) of water they simply tumbled to the bottom of the harbour and sat there in silence.

The bemused crew waited. Nothing. There was no choice but to try again. This time the crew attached some small floats to the depth charge to slow its descent in the hope that this would make it detonate. 'Tubby' Anderson lined up for a second attack run. He roared in towards the net, swung *Lolita* hard to starboard as they came up alongside the submarine and released a second charge. Again he raced off to get out of the way. Another agonising silence. Nothing. Two depth charges now sat on the bottom of the harbour, both 22 feet (6 metres) from detonating.

There is a school of thought which says this was a lucky escape for all concerned. If the depth charges had exploded and set off a sympathetic explosion in the sub's torpedoes and scuttling charges, then

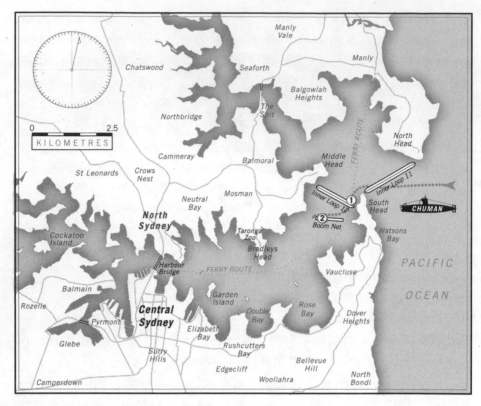

The track followed by Chuman's midget is still the subject of controversy. We know with some certainty that he crossed Inner Loop 12 at 8.01 pm, two minutes behind the Manly ferry. We also know with some certainty that he reversed into the Boom Net close to the Western Gate some time just before 8.15 pm. This diagram shows the track taken by the Manly ferry on the night of the attack, together with the best guess available at Chuman's movements: (1) 8.01 pm, Chuman crosses Inner Loop 12 two minutes behind the Manly Ferry, then heads across harbour, avoiding Sow and Pigs Reef, and enters via Western Gate; (2) 8.10–8.15 pm, reverses into Boom Net. At 10.37 pm, he fires scuttling charges, killing both crew.

a ton of military-grade high explosive would have gone up within a few metres of Sydney's harbour shore. This would have left nothing of the submarine. It would also have spelt the end for *Lolita*, probably *Yarroma*, and every window in Clifton Gardens.

Anderson prepared for his third attack. As *Lolita* headed towards the submarine for the final depth charge run, she was met by a deafening explosion, sending a gigantic column of flame and water towering over the patrol launch. The shock wave lifted *Lolita* out of the water, heeling her over and almost swamping her. As the water settled, a huge oil patch spread on the harbour surface. Realising that their position was hopeless, the midget's crew had fired one of their two sets of 135-kilo scuttling charges, killing themselves in the process. Lieutenant Kenshi Chuman and Petty Officer Takeshi Omori had chosen a warrior's exit. They were the first men to die in the Battle of Sydney Harbour. The time was 10.37 pm.

◆　　◆　　◆

On Garden Island, 18-year-old signalman Ian Mitchell had just worked the 'dog watch' from 4 pm to 8 pm. Instead of returning to his sleeping quarters at Rushcutters Bay after his watch ended, he stayed to eat in the mess. He was still on Garden Island when the excitement began. He was standing in the visual signal tower when a W/T operator from the wireless room below burst in. 'His eyes were sticking out like dog's whatsits,' Ian Mitchell recalls. 'He said: "Subs are in the harbour. We've got a red alert."'

Chapter 9

All hell breaks loose

The blast from Chuman's submarine reverberated around the harbour. Windows were flung open and curtains pulled back as people rushed to see what was going on. The first thought was an air raid. The anti-aircraft batteries woke up with a start. Searchlights snapped on and probed the clouds.

In his report dated 22 June 1942 Rear Admiral Muirhead-Gould lamented: 'Great difficulty has been experienced in making out any sort of chronological plot. A great many ships and boats and, therefore, people were concerned in these operations, and all were so busy that they had no thought for recording actual time of incidents.' It is hard to avoid the suspicion that this blurring of time suited Muirhead-Gould well. His account of his own preparedness does not match the recollection of others.

According to Muirhead-Gould's report, Captain Bode of the USS *Chicago* left the dinner party at 'Tresco' at 10.20 pm 'with suggestion that he should go to sea with *Perkins*'. At 10.27 pm, within a few minutes of *Lolita*'s signal that she was attacking an enemy submarine, Muirhead-Gould issued an order to all ships in Sydney Harbour: 'Take anti-submarine precautions.' He also closed the harbour to outward shipping. At 10.36, one minute before Chuman scuttled, Muirhead-

Gould sent out a general signal: 'Presence of enemy submarine at boom gate is suspected. Ships are to take action against attack.' Muirhead-Gould's orders will have been transmitted from Garden Island by W/T and visual signal, and repeated from the Port War Signal Station by the same means. As we have seen, this left large numbers of ships in the harbour uninformed. Any ship out of sight of both Garden Island and PWSS—the Channel Patrol boats tied up in Farm Cove, for instance—will have seen and heard nothing.

Nevertheless, Muirhead-Gould sets out in his report to present a picture of himself quickly grasping the nature of the threat and responding correctly and effectively. If other accounts are to be believed, it was not quite like that. The lights in the Garden Island construction site stayed burning brightly, outlining ships in the harbour including the *Chicago*. In fairness to Muirhead-Gould, this was not unreasonable. The construction of a massive graving dock at Garden Island was regarded as urgent war work, and it went on 24 hours a day. There were 1000 men on the site at any given time, and the night shift needed light. However, Muirhead-Gould's other orders were less defensible. He specifically ordered that commercial harbour traffic continue as normal, which meant fully lit. He prudently omits this order from his final report, but it appears in his draft report dated 22 June 1942. He wrote: 'Some comment has been made that the ferries were allowed to continue to run. This was done by my direct order as I felt that once there was a submarine, or more than one submarine in the Harbour, the more boats that were moving about at high speed the better chance of keeping the submarines down till daylight.' He could not have been more wrong.

◆   ◆   ◆

By 9.48 pm and the second indicator loop crossing, the anti-submarine specialist HMAS *Yandra* and the three NAP boats *Lauriana*, *Allura* and *Yarrawonga* had allowed two enemy submarines to slip into the harbour unchallenged. The blast from the direction of the boom net, however, alerted all four to the fact that all was not well. *Lauriana*'s log takes up the story.

2237. Large charge exploded Western channel Boom. Orange flash about 20 or 30 feet high followed by charge like depth charge. Water up about 40 feet. Watched searchlights and C.B. [Channel Patrol boat] who were showing on boom for signal. Received no signal from Port War or Channel Patrol boat, thought it was large practice charge.

2248. Proceeding in line towards South Reef from Inner North Head. Visibility fair only, clouds. Noticed flurry on water ahead to port. Thought it may have been paravane* from minesweeper, or shark broaching. Decided to investigate.

2252. Speeded up, put searchlight on at about distance 60 to 80 feet, immediately showed Conning Tower of sub about two points to port. Black in shape about 2′6″ diameter.

This was Matsuo's midget, finally entering the harbour almost four hours late. *Lauriana*'s log continues:

Sent flash to Port War (L.L.L.) also Channel Boat and in direction of Minesweeper. Put searchlight on and off and continued to send L's and AA to Port War, to Channel Boat in direction of Boom. No response to our signals.

Lauriana was totally unarmed. The NAP flotilla leader L.H. Winkworth later complained in his official report: 'Had we had our promised depth charges, we could have certainly sent the sub to the bottom. Had we had Verey lights or rockets, we could have immediately illuminated the area for the batteries to open fire.' Instead all *Lauriana* could do was send frantic light signals—'L's' and 'A's' to raise the alarm, 'C's' to attract the attention of the Channel Patrol boat. No one reacted.

---

* Paravanes are large, fish-shaped devices towed by cables extending from the bow of a minesweeper. The cable deflects any mine it comes across and cuts it from its mooring, after which the mine can be destroyed. Paravanes endlessly break away from their towing cables, and the bulk of 'sightings' of midget submarines are in fact sightings of wayward paravanes.

Unlike *Lauriana*, *Yandra* was well armed with depth charges and other anti-submarine weapons. While *Lauriana* was flashing and signalling, *Yandra* was heading back into the harbour from the heads. As she altered course towards the inner harbour, she saw a conning tower about 400 yards (360 metres) ahead and on the same 265-degree course. *Yandra*'s commander, Lieutenant James Taplin, estimated the sub's speed at 5 to 6 knots. *Yandra* increased speed to 8½ knots and set off in pursuit.

Matsuo now turned left onto a heading of 186 degrees, which would take him down the Eastern Channel and into the main shipping area of the harbour. Taplin continued to overhaul him. Unlike many of the defenders on Sydney Harbour that night, Taplin was no beginner: he had served 14 years in the navy, and knew what he was doing. He decided that ramming was his best course of action—he was cramped for space, and there were too many other surface vessels nearby to carry out a depth charge attack. (He complained in his official report that surface vessels 'frequently later on prevented an efficient investigation of suspicious objects'.) Let Taplin take up the narrative.

> 2257. Submarine appeared to be on steady course of approx 186 deg at same speed, hull slightly awash, no periscope visible, trimmed slightly by the stern.
>
> 2258. Submarine appearing to submerge a little when hidden from bridge by bow, but was definitely seen to be struck by 'Yandra'. This evidence was given by reliable ratings of foc'sle party. Slight impact felt on bridge. Submarine was seen to break surface on starboard side aft alongside of hull. Submarine was observed by myself and independent witnesses aft to be listed to starboard about 15 deg. and bow out of the water at approx. the same angle. Submarine . . . seen to submerge while turning to starboard when about 100 yards astern.

Yandra had clearly scored a hit with its ramming tactic. However, the sub and its attacker were both on a similar course, so it was a glancing impact. The port side of Matsuo's bow cage almost certainly took the main force of the collision. The only result appeared to be to make the submarine list to starboard. Taplin could see that the damage was not fatal. Depth charges would be needed to finish the job. Having overrun the submarine with his ramming attack, Taplin turned back, facing out towards the harbour entrance, and tried to pinpoint the submarine's position with his ASDIC gear. No contact. But Matsuo solved Taplin's problem for him. Matsuo had also turned back towards the harbour entrance in the hope of evading his tormentor. He surfaced again about 600 yards (550 metres) from *Yandra*, on a bearing 20 degrees to starboard. At this stage the submarine was moving very slowly from left to right across *Yandra*'s bow. *Yandra*'s ASDIC still showed nothing, but Taplin had a visual contact and he set off in furious pursuit, this time at maximum speed. He ordered a full pattern of six depth charges prepared, set to 100 feet (30 metres). The gap narrowed. At 400 yards (360 metres) the ASDIC was now picking up the sub. Taplin hurtled on. At 150 yards (140 metres) the ASDIC signal was very strong. Matsuo tried desperately to submerge while Taplin bore down on him. As *Yandra* passed directly over the disappearing submarine, Taplin dropped his pattern of six depth charges.

The result was not the one Taplin had been hoping for. His official report says simply: 'Submarine was not seen after explosions.' The implication was that it had been sunk. Not so. The main victim of the depth charge attack was the *Yandra* itself. Again, let Taplin take up the narrative.

> The shock of the D.C. [depth charge] explosions resulted in the instantaneous failure of steering gear, A/S [anti-submarine] gear, De-Gaussing gear [used to minimise magnetic interference and thereby foil magnetic mines], phone communication to aft, tunnel bearing covers fractured and partial failure of lighting throughout the ship.

As attacks go, this was not a rip-roaring success. Taplin hand-steered his crippled ship back out of the harbour to a position just off the Heads and set about repairing the damage. Fifteen minutes later he had restored the ASDIC and steering gear and was able to re-enter the harbour. Taplin's report concludes laconically: 'Anti-submarine sweep carried out in the vicinity of the depth charge attack but no contact obtained.'

◆　◆　◆

We can only speculate on Matsuo's next move. The standard Japanese instruction for midget submarines under attack after launching was to 'immediately flood tanks and submerge to a depth of 150 to 200 feet [45 to 60 metres] or deeper, and take evasive action on a course which is at right angles to that at the time of launching'. It seems highly likely that Matsuo did exactly that. He submerged into about 12 fathoms (72 feet or 22 metres) of water on a line between Inner North Head and Inner South Head. The highest probability is that he turned right towards the inner harbour, settled his submarine gratefully on the harbour bed, and tried not to make a noise.

◆　◆　◆

After crossing Inner Loop 12 at 9.48 pm, Ban made his way cautiously down the harbour towards Garden Island, delicately conserving his batteries. It took him an hour to travel 4 kilometres. By 10.52 pm he had crept to within range of USS *Chicago*, tied up at the no. 2 buoy off Garden Island. The orders governing Japanese midget submarine tactics were quite specific about the timing of an attack. 'If a large ship or transport anchors, a resolute attack should be executed immediately,' the commanders were instructed. 'Attack with the least possible delay. Opportunity to attack is lost if a vessel escapes to sea.'

According to *Chicago*'s action report, the first sighting of Ban's submarine placed him 300 to 500 metres off *Chicago*'s starboard side and at an angle of 45 degrees to *Chicago*'s stern, on a course towards the Harbour Bridge and parallel to *Chicago*'s position at anchor. It has always been assumed that at this point Ban was simply trying to make a positive identification of his target. But that overlooks the fact that Ban's torpedoes had been set to 60 degrees left deflection. Ban's orders were to attack at once, and his present course was taking him into a perfect firing position for his deflected torpedoes, with 183 metres of *Chicago*'s starboard side exposed at close range. At this point *Chicago* may have had seconds to live.

There are as many accounts of what happened next as there are people who took part. Taking only from first-person accounts available to the author, including *Chicago*'s action report, what followed went something like this.

The anti-aircraft gun crews aboard *Chicago* were doubly alert: William Floyd had read the riot act to them two days previously after they missed Ito's flight; and they had received Muirhead-Gould's 10.27 and 10.36 alerts. They will also have heard Chuman's scuttling charge, indicating that the threat was serious. So they were on the lookout for trouble in the water, particularly submarine trouble.

Floyd takes up the narrative: 'The sky-control personnel began searching to see if they could pick up anything in the harbour. Some little time later they saw what they believed to be a sub. A gun and a searchlight were trained there and the arcs were struck [the searchlight was turned on] so that by opening the shutters they would illuminate this object.' At this point the searchlight was alight but closed, with its beam trapped behind shutters. The crews asked for permission to open the shutters, and to open fire if what they found turned out to be a submarine. While the seconds ticked away, no orders came. After an agony of waiting—and with Ban moving into a perfect firing position, although they were in no position to know this—they decided they could stand it no longer. They opened the shutters. The conning tower of a baby submarine glistened in the searchlight beam.

The officer of the deck, Ensign Bruce Simons, was first to act. His response was not exactly devastating, but it was enterprising. He emptied his .45 automatic pistol at Ban's conning tower, while raising the alarm. All over the ship a gong sounded the general alarm, and the public address system made a difficult-to-understand announcement, something about a submarine.

George Kitteridge was a junior gunnery officer aboard *Chicago*.

I was in the duty section and my recollection of the whole thing was Gong! Gong! Gong! I ran up the ladder to the communications deck. We had a 1.1-inch mount or a Bofors and a quick-firing gun on the bridge there. Jimmy Mecklenberg [the senior officer on board at the time] jumped in the pointer's seat and I jumped into the trainer's seat and he yelled at me: 'Where's the trigger on this thing?' I said: 'Let's switch.' We switched. The trigger was in the foot pedal.

Kitteridge and Mecklenberg blazed away with the anti-aircraft pom-pom at the submarine's conning tower. Eyewitnesses recalled red tracer pouring into the harbour and shots 'falling all around' the submarine, which is a polite way of saying Mecklenberg and Kitteridge missed. They certainly inflicted no known damage.

The *Chicago* now tried some heavier metal. Two 5-inch guns at the stern of the ship joined the battle. However, they could not depress far enough to get Ban in their sights. This did not prevent the gun crews from opening fire anyway. Shells ricocheted across the harbour, miraculously doing no serious harm as they crashed into North Sydney. Chunks were blasted off the venerable stone walls of Fort Denison. Again there were no casualties. A few of the ricochets hit the armed merchant cruiser HMAS *Westralia* anchored in Athol Bay not far from Cremorne Point opposite, again doing no damage.

The searchlight beam and all of this wild firing may not have done Ban's submarine any immediate damage, but it had the effect of distracting him—and very likely temporarily blinding him—making a torpedo attack impossible. Instead, Ban submerged. Three minutes later, he surfaced again about 300 metres off *Chicago*'s starboard bow, having continued on course towards the Harbour Bridge underwater. It is impossible to know whether his disappearance and reappearance were deliberate, or whether the midget was pulling its regular trick of soaring and diving of its own accord. Whatever the explanation, it led to more pandemonium. *Chicago* opened fire again. A ferry pulled out of Circular Quay, to find shots from *Chicago*'s pom-pom falling all around it. The ferry skipper beat a hasty retreat back to the wharf. Red tracer whistled past the Garden Island launch *Nestor*, which had to swerve to avoid a collision with Ban. The sub's new position put it within sight of the Australian corvette HMAS *Geelong*, berthed on the Harbour Bridge side of Garden Island. *Geelong* opened fire on a 'suspicious object' in the direction of Bradleys Head, adding to the bedlam. Somewhere between Garden Island and the Harbour Bridge, Ban submerged again, leading some on the *Chicago* to think they had sunk their target.

Chicago's official action report plays down the amount of gunfire during this episode. Bode's report claims that at the first sighting only one round was fired, from the no. 3 5-inch gun. At the second sighting, according to the report, the 1.1-inch pom-pom fired 20 rounds and the 5-inch deck gun fired another single round. The report was signed by Bode and dated 5 June 1942. As Bode was nowhere to be seen aboard *Chicago* at the time, the first-person accounts from the officers who did the actual shooting, backed up by dozens of eyewitnesses all around the harbour, probably tell a more accurate story.

Meanwhile, plenty else was happening aboard *Chicago*. George Chipley was the duty engineering officer. The ship was on four-hour standby, meaning it had to be ready to sail in four hours. When Chipley heard pistol shots followed by shouting and the alarm gong, he went straight into action. 'I ran for the Main Engine Control in the after engine room, and soon both engine rooms and all four fire rooms reported manned and ready.'

Whatever Muirhead-Gould may have asked us to believe, at 10.52 pm when all the excitement began Captain Bode had not returned to his ship. It was anchored no more than a few hundred metres from 'Tresco', a couple of minutes away in the Captain's gig (launch). So 32 minutes after Muirhead-Gould claimed Bode left 'Tresco' 'with suggestion that he go to sea with *Perkins*', there was still no sign of the *Chicago*'s captain.

Lieutenant Commander H.J. Mecklenberg, fresh from his adventures with the anti-aircraft gun, assumed command. He ordered Chipley to do what he was doing already, and prepare the ship to get under way. 'Fires were lighted under the seven cold boilers, and the fire room crews used high rates of oil and air flow to raise steam pressure rapidly,' Chipley remembered. 'I went up on deck to look at the stacks and I could see large volumes of persistent white smoke pouring from both stacks.'

As well as ordering Chipley to get *Chicago* prepared for sea, Mecklenberg signalled his destroyer escort USS *Perkins*, tied up on the next-door no. 4 buoy, to get under way and conduct screening patrols around *Chicago*. At 11.15 pm *Perkins* did as she was bid.

◆　◆　◆

Chicago's guns marked the beginning of a restless night for 17-year-old secretarial student Margaret Hamilton. Her family's home overlooked Taylors Bay, on the northern side of Sydney Harbour. When the wind blew from the south-west, as it did on the night of 31 May 1942, sounds from Garden Island carried clearly across the water to her front balcony. Margaret could hear the distinctive American accents of the loudspeakers on *Chicago* calling orders to the gunners: 'Ready! Aim! FIRE!' She could see what looked like a fireworks display, as the red tracer from George Kitteridge's pom-pom whipped down the harbour. Searchlights reflected on the clouds, bathing the water surface in a pale and eerie white light. She watched for a while, uncertain of what was going on but excited by the whole spectacle. When the sounds of firing and depth charges faded, she went to bed but couldn't sleep.

◆　◆　◆

Sydney Harbour was now in pretty good uproar. Chuman's scuttling charge, fired at 10.37 pm, could be heard all over the harbour, and particularly loudly in the northern suburbs of Clifton Gardens and Mosman. *Yandra*'s six 180-kilo depth charges had detonated at 11.07 pm just off South Head, within good earshot of Vaucluse, Dover Heights and Rose Bay. A few minutes earlier *Chicago* had been blasting away with its 5-inch gun and anti-aircraft gun from just off Garden Island, followed by more firing from *Geelong*. The citizens of Sydney could be in no doubt that something serious was afoot. However an air-raid remained the most likely explanation, with some sort of navy exercise on the harbour as the next best candidate.

The sirens had still not gone off, but people started slipping into their prearranged air-raid countermeasures. It is a common psychological insight that humans reserve their clearest memories for their worst humiliations. Tess van Sommers was a young evening student at Sydney University, working by day for Associated Newspapers and hoping for a journalism cadetship there. She lodged in Double Bay with the formidable Margaret Dalrymple Hay, clerk of the university's Law School. She was within good earshot of the explosions.

'In the event of enemy attack from the air or sea,' she remembers

my role in our household was to nab the two pet dogs, stuff their ears with cotton wool and bind up their heads with scarves to protect their ear-drums from blast.

At the first terrific thump I bounded up, flung on a dressing gown, grabbed the cotton wool and the scarves—of an especially hectic tartan pattern—and stumbled down stairs. In the hall, the dogs' baskets were empty. A faint light showed from a part-open door, where a relative of Miss Dalrymple Hay resided after being evacuated from the Solomons, where she had experienced bombardment.

I dashed in. She was sitting up, a quivering dog under either armpit, smoking a small cigar and tending a large bottle of Gordon's gin. In my haste I had wrapped the lurid scarves over the dressing gown and around my own neck. Our refugee fixed them with a stare and raised eyebrow. 'Well, well, well,' she said, heavily sardonic, 'somebody got dressed in a hurry.'

It rankled for days afterwards. In my first test in the face of the enemy, I had been suspected of panicking.

At Riverview College, well up the harbour and away from the immediate gunfire, the schoolboys were determined not to miss any of the action. The priests had told them all to go to the air-raid shelters below. They would have none of it. Instead they climbed onto the roof. Jim Macken remembers:

> All we were able to see was searchlights, all over the sky. There were explosions coming from the harbour, which we assumed to be bombs. They were the depth charges. We didn't think there were any bombers there, because we could see in the searchlights that they weren't picking up any planes.
>
> We weren't scared. We were just excited. We wanted to know what was going on. It was the only time during the whole war that we went up on the roof.

Aboard the *Sea Mist*, Reg Andrew could hear firing and explosions up the harbour. He went up on deck to see if he could work out what was going on. 'We could hear firing in the distance,' he recalled. 'But after a while that all disappeared. When there was no more activity, I went back to bed.'

◆　◆　◆

At 11.14 pm Muirhead-Gould responded to the increasing tumult on the harbour by issuing his third and, by his account, final order of the night: all ships to be darkened. However, the floodlights remained burning at Garden Island, continuing to silhouette *Chicago* and other ships at anchor nearby.

At this point, things had become relatively calm. There was no actual firing on the harbour, and no depth-charging. The smoke was beginning to clear, as was the cloud, which now began to thin and allow a little moonlight through. Ban's submarine lay submerged in the harbour somewhere near the Harbour Bridge. Matsuo's submarine lay in wait, inert on the bottom of the harbour near the heads. The two submarine commanders will have heard Chuman's scuttling charge explosion (which they probably thought was either a depth charge or, much better, a torpedo at :ck) and both will have heard *Yandra*'s depth charges. So the submarines knew that the defences were alert, and some of the defences knew there were submarines on the loose. But the full reality was not available to either attackers or defenders. The defence did not know the correct count of submarines still alive in the harbour: Matsuo's submarine, which had gone quiet after *Yandra*'s depth charge attack, was presumed by the defence to be sunk somewhere near the Heads; and Ban's submarine, which had submerged while heading up the harbour near the Harbour Bridge, might have been sunk by *Chicago*'s and *Geelong*'s guns. The midgets' commanders did not know which submarines, other than themselves, had survived the depth-charging and gunfire. Nor did they know that Chuman had scuttled before he could inflict any damage.

At 11.30 the Australian anti-submarine vessel HMAS *Bingera*, which had been tied up near *Chicago*, reported ready to proceed. She was ordered to slip her moorings and carry out an anti-submarine search inside the harbour. In particular, she was asked to follow up a report of a submarine passing her position and proceeding towards the Harbour Bridge—Ban's midget. The two Australian corvettes *Geelong* and *Whyalla*, both tied up alongside each other at the oil wharf on the western side of Garden Island, began searchlight sweeps of the harbour, particularly in the direction of the North Shore from Cremorne Point to Bradleys Head. They all found nothing.

◆　　◆　　◆

It would be interesting to know where and how Rear Admiral Muirhead-Gould and Captain Bode of the *Chicago* spent the time between 10 pm and 11.35 pm that night. The first message suggesting something was amiss was transmitted to Muirhead-Gould's headquarters on Garden Island at 9.52 pm. This reported a suspicious object in the net. The second and stronger report from *Yarroma* was transmitted at 10.10 pm, and talked about a metal object with serrated edge, moving with the swell.

The first message would hardly warrant a phone call to the Admiral. It is credible that the second message, however, was alarming enough for Garden Island to contact Muirhead-Gould by phone at home.

Presumably Muirhead-Gould reacted with as much pleasure to this phone call as anyone else might when being disturbed on a Sunday night towards the end of a pleasant dinner party by a call from the office. From their subsequent behaviour it is apparent that neither Muirhead-Gould nor Bode believed a word of it. As far as Muirhead-Gould was concerned, all this talk about submarines came from a bunch of weekend sailors who wouldn't know a sub if it fell on their heads.

Matters were not improved by the mounting collapse of communications on the harbour. The Port War Signal Station on South Head simply did not cope with the flood of telephone, R/T, W/T and signal lamp messages pouring in from Garden Island, the loop station, Channel Patrol boats, Naval Auxiliary Patrol boats, *Yandra* and myriad others, all trying to pass on information or request it. Given that effective communication and accurate information are the bedrock of modern warfare, Muirhead-Gould was certainly at a disadvantage.

Muirhead-Gould's report paints a picture of the dinner party breaking up the minute the first alert came in, with Bode leaving at 10.20 to take *Chicago* to sea, escorted by *Perkins*. A more likely scenario would have Muirhead-Gould issuing his two precautionary orders, the first at 10.27 to all ships to take anti-submarine precautions, the second at 10.36 to take action against submarine attack, by telephone from 'Tresco' while allowing the dinner party to continue merrily on. Both these orders were issued before the first explosion on the harbour, the 10.37 detonation of Chuman's scuttling charges. Muirhead-Gould may even have issued his third order—at 11.14, to darken all ships—by telephone from 'Tresco' as well.

If this is so, and all the timing points this way, then the dinner party must have come to something of a pause at 10.37 when Chuman scuttled. The explosion could certainly be heard as far away as 'Tresco'. Whatever remaining fun was left in the party would have started to drain away around 10.53 pm when *Chicago*, which was anchored only a few hundred metres away from 'Tresco', opened fire with its pom-pom and 5-inch deck guns. All remaining fun would have evaporated 14 minutes after that with the six thunderous explosions from *Yandra*'s depth charges.

Communications on the harbour had by now well and truly broken down. There had been wild firing from nearby heavy guns aboard *Chicago*, and thumping explosions in the distance. It could no longer be ignored. Both Muirhead-Gould and Bode decided, some time around 11.20 pm, that they would have to find out for themselves what was going on.

Chapter 10

Men with black beards

It would be incorrect to say *Chicago*'s officers disliked their captain. Loathed would be the more appropriate word. Reading through their letters and recollections, all written 30 and 40 years after the event, their anger and bitterness towards him remain palpable. One officer likened him to Charles Laughton's Captain Bligh in the 1937 film of *Mutiny on the Bounty*. In 1942, Herman Wouk was still nine years away from publishing his classic novel *The Caine Mutiny*. If he had, *Chicago*'s officers might have found plenty of its unstable central character Lieutenant Commander Philip Queeg in their own Captain Howard Bode.

Bode and his executive officer Commander John Roper returned to *Chicago* from 'Tresco' aboard the Captain's gig some time around 11.30. Bode was in a towering rage. Jimmy Mecklenberg tried to brief him on the events of the night but Bode would not listen. There were no periscopes, he thundered, and no submarines. They were all insubordinate jittery fools. Mecklenberg must at once take the ship off 'general quarters'—its current high state of alert. Preparations to get under way were to cease at once. *Perkins* should come off patrol and return to her mooring. So much for Muirhead-Gould's assertion that Bode left the dinner party at 10.20 with the idea of putting to sea with *Perkins*.

Bode then ordered a message to be sent to Muirhead-Gould, flashed by signal lamp to the Garden Island headquarters. The text has long vanished, but William Floyd recalls that it said, in effect: 'I apologise for the ship opening fire in your harbour. It was done without my permission by some junior officers who mistakenly believed there were enemy midget submarines in the harbour.' Bode then retreated to his cabin, with an order that all officers were to assemble before him on the bridge.

Some time after midnight the officers gathered to meet their captain. According to George Chipley, that night Bode 'rose to new dramatic heights'. He accused all the officers of being drunk. (George Chipley commented: 'Our ships were dry and in two-and-a-half years I never saw alcohol consumed on the *Chicago*.') They were a bunch of incompetents. There were no submarines. They had been firing at shadows. Dire judgements would follow in the morning.

◆　　◆　　◆

Rear Admiral Muirhead-Gould was not the only commander anxious to find out at first hand what was going on in Sydney Harbour. The six Channel Patrol boats not on duty were all required to tie up at Farm Cove, two bays along from Garden Island. This put them out of sight of both Garden Island and Port War Signal Station, so they had no way of receiving visual signals. They carried no R/T or W/T. However, they were close enough to the *Chicago* and *Geelong* for the shooting to be heard loud and clear, never mind the depth-charging and scuttling which had taken place much further down the harbour. Curiosity got the better of *Marlean* and *Toomaree*. Without waiting for orders, they both slipped their moorings and headed off towards the sound of gunfire.

That left *Esmerelda, Leilani, Sea Mist* and *Steady Hour* as the reserve Channel Patrol boats still tied up in Farm Cove. *Leilani* was unmanned, however, and *Esmerelda* had engine problems. Only *Sea Mist* and *Steady Hour* could offer any additional firepower if required. At the stroke of midnight, with the smoke clearing and the thunder of the first round of explosions now fading, Reg Andrew officially took command of *Sea Mist*. He was asleep at the time.

♦　　♦　　♦

Rear Admiral Muirhead-Gould and his chief staff officer called for the Admiral's barge some time around 11.30 pm. They set off down the harbour at 11.36 in the direction of the boom net. Muirhead-Gould has been criticised for abandoning his headquarters and taking to the water at this juncture, but this criticism seems harsh. The collapse of communications meant that he was starved of reliable information. He was far from convinced that his harbour was under submarine attack. Going out and finding out for himself seems, in the circumstances, to be both an honourable and a defensible action, particularly as he did it during a lull in all the shooting and depth-charging.

According to his own report, Muirhead-Gould arrived at the boom net and boarded *Lolita* at midnight. At this point, accounts of what happened tend to diverge, and the various versions of the story seem to depend on both the diplomatic instincts and discretion of the teller. Were Muirhead-Gould and Bode both drunk? The reader will have to make up his or her own mind.

Muirhead-Gould's manner on board *Lolita* has been variously described as jocular, sarcastic, belligerent, frivolous, sceptical and, in one case, incoherent. 'Tubby' Anderson did his best to describe to him what had happened. Muirhead-Gould simply didn't believe him. Jim Nelson, from *Lolita*'s crew, remembers the Admiral opening the dialogue by asking: 'What are you all playing at, running up and down the harbour dropping depth charges and talking about enemy subs in the harbour? There's not one to be seen.' Nelson continues:

Muirhead-Gould was very sarcastic about our story. He asked us how we knew we had actually sighted a sub. Tubby told him that Jimmy Crowe [another *Lolita* crew member] had been a First World War submariner. Muirhead-Gould called Crowe over and asked him: was it a sub? Crowe verified it. Muirhead-Gould asked us if we had seen the captain of the sub. Did he have a black beard?

The grilling of *Lolita*'s crew lasted half an hour. By 12.30 Muirhead-Gould had heard enough. He was still unconvinced. As he was about to leave, he turned to the crew and said: 'If you see another sub, see if the captain has a black beard. I'd like to meet him.'

◆　　◆　　◆

Ban submerged near the Harbour Bridge some time around 11 pm. It is a matter of guesswork how he spent the next 90 minutes. The highest probability is that his first action was to do what submariners regularly do when under attack—head off underwater in what they hope is an unexpected direction, then make for the seabed and stay still and quiet. All Ban's behaviour up to this point suggests he was conserving battery power, so his every move will have been slow and calculated. The dashing Ban would have to wait his turn: this was a time for cool and calm.

It is worth standing back and trying to see the situation through Ban's eyes (and hear it through his ears, because sound was one of his most important sources of information). He will certainly have heard the thump of Chuman's scuttling charge: Ban was not far away at the time. He probably heard *Yandra*'s six depth charges. Although they were fired several kilometres away, sound carries well under water. The fact that there were six explosions meant they could not be Japanese torpedoes: there were only four other torpedoes in the harbour that night, two each aboard Chuman's and Matsuo's midgets. If the explosions weren't from torpedoes, it was very likely at least one of his fellow submariners was under depth charge attack elsewhere.

Anti-submarine detection gear like ASDIC sends out a sound 'ping', which can be heard by the submarine as it bounces off the sub's hull. The anti-submarine specialist HMAS *Bingera* began patrolling near the Harbour Bridge around 11.30, so from his hiding place nearby Ban will have heard the pinging of her ASDIC. Clearly the harbour was becoming an increasingly dangerous place for submarines. As well, each of the midgets carried a hydrophone to pick up other ship movements through the sounds of their engines and propellers. As well as *Bingera*, the destroyer USS *Perkins* had got under way and was carrying out an anti-submarine patrol near Garden Island to screen *Chicago*. Both *Marlean* and *Toomaree* had slipped their moorings and headed down the harbour. Their propellers will have been less noisy than *Bingera*'s or *Perkins*', but from where Ban sat they will have added to the impression of turmoil all around and above him.

Nevertheless, Ban had a job to carry out. If he went to periscope depth, he could see *Chicago* silhouetted against the Garden Island floodlights. She was still tied to no. 2 buoy, but with smoke belching from her funnels she must be about to get under way. There was no time to lose.

◆　◆　◆

G. Hermon Gill's official history of the Royal Australian Navy contains a diagram, drawn by Hugh W. Grosser, depicting Ban's attack. This diagram is universally reproduced in accounts of the raid, whether in books and magazines or on television. It is reproduced here on p. 141. It is simply wrong.* It flies in the face of eyewitness accounts, as well as defying common sense. However, it is fatally tempting for writers and television directors, because it allows everyone to marvel at the fact that Ban had a sitting duck for a target. Almost every account talks about 183 metres of *Chicago*'s hull broadside on to Ban's submarine and impossible to miss from 500 metres. That is not how it was.

Chicago's action report records that the cruiser was facing 265 degrees (almost due west) at the time of the attack. She was tied up to no. 2 buoy, which put her about 400 metres due east of the north-east corner of Garden Island. It does not require an elaborate Admiralty nautical chart to work out the firing positions: a Sydney street directory will do the job nicely. The best position to attack would be from north of *Chicago* just off Cremorne Point (or Robertsons Point, to give its less-used but

---

* Alert readers will notice that Grosser also places Chuman's sub on the wrong side of the net. His diagram has much to answer for.

technically correct name). A torpedo fired from Robertsons Point would have as its target the whole 183 metres of *Chicago*'s starboard side. Ban's problem with this ideal firing position was the bristling collection of warships already manoeuvring in the area, plus the armed merchant cruiser HMAS *Westralia* tied up in Athol Bay. If he took up a firing position there, he could expect a hot time from them all, especially *Westralia*.

Instead of stopping at Robertsons Point, Ban opted to move further down the harbour. He looked for a firing position less visible from Athol Bay, which took him to a point south of Bradleys Head. This put him facing *Chicago*'s stern, not her starboard side, and therefore offering a much narrower target. The *Chicago*'s beam (width) was 20 metres. But the hulls of fighting ships are generally 'V' shaped, and 20 metres refers to the ship's beam at its widest point, usually on the main deck. The hull sat 7 metres deep into the water. At 5 of those 7 metres below the surface— the depth at which Ban's torpedo was set to run—the hull will have tapered off to less than 10 metres. *Chicago* lay at a slight angle to Ban's line of fire, presenting a target less than 20 metres wide at a range of 500 metres. To add to the problem, Ban would have to align his submarine to allow for the 60-degree left deflection pre-set on his two torpedoes. Torpedoes do not snap into a turn the instant they leave the tubes: they follow a leisurely curve. It would require fine judgement to position the moving submarine in such a way that the torpedoes would curl into the precise line needed to attack a 20-metres-wide target 500 metres away.

The reader might like to think of it this way. A common way of describing an easy shot is to say it's like hitting a barn door from 10 paces. That would indeed be hard to miss. But if the barn door swings open, so that only the door's edge is almost facing the marksman, then it becomes a lot more difficult. Now add the fact that the rifle is not up to the marksman's shoulder and being aimed directly along the barrel through the sight: instead it is being held at arms length and angled at 60 degrees to the marksman's body, and being sighted through a mirror. It becomes a circus trick shot. That is some measure of Ban's difficulties.

Ban had a further problem. The torpedoes were driven from their tubes by a blast of compressed air. In the instant after firing, the whole trim of the submarine would be lost as the heavy torpedo was replaced by the light air in the torpedo tube, then by water flooding into the tube. The bow of the submarine would rear up sharply, and the crew needed to retrim before the second torpedo could be fired. This job took time— a matter of 30 seconds if the crew were lucky (and skilful), but two or three minutes if the submarine proved obstinate.

Ban took up position off Bradleys Head some time after midnight. There he had a stroke of bad luck followed almost at once by a counterbalancing stroke of good luck. At 12.25 am the lights at Garden Island were doused. *Chicago* was no longer silhouetted against them. The target was now much harder to see. Then Ban's luck bounced straight back: at about the same time as the lights went down, the full moon finally broke through the cloud. His target was now bathed in moonlight.

At 12.29 Ban fired his first torpedo.

Allowing time to accelerate to 44 knots, the torpedo will have taken about 30 seconds to cover the 500 metres or so between Ban's midget and *Chicago*. Even as they struggled to retrim their submarine and fire the second torpedo, each second must have been an eternity for Ban and Ashibe. The 30 seconds passed. No explosion.

Never mind. They fired the second torpedo.

On the USS *Perkins*, now back secured on the no. 4 buoy on Bode's orders, a lookout saw the first torpedo's wake coming from the direction of Bradleys Head. It passed between *Perkins* and *Chicago*, about 25 metres off *Perkins'* starboard bow. Running at 5 metres below the surface, it continued towards Garden Island, passed under the Dutch submarine *K9*, passed under the converted harbour ferry HMAS *Kuttabul*, and slammed into the Garden Island sea wall immediately below *Kuttabul*. Instead of crossing the 500 metres between Ban's midget and *Chicago*, the torpedo had to travel a total of 1100 metres for a full 60 seconds before coming to its jarring halt against the stone wall.

◆　　◆　　◆

On the bridge of the *Chicago*, Bode was still haranguing his officers. He was particularly hard on Jimmy Mecklenberg, but he made it clear they

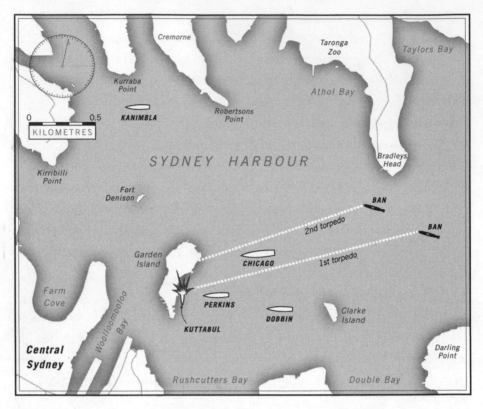

Ban's two torpedoes were fired about 30 seconds apart. The first torpedo passed between USS *Chicago* and USS *Perkins* and exploded against the Garden Island harbour wall, underneath HMAS *Kuttabul*. The second torpedo passed down *Chicago*'s starboard side and came to rest unexploded on Garden Island. The two tracks converged slightly, indicating that Ban changed position between firings. Note that the *Chicago*'s stern is facing Ban, not her long starboard side.

The diagram on the opposite page, drawn by Hugh W. Grosser for the official history of the Royal Australian Navy, is universally used to describe the midget submarine attack. It is simply wrong. Because the diagram shows USS *Chicago* facing north-west rather than a little south of west, it leaves the impression that Ban was firing at *Chicago*'s side, not her stern. As well, it shows Ban's two torpedoes fired on diverging tracks from the same static position, whereas eyewitness accounts make it clear that Ban's two torpedoes were fired on converging tracks. This is possible only if Ban changed position between shots.

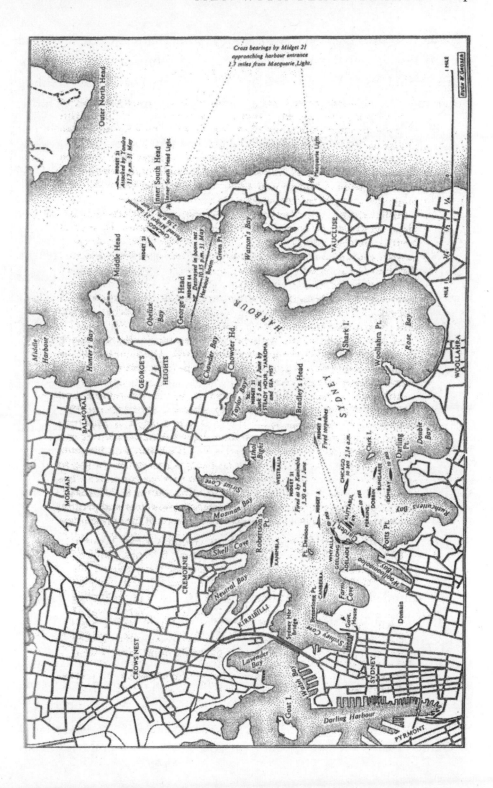

were all to blame. They were young fools. They'd got excited. They had opened fire at something in the water, not a submarine. At this point Ban's second torpedo appeared on *Chicago*'s starboard side, running along the surface and crossing *Chicago*'s bow from starboard to port. George Kitteridge remembers that it was spotted by several officers on the bridge, who interrupted Bode's tirade. 'It was obviously a torpedo wake and everybody said: look at that, look at that. Bode looked over and said: Hmp! It's just a motor launch going by.

'Just when he said that he faced us again. His back was towards the bow, and boom!'

Bode's next words were drowned by the biggest explosion of the night, only 500 metres away. Ban's first torpedo, containing 350 kilos of high explosive, detonated in the trapped space between the harbour wall, the harbour bed and the steel hull of the *Kuttabul*. The effect was devastating. The old ferry was lifted bodily from the water and brutally smashed. A ball of orange flame billowed from below the surface and lit the surrounding area, while a massive column of water spouted scores of metres in the air. An eyewitness told the *Sydney Morning Herald:* 'I saw the whole ferry lift as though she were on top of an enormous wave and then settle down again, sinking at the stern.'

In the nearby blocks of flats in Potts Point and Elizabeth Bay, crockery crashed from shelves, windows rattled, pictures fell off walls. People rushed to see what had happened. It had to be an air raid. Not a drill, either. The real thing.

◆　◆　◆

At the sound of the explosion, Captain Bode hesitated. His officers thought they detected a flicker of doubt as the monstrous roar of the torpedo's blast echoed and rumbled around the harbour. Bode's first response was to return to the attack with a new accusation. 'There you are', he snapped, 'you've got the shore batteries opening up'. However, the doubt must have been real. He turned to Jimmy Mecklenberg and said: 'Commander Mecklenberg, I want you to take my gig and go over to Garden Island. Present my compliments to Rear Admiral Muirhead-

Gould and say there's been an explosion reported and I request the nature of the explosion.'

✦   ✦   ✦

On board *Lolita* near the boom net, Rear Admiral Muirhead-Gould was about to climb back aboard his barge when he heard the explosion. 'What the hell was that?' the Admiral demanded.

Tubby Anderson knew the answer: 'If you proceed up harbour, sir, you might find your Japanese captain with a black beard.'

✦   ✦   ✦

The depth-setting mechanism failed on Ban's second torpedo. It ran along the surface instead of finding its correct depth of 5 metres. As a result, the 'arming' propeller did not spin through the required number of revolutions, and the torpedo failed to arm. It came to rest harmlessly on the shore next to Gun Wharf on Garden Island, spilling its brownish-yellow explosive innards onto the rocks.

For all Ban's undoubted courage and skill, for all his years of training and preparation, for all the meticulous planning which had gone into the raid, his attack had failed. The two torpedoes missed *Chicago* because, at the last minute, Ban's firing position off Bradleys Head made the shot impossibly difficult. The fact that the second torpedo failed to arm was neither here nor there: if it had armed correctly, a few rocks and an old wharf on Garden Island might have been violently rearranged. Yamamoto's dream of the total destruction of the American Pacific Fleet, however, would have remained as distant as ever.

Chapter 11

Sudden death

The *Kuttabul* had a slightly bizarre history. She was one of the first victims of the Harbour Bridge. *Kuttabul* was completed in 1922, destined for big things. She could carry up to 2250 passengers. She shuttled them on one of the busiest routes in the harbour: the short distance between Milsons Point at what became the northern end of the Harbour Bridge and Circular Quay ferry terminal near the southern end. When the bridge opened on 19 March 1932, *Kuttabul* was out of a job. She joined 16 other harbour ferries in the redundancy pool.

When she came off her Milsons Point route, she was used for a time as a concert boat. The concert boats and showboats were a Sydney institution right up until the 1960s. They were invariably big, and offered live entertainment as part of a three-hour cruise on the harbour. The concert boats entertained their packed passenger decks with live music, while the showboats offered a full vaudeville line-up. *Kuttabul*'s show-business career came to an abrupt end on 26 February 1941 when she was taken over by the Royal Australian Navy, to be re-born as HMAS *Kuttabul*. The navy tied her up permanently to a mooring at the south-east corner of Garden Island, and used her as a dormitory for sailors who found themselves without a current ship.

Like Sydney ferries to this day, she had two passenger decks. Passengers—or re-housed sailors—entered via a gangplank bridging the shore to the lower deck. They could then climb an internal staircase to the upper deck. There was no exit from the upper deck to shore other than by going back down the stairs. Below the lower deck were the engines. Sailors slung their hammocks on both passenger decks. Their quarters were totally spartan. Cooking and eating facilities were all ashore, as were showers and washrooms. They had card tables and a ping-pong table, but not much else—just a locker, a few lavatories and wash basins, and a place to sling their hammocks.

Kuttabul was fairly loosely controlled, so that it is not possible to say with certainty how many sailors were aboard at any given time, nor who they were. The only certainty from that night is the number of casualties. At 12.30 am on 1 June 1942, *Kuttabul* was home to at least 31 sailors from three navies—Australian, New Zealand and British.

◆   ◆   ◆

The Japanese Type 97 Special torpedo was designed to tear a large hole in the armour-plated steel hull of a battleship or aircraft carrier. Its effect on an unprotected 20-year-old civilian ferry largely built of wood was catastrophic. Ban's torpedo blasted a massive hole in *Kuttabul*'s hull towards the ferry's stern, almost breaking the ferry in two. After being tossed in the air by the initial explosion, *Kuttabul* crashed back into the water and slid straight to the harbour bed. Wintry sea water roared in through the hole in the hull, sinking the ferry instantly by the stern and engulfing the lower passenger deck. The bow remained clear of the water. Any sailors sleeping near the blast on the lower deck were probably dead by the time *Kuttabul* slammed back onto the harbour surface. The force of the blast from 350 kilos of high explosive detonating at unprotected close quarters was simply not survivable. The explosion blacked out all the lights on Garden Island, and cut the telephone cable. It started a small fire on the wharf.

At the Australian National Maritime Museum in Darling Harbour, Sydney, there is a dramatic voice tape from one of the survivors, painting a vivid word picture of the scene on board. He was quartermaster aboard the *Kuttabul* that night, and the tape tells us nothing about him other than that his name was Ed. He was lightly injured in the explosion. Here are his words:

All I can remember was when I was hit I went down on the deck. You couldn't see your hand in front of your face. I just covered up. I'd just come back from the Middle East and I thought: this is an air raid. I heard water running and I said gee, it's time I got out of here.

We all sort of made a move then. I don't know what window we got out of. Three or four of us scrambled through and we pulled ourselves up onto the wharf. Next thing we looked around and the *Kutta* was more or less right on the bottom. So there was nothing much we could do, only turn around and help get the injured.

We took them up to the sick bay on Garden Island. The Petty Officer came and said: 'Ed, you're the quartermaster here. You should know all the chaps on board.' I said: 'I'll give it a go, but they're coming and going like flies. They might be here 24 hours and they get a draft straight away.' He said: 'I'd like you to come up and try to identify some of the bodies up there in the sick bay.'

He took me up there. This will stick in my mind the rest of my life. There was one chap there: all the skin of his face, you could just lift it up, straight off. Embedded itself in my mind, that did.

There were extraordinary acts of courage that night, and extraordinary tales of luck, good and bad.

Bandsman M.N. Cumming was, as his rank implied, not a fighting sailor. He was a musician. He had boarded the *Kuttabul* only five minutes before the explosion. The blast itself caused him a few cuts, but he was otherwise uninjured. He thought the ship had been hit by a bomb. Instead of heading for the safety of shore, then only a metre or so away, he stripped off and dived repeatedly into the bitterly cold, watery wreckage, ignoring shattered glass and jagged woodwork in a frantic search for survivors. He is credited with rescuing three critically injured sailors.

Engineer Captain A.B. Doyle and Commander C.C. Clark had been ashore on Garden Island when they heard the explosion. They raced to the scene and waded straight into the deep water. In pitch darkness they ignored the dangers of splintered decks and other lethal hazards to rescue shocked and dazed sailors, and lead them to safety. Cumming, Doyle and Clark were all singled out for mention by Rear Admiral Muirhead-Gould in his report, with the implication that they all deserved medals. They did.

They had no monopoly on courage. Ordinary Seaman L.T. Combers was below decks when the explosion knocked him off his feet. He smashed through a window to safety outside the ferry. Then he heard a cry for help, and saw a sailor slipping below the surface with the sinking wreckage. Although he was now safely clear, he dived back into the danger area and managed to drag the stricken sailor to the safety of a nearby motor launch.

Petty Officer J. Littleby usually slept aboard the *Kuttabul*. That night he had accepted a friend's invitation to bunk down in a small motor boat tied up nearby. The blast and shock wave almost swamped the tiny boat. However Littleby managed to keep it afloat and bring it up alongside *Kuttabul*. Three injured sailors owe him their lives. Littleby's regular sleeping quarters on the *Kuttabul* were totally demolished in the blast. If he had been asleep in his regular place that night, the death toll might have risen by four.

Others were plain lucky. Able Seaman Neil Roberts had been on sentry duty on land. He was due to be relieved at midnight. When his relief failed to materialise, he went to look for him aboard *Kuttabul*. As a way of apologising for failing to turn up for duty on time, the chastened relief offered Roberts his bunk on the more pleasant upper deck, instead of Roberts' usual bunk on the lower deck. Roberts accepted. And lived.

Able Seaman Charlie Brown had also been on sentry duty. He had heard the gunfire and explosions on the harbour, and wondered what was happening. He went off duty at midnight and by 12.10 was asleep in his bunk on the lower deck near the bow. His next memory is of a gigantic orange ball of fire, and of being blasted between a row of wash basins through the ship's side and into the water. Debris rained down on him, trapping him. He was slipping into unconsciousness when someone saw his hand flailing in the water. He was dragged to safety.

Able Seaman Colin Whitfield, a New Zealander, had one of the most remarkable stories of the night. He was climbing out of his hammock, with his feet on the deck, when the torpedo struck. When he tried to move he found his legs were useless, although he could see no injury. He had to descend the staircase to get to safety, which he managed by bumping down on his backside. At this point he blacked out, and remembers only that somebody helped him to the jetty, then carried him to the sick bay.

His next memory is of waking up in hospital at 3 am, with the surgeon bending over him saying something like: they'll have to come off. The surgeon then told a colleague that the anaesthetist had gone home for the night so they'd have to come off in the morning. In the meantime an orderly was told to make Whitfield comfortable. The orderly took it upon himself to bind up Whitfield's feet. Although the skin was unbroken, every bone inside was smashed. In the morning the surgeon was fulsome in his praise for the orderly. He had done exactly the right thing. Whitfield's feet had been bound in such a way that the bones might re-knit. The surgeon thought the feet might be saved. They were.

Others were less lucky. Petty Officer Leonard Howard, from Penrith west of Sydney, wanted to meet his wife next day. So he swapped duty with another sailor, and stayed aboard *Kuttabul*. He was killed.

Stoker Norman Robson was due to go on leave later that morning. Before going to sleep, he posted a letter to friend, including the words: 'You can never tell with this place. Anything might happen.' The friend received the letter three days after Robson's death.

Ordinary Seaman David Trist had survived the sinking of HMS *Repulse* six months earlier, on the second day of the Pacific war. He did not survive the sinking of the *Kuttabul*.

In all, Ban's torpedo led to the death of 21 sailors aboard the *Kuttabul*, 19 Australian and two British. Of those who died, 19 were killed aboard the ship; one died later in hospital; one sailor was missing. There were 10 injured, some seriously. The death toll in the Battle of Sydney Harbour had now risen sharply, from two to 23.

At about 1 am, half an hour after the torpedo struck, *Kuttabul's* bow slid under the water, leaving only her wreckage-strewn upper deck slightly exposed.

◆　　◆　　◆

In the wake of the blast, bedlam returned to Sydney Harbour. There was wild shooting from all directions. It was a bad night for floating bits of wood, old packing cases, buoys, broaching fish, and fleeting shadows: all were sent ruthlessly to the bottom in a hail of tracer fire and heavier shells.

Some ships fired aimlessly into the air, believing this was an air raid and they might as well be seen to be doing something. Others felt obliged to sound off with klaxon horns or sirens, adding to the mindless pandemonium. The crew of the Channel Patrol boat HMAS *Marlean*, which had slipped its mooring earlier in the night and moved down the harbour to see what the fuss was all about, sheepishly admitted they had fired at their own shadow in Athol Bay, which they saw projected onto the harbour shore by the roving searchlights. Next day they scoured the papers for any report of casualties among the animals at Taronga Park zoo, which had been right in their line of fire.

This had no effect whatsoever on the two Japanese midget submarines still alive in the harbour. Matsuo continued to hide on the harbour bed just inside the entrance, awaiting his chance. He must have heard the detonation from Ban's attack, but he will not have known whether it was caused by another midget's torpedo or by some other explosive device like a depth charge. If it was a torpedo, he will not have known what damage resulted. He must have hoped that whoever had triggered the explosion had left him some worthy targets to pursue when he could finally get under way.

Meanwhile, Ban continued to creep towards the harbour exit and safety. From his periscope Ban could see the *Chicago* still serenely tied to her moorings. With both torpedoes spent, he had nothing left to fire at her but an 8 mm pistol. Time to say farewell to Sydney Harbour, and head for the open sea.

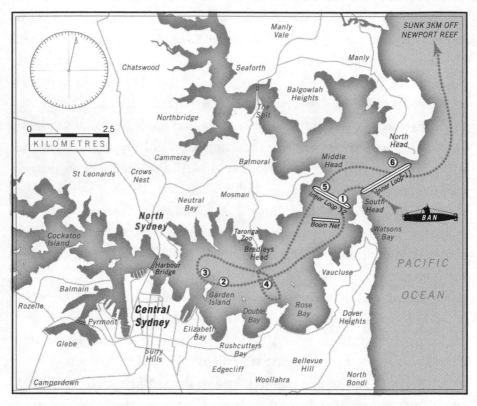

The track followed by Ban's midget is fairly well established. The timings are: (1) 9.48 pm, crosses Inner Loop 12, leaving a clear trace; (2) 10.50 pm, fired on by USS *Chicago*, and submerges; (3) 11.10 pm resurfaces, fired on by USS *Chicago* and HMAS *Geelong*, submerges; (4) 12.29 am fires two torpedoes at USS *Chicago*, both of which miss, but one sinking HMAS *Kuttabul*; (5) 1.58 am crosses Inner Loop 12; (6) 2.04 am crosses Inner Loop 11 and exits Sydney Harbour.

◆ ◆ ◆

The bedlam in the harbour was well mirrored by chaos on land. Radio stations broadcast urgent appeals to sailors to return to their ships. Taxi drivers were asked to scour the streets, cinemas, theatres, pubs, bars, nightclubs and brothels in a hunt for sailors to be rushed back to their stations. Police cars joined in the hunt for roistering crews.

Among the civilians, wild rumours spread at amazing speed. The invasion had started. The Japs were here. Even those who should have known better joined in the madness. A caller to a Sydney radio station remembered a particularly hysterical air-raid warden on his street, knocking on doors and rousing the occupants with an urgent message: 'There's an armada of aircraft. They're coming down. They've flattened Brisbane and they're now over Gosford, and soon they'll be bombing Sydney. Get the children under the table, in the hall, with a mattress on top. Good luck! Good luck!'

The 19-year-old Dorothy Levine had been on duty at the American Service Club in Phillip Street in Sydney's Central Business District. She was trying to make her way home by taxi to Vaucluse. Just as she was passing Rose Bay Police Station she saw tracer fire on the harbour followed by booming explosions.

I said to the taxi driver: my goodness, fireworks in the middle of wartime. I think it's ridiculous.

Then people came running out of all the units along the waterfront. We were told to go immediately to the nearest air raid shelter. We could hear boom, boom, boom, then a huge, loud explosion.

We were very frightened because it just wasn't natural to have all that light. The whole sky was lit up with searchlights. There seemed to be a lot of people. They just came from nowhere. Everyone was running all over the streets, not knowing what was going on.

◆　◆　◆

Rahel Cohen, a 23-year-old secretary serving in the Women's Auxiliary Air Force, had come to Sydney from Wagga Wagga on leave. At 12.15 am she caught the last ferry from Circular Quay to Athol Wharf near her parents' home in Mosman. There were only four people on board—

Rahel, an army officer Captain Ross Smith, the ferry captain and the ferry's engineer.

The ferry captain decided to take a slightly longer route this night. The Athol Wharf ferry normally tracked north-east from Circular Quay, passing to the north of the small harbour island of Fort Denison. However, an hour earlier the captain had heard shooting and general uproar from the direction of Garden Island and the USS *Chicago,* so he decided to take his ship south of Fort Denison and close to Garden Island to see what was going on.

The ferry had passed both Garden Island and *Chicago* and was about to turn left towards Athol Wharf. 'I was standing on the lower deck talking to the army man when I said: what's that? It looked like a silver thing, going under our ferry,' Rahel recalls. It was Ban's first torpedo, 5 metres below the surface and well under the ferry's hull, on its way to the *Kuttabul*. 'The Army captain saw it too. He pushed me down on the deck and fell down on top of me to protect me. Then there was a crash, of course. The torpedo had come up on the other side of our ferry and killed all the sailors. I remember the army fellow said to me: don't look.' Within seconds all hell broke loose. Searchlights flashed on all over the harbour. Rahel heard the ferry captain poke his head out of the wheelhouse and say: 'Let's get to hell out of here. Get inside. We're going to try to rush across.'

The ferry raced across the harbour to Athol Wharf. By the time it tied up, the tram which normally met it and carried the ferry passengers up the steep hill to the suburb of Mosman had fled. That night Rahel Cohen walked home, escorted in the darkness by the gallant Captain Smith.

◆ ◆ ◆

Muirhead-Gould left the boom net in his barge and went straight to his headquarters on Garden Island. Clearly his first job was to find out what had happened. This will not have taken long. By now there were plenty of people who knew it was a torpedo attack.

Jimmy Mecklenberg arrived on Garden Island in the *Chicago*'s Captain's gig at about the same time as Muirhead-Gould. His account of his encounter with Muirhead-Gould is a masterpiece of tact. 'The Admiral was well aware that there were submarines in the harbour,' Mecklenberg recalled. 'He suggested that I should tell my commanding officer to take the US forces to sea.' There is another version of this story, which suggests that Muirhead-Gould's words were a great deal more terse and to the point. In this version, his message to Bode was only five words long. 'Get out of my harbour.'

However it was expressed, the order to get under way was repeated around the harbour. The Indian Navy corvette HMIS *Bombay* and the Australian Navy corvette HMAS *Whyalla* were ordered to get moving, while the long-suffering USS *Perkins* once again slipped her mooring and set out to screen *Chicago* while the cruiser built up steam ready to head out to sea. The anti-submarine vessel HMAS *Bingera* was ordered to switch her search from the Harbour Bridge area and sweep the harbour between Garden Island and Bradleys Head, offering further protection to *Chicago*.

None of this was easily achieved. With the general overload of communications, very often there was no way to pass orders to the ships by radio. An officer was dispatched in a speedboat from Garden Island to go around the harbour advising all ships to make ready to go to sea, or to take up anti-submarine duties in the harbour.

At 1.10 am Muirhead-Gould sent out a general message: 'Enemy submarine is present in the harbour and *Kuttabul* has been torpedoed.' It was now five minutes short of five hours since Jimmy Cargill had spotted Chuman's sub in the net. Yet this message from Muirhead-Gould was the first to ships in the harbour giving them any accurate information about what was going on.

◆　◆　◆

At 1.58 am Inner Loop 12 recorded its third small, unexplained blip of the night. This was immediately taken to be a third submarine entering the harbour. In fact it was Ban on his way out.

◆　◆　◆

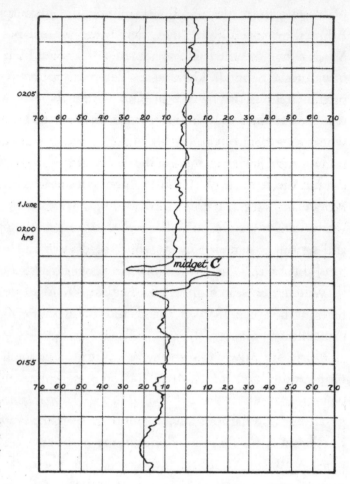

0205

70 60 50 40 30 20 10 0 10 20 30 40 50 60 70

1 June

0200
hrs

midget C

0155

70 60 50 40 30 20 10 0 10 20 30 40 50 60 70

Trace left by Ban
(I–24's midget) on
Inner Loop 12 as he
leaves the harbour
at 1.58 am.

More and more ships got under way. HMAS *Canberra*, on four hours'
notice at no. 1 buoy, was ordered to sea at 1.15 am. The Dutch
submarine *K9*, moored alongside *Kuttabul*, where she had taken a lot of
damage but injured only one sailor, was towed up the harbour and out
of harm's way at 1.20. The Australian minesweeper HMAS *Samuel
Benbow* moored off Watsons Bay reported at 1.25: 'Crew at action
stations. Raising steam.' At 2.14 *Chicago* reported: 'Proceeding to sea.'
The Australian corvette HMAS *Whyalla* informed Garden Island at 2.30:
'Slipped and proceeding to sea.'

It is worth standing back a moment and considering these decisions. Large ships like USS *Chicago* and HMAS *Canberra* are at a massive disadvantage in the tight space of a harbour, particularly a narrow harbour like Sydney's. There were enemy submarines on the loose, so the natural response of both Muirhead–Gould and the respective captains was to take their ships away from the immediate danger and out to sea where they could fight. But that raised a massive question: if there were midget submarines in the harbour, how did they get to Sydney? And if the answer was: on the backs of larger submarines as they had done at Pearl Harbor, then where did that leave the escaping ships? The answer was: in huge trouble. There were five massive 'I' class Japanese submarines, all armed with an arsenal of their justifiably feared Long Lance torpedoes, lurking in the deep water outside Sydney Harbour.

We can only guess at Sasaki's motive in not leaving at least one or two of his mother submarines outside the harbour entrance with orders to pick off any large ships trying to escape. After all, that had been his tactic at Pearl Harbor six months earlier. In his official account of the raid G. Hermon Gill concluded: 'Luck was certainly on the side of the defenders.' Luck was surely with them now. As the ships steamed towards the open ocean, the mother subs had moved off south towards the rendezvous point at Port Hacking. So no Long Lances lay in wait for *Chicago*, *Perkins*, *Canberra*, *Whyalla* and all the other warships racing for the open sea.

Chapter 12

Matsuo's turn

Chicago's departure from the harbour was scarcely dignified. From earlier cancelling Mecklenberg's orders to prepare the ship to get underway, Captain Bode was now in a tearing hurry to get out. Following the torpedo explosion, he had ordered the engine room crews to resume building up steam. The crews responded with frantic efforts. At 2.14 the cruiser was ready, and Bode signalled Garden Island: 'Proceeding to sea.' Crew members had to be sent down to the buoy to unshackle the cruiser from its mooring. *Chicago* slipped with such indecent haste that at least one crew member was left behind, stranded on the buoy and shouting to his ship to wait for him. The telephone line to Garden Island via the buoy was not disconnected, and snapped as the giant cruiser backed off her mooring. Jimmy Mecklenberg, sent to Garden Island on the captain's gig, had to race up the harbour to catch up with his departing ship. *Chicago* paused briefly in mid-harbour to gather him up, then continued her charge towards the open sea and hopes of safety.

At 2.43 am the Port War Signal Station reported: '*Perkins* to sea.' At 2.56 they followed up with: '*Chicago* to sea.' Both American ships had passed through the boom gate, crossed Inner Loop 12 and were on their way out of the harbour.

On the bridge of the *Chicago* Captain Bode was still not convinced by his officers' account of sighting and firing at a midget submarine. As the cruiser steamed up to the harbour entrance Bode turned to Jimmy Mecklenberg and said: 'You wouldn't know what a submarine looks like.' In life it is seldom given to anyone to have a perfect riposte to this kind of remark, but this was Jimmy Mecklenberg's lucky night. 'They looked like that, Captain,' said Mecklenberg, pointing to a midget submarine passing down *Chicago*'s starboard side, too close for the guns to depress and fire at it. The midget was so close that it probably collided with *Chicago*, though nobody aboard *Chicago* felt any impact.

There was now no room for doubt. At 3 am Captain Bode ordered a fresh signal to Garden Island: 'Submarine entering harbour.' At 3.01 Inner Loop 12 recorded its fourth enemy blip of the night. After almost four hours of sitting patiently on the ocean bottom near the Sydney Harbour heads, Matsuo and his two torpedoes were on the move and inside Sydney Harbour.

◆　　◆　　◆

The Lieutenant in the speedboat criss-crossing the harbour with instructions to ships to get under way finally reached the remaining Channel Patrol boats in Farm Cove at around 3 am. His message to Reg Andrew and *Sea Mist* was scarcely a detailed set of orders. 'I think you'd better get under way,' the Lieutenant called out. 'There are subs in the harbour.' That was the first indication Reg Andrew had of what the firing was all about, and what was going on.

At this point Lieutenant Athol Townley appeared on the deck of the Channel Patrol boat *Steady Hour*, tied up behind *Sea Mist*. Townley had officially relinquished his command of *Steady Hour* at midnight (at the same moment that Reg Andrew took over command of *Sea Mist*). However, he had agreed to stay on board to allow the new skipper a night ashore. He was senior to Reg Andrew and the other Channel Patrol boat skippers on the harbour, and he assumed command. Was Reg Andrew ready to move? Yes. Okay, said Townley, go to Bradleys Head. Set your depth charges to 50 feet (15 metres).

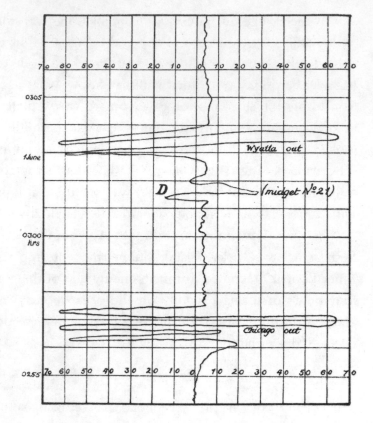

Trace left by Matsuo (I-22's midget) on Inner Loop 12 as he enters the harbour at 3.01 am.

After ordering the motor mechanic Winstanley to start the engines and the coxswain Potter to rouse the crew, Reg Andrew changed into his uniform and collected the vital paper with the code letter of the day on it. Now prepared, he ran to the upper deck and took over the throttles and wheel, ordered the mooring lines cast off, and set off down the harbour. *Sea Mists*'s new skipper was not exactly brimming with confidence. He was not alarmed by the prospect of enemy submarines: he was much more afraid of being mistaken for one of them and shot at by his own side. There had been plenty of wild firing earlier in the night. In the now darkened harbour he threaded his way cautiously through the unlit warships to his allotted station off Bradleys Head.

There was plenty to think about on the way. He had no idea how to fire a depth charge, let alone set it to 50 feet. There was also the Very pistol. Orders required the firing of two red Very flares before launching an attack, to warn other ships to stay clear. There was a Very pistol with red, green and white flares in the darkened wheelhouse. Which were which? The green ones had no serrated edge, and they felt greasy. That was a start.

The order to set depth charges to 50 feet carried serious implications. A depth charge takes about four seconds to drop 50 feet through water. The best *Sea Mist* could hope for was a speed of 10 knots. At that speed, a boat travels 20 metres in four seconds. So *Sea Mist* would have, at most, 20 metres between her and the blast from 180 kilos of military-grade high explosive. It was not a prospect to relish. For a young naval Lieutenant three and a half hours into his first command, working in a boat and with a crew he had met less than 24 hours earlier, carrying weapons he neither knew nor had practised with, going into battle must have been a daunting prospect.

When both *Sea Mist* and *Steady Hour* reached Bradleys Head, Townley ordered *Sea Mist* to patrol between Bradleys Head and the west boom gate. This gave Reg Andrew about 2500 metres of harbour shore to cover, including two bays, Chowder Bay and Taylors Bay. He decided to hold *Sea Mist* on a course following the shape of the shoreline, standing off about 150 metres as he tracked slowly between his two turning points.

It was now 3.35 am and six Channel Patrol boats swarmed around the boom net: *Toomaree* guarded the east boom gate; *Marlean* and *Sea Mist* patrolled the west boom gate and back into the harbour; *Yarroma*, *Steady Hour* and *Lolita* roamed freely throughout the area. *Yarroma* was now a key player: she carried ASDIC, and could look for submerged submarines as well as any sub foolish enough to broach the surface.

◆　　◆　　◆

At 1.05 am Licensed Fishing Boat no. 92 (the trawler *San Michele*) sighted a large submarine off Cronulla, a Sydney beach suburb well south of the harbour entrance. At 3.40 am she reported her sighting, probably to the Port War Signal Station. The mother subs had begun to arrive at the rendezvous point.

◆ ◆ ◆

We can only speculate on Matsuo's progress after entering the harbour. He probably began by picking his way carefully towards the Harbour Bridge. We know that he intended to head for Garden Island and the warships tied up there. By now his principal target USS *Chicago* was well out to sea. That left the cruiser HMAS *Canberra*, still tied up at Bennelong Point, the armed merchant cruiser HMAS *Westralia* moored in Athol Bay off Robertsons Point, and another armed merchant cruiser HMS *Kanimbla* moored at Birts Buoy near Kirribilli Point. All were worthy targets. After that, the harbour was plentifully stocked with smaller warships. If Matsuo made it as far as mid-harbour, and there is evidence that he did, then he will not have wanted for ships to attack.

At 3.50 am *Kanimbla* switched on her searchlight and opened fire on what she thought was a submarine. The anti-submarine vessel HMAS *Bingera*, patrolling between Garden Island and Bradleys Head, raced over towards Kirribilli to join the fray but found nothing. The timing of *Kanimbla*'s sighting—50 minutes after Matsuo crossed Inner Loop 12—suggests that the *Kanimbla*'s lookouts may well have spotted the real thing.

The harbour stayed quiet for the next hour. As Matsuo had something of a track record for lying low, this too is consistent with a genuine sighting. At 4.40 am HMAS *Canberra* sighted what she thought was a torpedo track coming from the direction of Bradleys Head. At 4.50 am the minesweeper HMAS *Doomba* signalled to *Bingera* that they had a submarine contact off Robertsons Point, the next big headland after Bradleys Head on the north side of Sydney Harbour. Again *Bingera* raced to the spot, and again found nothing.

Most accounts of the raid assume that the 'torpedo track' sighted by *Canberra* was a false alarm, in a night when false alarms were in plentiful supply. There is, however, a much more sinister explanation which needs examination. We know from subsequent events that at some time during the night Matsuo fired both his torpedoes, though we have no way of knowing when. Both failed to leave their tubes. The midget's crew had operated the bow cap releases from inside the submarine, but both torpedo tubes remained blocked. The submarine's bow cage had been crushed inwards from both sides as the result of collisions, depth charges or both. This prevented the bow caps from dropping clear. The lower bow cap was damaged as well as blocked. Finally, the lower torpedo tube had been fired while the external adjustment fittings were still engaged, though these sheared off when the torpedo moved inside the tube. The failure of both torpedoes to launch correctly was the result of external damage to the submarine. The question is: when and how was the damage done?

We know for sure that Matsuo's sub was rammed by *Yandra* at 10.58 pm, and that the impact probably was felt in the submarine's bow area. That alone could account for the buckled bow cage, the damaged lower bow cap and the jamming of both caps. *Yandra* then dropped six depth charges from close range, and any one of these might have done the damage, or exacerbated it. There is the possibility that Matsuo collided with *Chicago* on his way into the harbour. This would have been a harsher impact than *Yandra*'s, because Matsuo and *Chicago* were travelling in opposite directions. This impact, if it happened at all, would have been felt mostly by the midget's bow. So it, too, might account for some of the damage. Whatever the reason, it appears certain that Matsuo's torpedoes were unable to launch by the time he made his way down the harbour and prepared to attack. He had no way of knowing this until he tried to fire his weapons.

If he crept down the harbour then went to periscope depth some-where around Bradleys Head, HMAS *Canberra* would be the sitting duck of legend, tied up to no. 1 buoy in the entrance to Farm Cove off Bennelong Point. Any reader who finds himself or herself in Sydney and who cares to take the attractive bushland drive down to Bradleys Head lookout and ask how easy it would be to fire a shot at the Sydney Opera House from there will know how simple Matsuo's task looked. Matsuo's shot would be from a range of well under 2000 metres aimed at a stationary target, with his torpedo passing between Garden Island and Fort Denison on its way to *Canberra*'s exposed flank.

It is easy to imagine Matsuo lining up his submarine facing *Canberra*, sending his crewman Tsuzuku forward to release the bow caps, then giving Tsuzuku the order to fire. It is even easier to imagine Matsuo's legendarily volcanic temper exploding when the torpedo failed to leave the tube. What had gone wrong? There was no way of knowing from inside the submarine. Okay, let's try the second torpedo. This shot was probably fired in a fury, because the crew forgot to disengage the external adjustment fittings. The problem, however, was the buckled bow cage and the jammed bow caps, not the adjustment fittings. The result was the same—a hiss of compressed air followed by the dismal realisation that the second torpedo also remained firmly stuck in its tube. The long streak of compressed air bubbles released by the two firings might easily account for HMAS *Canberra*'s 'torpedo track'.

If this sequence of events, or something like them, did indeed take place then two things follow. An Allied ship, most likely *Canberra*, just had the escape of a lifetime. And Matsuo's logical next step would be to see if he could fix his problem and still salvage something from the attack. He was in the middle of a hostile harbour so he would need to find somewhere quiet, away from the searchlights and sheltered from the south-westerly wind, where he could risk surfacing and attempt to free the torpedoes. The quietest and darkest parts of the harbour were on the northern side, where bushland rather than houses lines the shore. Taylors Bay, just behind him, would be ideal.

◆　　◆　　◆

Reg Andrew's first impression as he began his patrol was the profusion of ships now active on the harbour. There were minesweepers, corvettes, Channel Patrol boats, Nappies, all swirling around him. Why hadn't the reserve Channel Patrol boats been called in earlier?

Sea Mist cruised her way between the western boom gate and Bradleys Head, scouring the harbour surface for periscopes and other danger signs. She showed no lights, and the crew had only intermittent moonlight to guide them. Sydney Harbour in the early hours of the morning is an eerie place at the best of times. When the wind is up, waves crash on the rocky shores and fling spray high in the air, while the sounds of wind and sea in the darkness can be ominous rather than soothing. The darkened headlands and bays look alike to all but the most experienced. There are reefs and hidden rocks to avoid. In the early hours of 1 June 1942 there was also the small matter of a lethal enemy lurking below the surface, hell bent on inflicting more death and destruction.

◆　◆　◆

Margaret Hamilton couldn't get to sleep in her second-floor bedroom overlooking Taylors Bay. She had heard the loudspeakers on *Chicago* barking out orders, and the sounds of *Chicago*'s and *Whyalla*'s guns, followed 90 minutes later by the blast which sank *Kuttabul*. The events of the night were too exciting for sleep. Some time in the early hours of the morning she left her bed to take a look from her balcony and see if anything new was happening.

Her eyes were already adjusted to the darkness, and she had the help of a little light reflected into the bay from anti-aircraft searchlights shining into clouds over the harbour. In the calm water she saw a submarine periscope making its way gently into Taylors Bay, heading towards the sandy beach 100 metres west of her vantage point.

Beyond the periscope she could see the harbour swarming with patrol boats and larger warships, so clearly the navy had it all in hand. When the periscope disappeared from sight, she went back to bed.

◆　◆　◆

Reg Andrew and his crew patrolled their stretch of the harbour without incident for an hour. Then, at 4.30 am the minesweeper HMAS *Goonambee* called to them through a loud-hailer. There was a suspicious object in Taylors Bay. Could *Sea Mist* please investigate and report? *Sea Mist* made a thorough search of the area and found nothing but an old boomerang buoy. This particular design of permanent buoy was prevalent in Sydney Harbour in the 1940s. It was huge and metallic, designed to give a secure mooring to bigger harbour boats, particularly large yachts. A boomerang buoy was big enough for a man to stand on comfortably if he was so minded. *Sea Mist* moved back closer to *Goonambee* and announced through her loud-hailer that Taylors Bay was clear of submarines.

Reg Andrew resumed his patrol. He was now on his second round trip between Bradleys Head and the west boom gate, and he still had nothing to show for it. At around 5 am, with dawn not far away, *Sea Mist* was on a south-westerly heading on the leg from the boom gate to Bradleys Head. She had just passed Chowder Head and was moving across the entrance to Taylors Bay when the skipper spotted a black object in the water about halfway between the patrol boat and the shore. Reg Andrew turned *Sea Mist* to starboard and set off to investigate. As he drew closer, the answer became clear even in the darkness. He was closing in on a submarine, its bow pointing down the harbour towards the boom net, with a metre of its conning tower protruding from the water. It was, in Reg Andrew's own words, 'a shattering experience'.

Andrew brought *Sea Mist* around behind the submarine, still in a right turn. He was now between the submarine and the Taylors Bay shore, about 50 metres from the water's edge, with both vessels pointing north-east towards the boom net. As he circled he called orders. Did anyone know how to set depth charges? Yes, said Coxswain Potter. Okay, prepare charges and set them to 50 feet (15 metres). By rights the depth charges should have had their safety lashings removed on the way from Farm Cove, but nobody had told the coxswain to do this. Potter now worked frantically to free the charges before he could set them to the required depth. Next the Very pistol. Bring me the Very pistol and two red flares, the new skipper demanded. 'Which cartridges are the red ones?' a plaintive voice called from below. More shouting. Andrew continued his circle.

Sea Mist had completed its first circle and returned to its original starting position when Coxswain Potter reported that depth charges were

Rear Admiral Gerard
Charles Muirhead-Gould,
photographed in Sydney.

An excellent aerial picture of USS *Chicago,* showing the four Curtiss Seagull aircraft strapped to her deck.

Japanese midget submariners photographed in an informal moment during training. Matsuo is front row, left, while Chuman, rear left, peers over his shoulder.

The Japanese midget submariners in formal pose before the raid. Commanding officers are in the front row with their crewmen behind them. Ban is front left, Chuman is third from left and Matsuo is fifth from left.

Lieutenant Reginald Andrew, commander of the channel patrol boat HMAS *Sea Mist*.

Warrant Officer Herbert ('Tubby') Anderson, commander of HMAS *Lolita*.

Jimmy Cargill, the Maritime Services Board nightwatchman who first raised the alarm.

The boom net after completion, viewed from the western side. On the night of 31 May 1942 the curved boom gate on the centre right of the picture had not been fitted. Only the centre section stood ready to block ships and submarines. Note the Pile Light just to the left of the Western Gate and on the harbour side. Chuman's propellers became tangled in the net opposite the pile light, in 13½ fathoms of water.

Roy Coóté (left) 'suited up' and ready to dive. The identity of the second diver is not known, but it may well be Lance Bullard. *(Photograph courtesy Coóté family collection.)*

This picture has never previously been published. It shows Chuman's midget seconds after it was raised from the harbour bed, with the coils of the boom net clearly shown tangled around the sub's propellers. *(Photograph courtesy Coóté family collection.)*

Postcard produced by the Royal Australian Navy and sold as a souvenir of the submarine attack. This particular postcard shows the fearful beating from depth charges suffered by Matsuo's midget. The massive dent behind the conning tower is clearly the result of a depth charge detonated at very close range. It may well be the outcome of Reg Andrew's first attack in Taylors Bay.

A dockyard worker clearing wreckage from the devastated depot ship HMAS *Kuttabul*. *(Photograph courtesy Cooté family collection.)*

Matsuo's midget shortly after it had been recovered from Taylors Bay. This photograph clearly shows the bow cage bent inwards on both sides, with the bow caps jammed and blocking any possible release of the two torpedoes.

Channel patrol boat HMAS *Sea Mist,* whose crew dropped the first depth charge on Matsuo's midget in Taylors Bay. Note the lone machine gun, and depth charges strapped to the rear deck.

The scene on 8 June 1942 after the shelling of the Eastern Suburbs of Sydney. This photograph was taken at the corner of Fletcher and Small streets, Woollahra. The map given to the author by the Australian War Memorial records this shell as 'exploded, no damage' but the contemporary photograph suggests the outcome was rather more destructive.

The centre section of Chuman's submarine on its trailer journey around Australia. The navy chose to fly the White Ensign naval flag over their trophy.

The composite submarine, assembled from Matsuo's bow and the mid and stern sections of Chuman's midget, is the centrepiece of the most popular display in the Australian War Memorial in Canberra. It is just possible to see the denting of Matsuo's bow caused by the steel cable used to haul it up from the bottom of Sydney Harbour. Although much of the exterior of the submarine has been restored, the War Memorial has left the centre section as it was found, ripped open by the force of Chuman's scuttling charges.

The stern section of Matsuo's midget. This section broke away from the main body when the submarine was being dragged along the harbour bed to shallower water in Taylors Bay.

The bow of Matsuo's submarine, part of the special display at the Australian War Memorial. The bow cage has been straightened and the bow caps have been repaired and locked back into place.

This contemporary photograph, taken just off Bradleys Head on Sydney Harbour, shows Garden Island as it might have looked through Ban's periscope. The *Kuttabul* was moored in front of the low pink building on the centre left. The buoys' positions have changed since 1942, but the large white buoy on the extreme left of the picture is not far from the position of No. 4 buoy, where the USS *Perkins* was tied up on the night of 31 May 1942. From this position, Ban would have faced *Perkins'* stern.

Ban's midget at rest on the seabed off Newport Reef, Sydney. A diver's light illuminates a shoal of fish below the wrecked conning tower. The large hole in the hull is caused by corrosion after 64 years under water, and indicates the fragility of the wreck. Two lines can be seen on either side of the conning tower, both left behind by commercial fishing boats snagging their fishing lines and nets over the years. *(Photograph courtesy* 60 Minutes *and No Frills Divers).*

The graceful 'Tresco' still adorns Sydney Harbour's foreshore at Elizabeth Bay. Rear Admiral Muirhead–Gould could walk down the cliff path to a small wharf, where his barge would deliver him to his headquarters on Garden Island, a few hundred metres away.

Margaret Coote (*née* Hamilton) peers intently at the conning tower of Matsuo's submarine, on display at the Naval Heritage Centre on Garden Island, Sydney. This picture, taken in October 2006, records her first sighting of the submarine for more than 60 years: it last appeared in her life in June 1942, when she watched it being dragged to the surface in Taylors Bay. Previously she had seen its periscope gliding into Taylors Bay, and had watched the depth charge attack that led to its destruction.

This photograph of the western Pile Light was taken from the deck of the Manly ferry on its regular route via the Western Channel from Manly to Circular Quay shortly before its collapse at 4.30 pm on 12 December 2006. Its role in the Battle of Sydney Harbour—Chuman reversed into the boom net while submerged, almost certainly after colliding with the Pile Light—has never been given proper recognition. The old light, rebuilt in 1947, was at least as effective as the newfangled net in foiling Chuman's attack.

Sydney is packed with reminders of its World War II past. This concrete slab on Laings Point, an easy walk from the Watsons Bay ferry wharf and Doyle's Restaurant, was the anchor for the eastern end of a boom net that stretched across the harbour to Georges Head. Today it is marked by a small plaque, including a brief description of the net's role in the Battle of Sydney Harbour.

ready. Someone handed Reg Andrew the Very pistol and a single cartridge of unknown colour. This would have to do. At this point Matsuo must have realised he was in deadly danger. His midget submerged, leaving only a swirl of water on the surface. Reg Andrew knew he had to act straightaway or he would lose his quarry. *Sea Mist's* twin engines bellowed to maximum revolutions. Andrew simultaneously ordered the first depth charge dropped on the spot where the sub had disappeared and fired the Very pistol and its mystery flare. To his relief and mild surprise the flare bathed Taylors Bay in weird red light. This was followed by a tremendous explosion. According to Andrew: '*Sea Mist* rode the resulting wave like a surf boat.' A huge column of water was hurled into the air by the detonation and temporarily blacked out the night sky.

♦ ♦ ♦

Reg Andrew died in July 1984. He went to his grave stubbornly believing the version of events which follows. His refusal to budge from it cost him the sole credit he almost certainly deserved for sinking Matsuo's midget. Andrew's version cannot be correct, and it may be possible after all these years to come up with an explanation which both fits the facts and confirms his place as the hero he surely was.

In Reg Andrew's version, *Sea Mist* continued to circle, once again reaching her original starting point. Andrew could hear splashing coming from the spot where he dropped his first charge. Soon he could see the source of the splashing: Matsuo's twin propellers were rising slowly out of the water, the blades turning in opposite directions inside their metal cage. Andrew called for a second red Very cartridge, and ordered the coxswain to prepare a second depth charge.

Sea Mist continued in a tight circle to starboard. Let Reg Andrew now take over the narrative. He had the unnerving habit of writing about himself in the third person, which did him no good a few days later when he came to submit his action report. These are his words:

The commanding officer of *Sea Mist* now turned his charge to once again come between the midget submarine and the shore.

This time he ventured closer to the hull, which was now clearly visible and upside down. So close was *Sea Mist* that he could have easily stepped off the deck onto the hull of the submarine. At this time *Sea Mist* saw the inverted submarine with its bottom painted red, possibly of red lead origin.

Maximum revolutions were ordered for the engine when there was a shout from the coxswain aft: 'There are two more behind us.'

This amazing sight was probably witnessed as well from the wheelhouse as he remembers confirmation. He took a quick look himself and sure enough there were two more astern with their conning towers clearly outlined not 45 metres away. He had time to note the nearest was in the process of crash diving, but the aspect was peculiar. The submarine was not moving forward and the conning tower was boiling with escaping air. It was slipping below the sea, sinking.

Back to the job in hand, he fired another Verey flare which miraculously turned out to be red. He ordered another depth charge to be dropped. The commander of *Sea Mist* waited with bated breath for the tremendous upheaval from 180 kg of TNT, which was about to explode. Explode it did and *Sea Mist* seemed to receive as much of a shock as the stricken midget. At once its 10 knots were reduced to five knots and the motor mechanic reported one engine had stopped. The attack on this Japanese midget submarine by *Sea Mist* took place at approximately 5.15 am on the 1st of June.

Now we can be absolutely certain of one thing: at no time were there three midget submarines in Taylors Bay that night. Only three submarines took part in the attack. One had long ago scuttled in the net, and one had escaped to sea. That left only Matsuo in Taylors Bay.

The first clue is the red lead. Japanese midget submarines did not have red lead paint on their hulls: boomerang buoys did. On Reg Andrew's own description, we can be fairly certain his second depth charge did nothing to improve the health of the blameless buoy. The tide was low at 5.15 am that morning in Sydney Harbour, so the buoy's chain will have had plenty of slack. The most likely explanation is that *Sea Mist's* first depth charge, which caught Matsuo squarely, also flipped the buoy on its back. Darkness and disorientation did the rest.

That leaves the question of the 'two' submarines sighted. The propellers which Reg Andrew saw emerge from the water could only be Matsuo's sub in its death throes. Nobody on the Allied side knew that these submarines had cages around their propellers, an alteration made after the Pearl Harbor attack. So the crew of *Sea Mist* could only have known this through a genuine sighting. That leaves two conning towers to be accounted for. From Reg Andrew's description, it is clear that one conning tower was closer to *Sea Mist* and was seen more clearly than the other, so the second conning tower is the problem.

I am indebted to the author Steven Carruthers for an ingenious thought. It came too late for inclusion in his book, *Japanese Submarine Raiders 1942: A Maritime Mystery*, and he generously passed it on.

As we shall see, when salvage operations began on Matsuo's submarine there was an attempt to drag it along the harbour bed to shallower water, away from the main shipping channel. During this process the rear section of the sub, containing the electric motor and propeller shaft, broke off just behind the rear watertight bulkhead. Steven's suggestion is that *Sea Mist's* first depth charge broke the midget's back, causing a partial separation of the rear section. First the stern appeared above the water, with its propellers turning. Then, as the stern began to fall back to the bottom, the bow and conning tower swung up and broke the surface separately, giving the impression of two more submarines.

This author is inclined to place his trust in a law of science known as Ockham's razor. It is named after the 14th-century philosopher William of Ockham, who spent most of his life denouncing the temporal powers of the papacy. In his spare time William came up with one of science's most fundamental rules, which has stood the test of seven centuries. It states that when there are several possible explanations for something, the simplest explanation is correct.

In this case, the simplest explanation is that Reg Andrew and his coxswain made a mistake. If the great William of Ockham were with us today, he would probably agree that the first depth charge caught Matsuo's sub squarely and blew it out of the water, stern first. The sub then slid back into the water out of sight while *Sea Mist* continued its tight circle. *Sea Mist* then locked onto the boomerang buoy and positioned to attack it. At this moment the submarine resurfaced 45 metres away—they had an impressive track record for doing this sort of thing unasked—showing its conning tower and plenty of bubbles. So in the split second glimpse in poor light, and after the confusion of endless circling, what Reg Andrew and his coxswain saw and correctly identified was the conning tower of Matsuo's submarine, while they prepared to attack the boomerang buoy. And the second conning tower? Very likely a projected shadow of the real thing—after all, Reg Andrew's fellow Channel Patrol boat *Marlean* had fired at her own shadow only a few hours earlier. On a dark night and in the heat of battle, it would be an easy mistake to make.

Whatever the truth, it is clear there was no fight left in Matsuo's submarine after Reg Andrew's first depth charge. First the stern appeared above the water, the propellers thrashing aimlessly, with the submarine clearly out of control. Then a conning tower of a sinking submarine was seen 'bursting with escaping air'. Finally, after the attack divers found a sunken Japanese midget submarine at the precise location of *Sea Mist*'s attack.

◆　　◆　　◆

The scene aboard the submarine after Reg Andrew's first depth charge must have been appalling. Both crewmen would now be deaf, their eardrums ruptured and bleeding from the shock of the blast. The submarine would be taking on water through sprung plates on its hull. The violence of the blast followed by the submarine's contortions in the water will have flung the crew heavily against the hard and jutting metal controls. However, we know from the salvaged wreckage that the waterproof bulkheads appear to have held, so harbour water would not be gushing into the crew area with drowning force just yet.

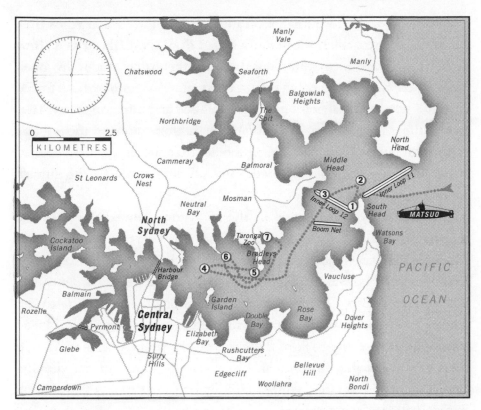

Matsuo's track inside Sydney Harbour remains a matter for conjecture. This diagram assumes that the various sightings and alarms between 3.40 am and 4.50 am were genuine. If they were, then Matsuo followed a complicated path between Bradleys Head and the Harbour Bridge, making two forays into the inner harbour north of Garden Island. His movements were: (1) 10.54 pm seen by HMAS *Lauriana* and HMAS *Yandra* entering the harbour, and subsequently rammed by *Yandra*; (2) 11.07 pm, attacked by *Yandra* with six depth charges at close quarters; (3) 3.01 am crosses Inner Loop 12 and enters harbour via the Western Gate; (4) 3.50 am, HMS *Kanimbla* fires at submarine contact in mid-harbour; (5) 4.40 am, HMAS *Canberra* sees 'torpedo tracks' fired from the direction of Bradleys Head, possibly plume of compressed air from Matsuo's jammed torpedo tubes; (6) 4.50 am HMAS *Doomba* signals to the anti-submarine specialist HMAS *Bingera* submarine contact off Robertsons Point, but nothing found; (7) 5.15 am Matsuo attacked and sunk by HMAS *Sea Mist* in Taylors Bay.

The submarine dived when it heard *Sea Mist* first approaching, so it must have been under the crew's full control up to that moment. At some point the crew attempted to fire both sets of scuttling charges, but the wicks were damp and the charges failed. The most intriguing action involved the access hatch on the bottom of the submarine's hull. It was wide open when the sub was raised from the harbour bed a few days later. There are endless reasons why the hatch might fly open without the help of the crew: one of the depth charges may have forced it, or it could have snagged on the harbour bed and burst open days later when the sub was dragged along the bottom during the salvage operation. But there remains the possibility that one of the crew opened it deliberately with the intention of trying to swim to the surface and survive.

Tsuzuku's body was found in the aft battery compartment of the submarine, with his shoes removed. This gave rise to a suggestion in Muirhead-Gould's report that he might have been planning to escape. If he was, then he was heading the wrong way: the access hatch was in the forward battery compartment, just in front of the conning tower. There was no escape route from the rear of the submarine. He was killed by a single shot to the back of the head, clearly fired by Matsuo. Matsuo then turned the gun on himself. His body was found in the conning tower. As the sun rose on Sydney Harbour on 1 June 1942, the death toll in the Battle of Sydney Harbour also rose—to 25.

The skilful Matsuo did a good job preserving his batteries: his electric motor was still turning gently eight hours later when the divers found the wreckage. The upper torpedo's 10,000-kilometre odyssey from Japan to Truk Island, then on to Sydney and finally into Sydney Harbour itself, ended with a journey of about a metre inside the tube where it had jammed. The lower torpedo fared worse—its entire journey after firing had taken it a mere 45 centimetres.

Chapter 13

Examining the wreckage

One of the more bizarre document folders in the Australian War Memorial's collection in Canberra is AWM 6945/27. It contains two letters, one dated 5 October 1948 addressed to the official navy historian, Commander G. Hermon Gill, from Ric Breydon, the commander of the Channel Patrol boat flotilla, and a second letter from Gill replying to Breydon, dated 29 November 1948. It is apparent from the tone of the correspondence that the row over who sank Matsuo's submarine still had a good head of steam six and a half years after the event.

There are two claimants: Reg Andrew and the crew of *Sea Mist*; and Athol Townley and the crew of *Steady Hour*. It is easy to take Reg Andrew's side, if only because we have more access to it. He left behind long taped interviews, several written accounts and some detailed correspondence. Persistent efforts by the author have failed to turn up the action reports filed by *Steady Hour* and *Yarroma*, or their log books, despite thorough searches in all the archives, libraries and institutions named in the acknowledgements to this book. Previous researchers on this subject have obviously come to the same dead end.

Let us therefore begin with Reg Andrew's account. Just to recap: he had dropped two depth charges on what he at first believed was the same submarine (though he would later claim he attacked two different submarines). He had sighted two submarines behind him while attacking the third. One of the two submarines behind him appeared to be sinking, though his first reaction is that it was crash-diving. The long and short of it is that, as far as he was concerned, he had sunk at least one submarine in Taylors Bay, but there were still two enemy submarines alive and kicking in the bay. Both were in urgent need of attention, and his half-powered and crocked boat could do nothing about them.

His first action was to signal with his Aldis light to his fellow Channel Patrol boat *Steady Hour*, standing off the entrance to Taylors Bay about 200 metres away. On board *Steady Hour*, Lieutenant Athol Townley was acting commander of the whole Channel Patrol boat flotilla, as well as acting skipper of *Steady Hour*. He was older than Reg Andrew and had been an officer of the Channel Patrol boat flotilla a great deal longer than Reg Andrew's five hours. Andrew had two urgent messages for Townley: first, there were still two enemy submarines in Taylors Bay; second, *Sea Mist* was crippled and could no longer take part in any attack. Townley needed to get more Channel Patrol boats into the bay before the two submarines escaped.

In Andrew's account, there was no response from *Steady Hour* to *Sea Mist*'s Aldis lamp signals. Andrew then set off to crawl on his single surviving engine across the 200 metres separating the two Channel Patrol boats. He called to Townley through a loud-hailer. Townley was more interested in cross-examining the very junior new commander than he was in hunting for submarines.

Had Andrew fired any flares? Had he dropped any depth charges? These were fairly fatuous questions, given that the depth charge detonations could be heard for kilometres around, and the Very flares had lit up the entire neighbourhood. Andrew is happy to admit that he had been feeling pretty pleased with himself up to this point. Now he found himself on the receiving end of a whole lot of sceptical and antagonistic questions. He turned angry. He had explained to Townley that *Sea Mist* was crippled. 'If you don't renew the attack, the subs will get away,' he shouted at Townley through the loud-hailer. Townley's response was dismissive. 'You're no fucking use around here,' he shouted back through his loud-hailer. 'Fuck off to base!'

The crestfallen Reg Andrew retreated a few hundred metres towards the centre of the harbour, but hung around to watch the action. Meanwhile, Townley began a search of Taylors Bay. Having seen and heard nothing, he signalled to *Yarroma*, patrolling the boom net area, to come and join him. *Yarroma* carried both ASDIC and hydrophone, and could hunt for submerged submarines without the need for a visual contact. For 80 minutes the two Channel Patrol boats scoured Taylors Bay, with *Yarroma*'s ASDIC pinging fruitlessly. Then at 6.40 am, an hour and 25 minutes after Reg Andrew's attack, *Steady Hour* had a contact and dropped her first depth charge of the morning.

Eighteen minutes later *Yarroma* picked up an ASDIC contact from the same submarine, and more depth charges tumbled into Taylors Bay. This pattern continued for the next two hours. *Steady Hour* and *Yarroma* scoured the bay, dropping depth charges on contacts. In all, nine depth charges exploded in Taylors Bay that morning. *Yarroma*'s final depth charge, dropped in broad daylight at 8.27 am, was the final shot in the Battle of Sydney Harbour.

◆   ◆   ◆

Reg Andrew's first depth charge detonated about 150 metres from Margaret Hamilton's bedroom overlooking Taylors Bay. The force of the explosion rocked the house—there is still a large crack today in the brickwork of the balcony—and threw her brother Bob out of bed. The whole household rushed to the window to see what was going on. 'There were a lot of searchlights going. They were criss-crossing, flying around the sky. They didn't know where to look,' she recalls.

The bay rapidly filled with patrol boats. 'The whole harbour seemed to be alive. The sea was white froth. They weren't just whizzing round—they were going with a purpose. They were charging, and we could see them rolling the depth charges off the back. Then, of course, they got the hell out of the way as fast as an express train. Then they'd turn, be curious. How did we go?'

Margaret and family watched the unfolding attack while dawn slowly lit the bay. Then she had a ferry to catch. After all, the ferry service and secretarial college had no cause to take a day off just because Sydney Harbour was under attack.

◆   ◆   ◆

The row over who sank Matsuo's submarine is, in the overall scheme of things, a trivial matter. More than 60 years later, who cares? But insofar as it led to a clash with authority by Reg Andrew and an unjust sidelining of *Sea Mist*'s new commander for most of the war, it is an important illustration of how awkward heroes can often suffer cruelly for their stubbornness.

In fairness to Athol Townley, we need an objective look at his version of the morning's work in Taylors Bay. In the absence of his action report, we can make a start by relying on Breydon's letter to Gill, which is based on Townley's vanished report and which tells Townley's story in good detail. In Townley's recollection, Andrew reported to him that he had attacked one submarine and believed he had sunk it. At the same time, Andrew had also sighted two other submarines about 50 yards (45 metres) away but had not attacked either of them. In the course of the attack on the first submarine, his port engine was put temporarily out of action and he could not carry out another attack for some time. Townley then ordered *Sea Mist* 'to patrol at a safe distance from the area'.

Townley's *Steady Hour* now entered Taylors Bay, and called on *Yarroma* to join the hunt. For 70 minutes the two Channel Patrol boats searched without result. Then, in Breydon's narrative: 'The submarine which Townley attacked was visually sighted (by *Yarroma* and *Steady Hour*) as she was surfacing, and was immediately attacked by *Steady Hour*. The C.O. of *Yarroma* did not give any directions regarding the attack.'* Breydon continues: '*Yarroma* did not, in fact, get any ASDIC results until 18 minutes later. Immediately after the attack, and whilst large bubbles, oil, and debris were still rising, Townley dropped a marker buoy on the spot, and subsequently secured his anchor to the submarine until divers descended and fixed wire cables to her hull.' Breydon then describes *Yarroma*'s role. '*Yarroma* did not get any ASDIC contact until 0658, after the submarine had been sunk; he was then ordered by Townley to drop three depth charges as a precaution.'

Breydon now sets out to argue that any submarine sunk by *Sea Mist* and Reg Andrew cannot have been the same as the one attacked by Athol Townley. Reg Andrew had written: 'As I was responsible for . . . finding . . . No 21 [Matsuo's midget] . . . but also in sinking No 21 and another . . .' To this Breydon retorts: 'The weight of evidence is against this claim. There was a lapse of 70 minutes between the attacks by Andrew and Townley. Townley attacked a submarine which was under way and surfacing—it could not therefore have been sunk more than an hour earlier.'

The problem with each story is that both Townley and Andrew accept the completely false premise that two Japanese midget submarines were sunk in Taylors Bay that morning, not one. In Reg Andrew's version, *Sea Mist* sank them both. One was recovered, the second has never been found. In Townley's version, Reg Andrew sank

---

* Breydon says this to support the proposition that *Steady Hour* acted alone and on the basis of her own visual sighting, so that sole credit for the sinking of Matsuo's midget should go to Townley and *Steady Hour*, and should not be shared with Sub-Lieutenant Eyers and *Yarroma*. There is an interesting discrepancy between Breydon's version and Muirhead-Gould's, although both are presumably based on *Steady Hour*'s action report. In his first draft report Muirhead-Gould says *Steady Hour* attacked a definite ASDIC contact. The word 'ASDIC' is crossed out and replaced by the handwritten word 'hydrophone'. The handwriting looks like Muirhead-Gould's. Either way, this meant *Yarroma* and not *Steady Hour* had the contact: only *Yarroma* carried a hydrophone and ASDIC. However, this is not the main point of interest. The important distinction is that *Steady Hour*'s target was not, in Muirhead-Gould's version, sighted visually but instead located below the surface by detection devices.

one submarine and Townley sank the other. Reg Andrew's submarine was never found. Townley's was. Matsuo's midget was his. In fact there was never more than one submarine, so only one skipper deserves the glory. Which?

Townley's claim to have sunk Matsuo's submarine single-handed rests on two propositions: the submarine he attacked was visually sighted, surfacing and under way; and he dropped a marker buoy and secured his anchor chain to the submarine he had successfully attacked. As we have already seen, there is good cause to doubt the first proposition. As we shall shortly see, there is even better cause to doubt the second.

◆　◆　◆

To 10- and 12-year-olds Jeff and Kevin Co\u00e9oté, their father Roy was already a hero. A certain magic attached to divers, and the boys knew that Dad was one of the best in the Royal Australian Navy. His status in their eyes received a sharp boost around 6.30 am on the morning of Monday, 1 June 1942. There was a thunderous pounding on their front door. When they opened it, a policeman in full uniform from the local Mosman police station was looking agitated on the doorstep. His motorcycle and sidecar were parked outside. Roy Coté was needed urgently at Garden Island. He should jump in the sidecar straightaway and the policeman would whisk him there.

Other members of the dive team arrived at Garden Island by more conventional transport. Lance Bullard caught the 7.30 am ferry to work. The dive team which now assembled on Garden Island contained no raw recruits. The diving officer, Lieutenant George Whittle, was 54 years old and had joined the navy in 1927. Lance Bullard, then 40, was the most experienced. He had joined in 1917. Roy Coté was also 40, and had joined in 1920. James Munn was the youngest at 34. He had joined in 1929. They were all familiar with wrecks, and with the recovery of bodies. Nothing prepared them for what they now saw. The cosy and familiar HMAS *Kuttabul* lay shattered in front of them, with only her funnel and wheelhouse out of the water. A high-voltage underwater cable had snapped in the blast. Their first task would be to make this cable safe.

Then they could see if, by some miracle, there were any survivors trapped in the wreckage. Their final task would be to find bodies.

They had their own immediate disaster to contend with. The dive team had finished work the previous Saturday at 1 pm. They tied up their dive boat between *Kuttabul* and the stone wall of Garden Island, and removed the woollen gear, helmets, diving suits and telephones to the diving shed. However, the vital heavy gear including two pumps, air hoses, breast lines, boots, weights and ladders remained on the boat. It had taken the full force of Ban's torpedo. All their heavy gear now lay wrecked at the bottom of the harbour.

With some ingenuity and resourcefulness they tracked down a new dive boat, plus pumps and other heavy diving gear. This had to be fitted up and tested before anybody could enter the water. Lance Bullard reported afterwards: 'We were in business again and under water by about 9.15 am, which was fast work.'

Roy Cooté's dive log tends to be pretty terse. His record of this phase of the operation is a miracle of brevity. 'Dived under wreckage of *Kuttabul* examining High Power cables. Dived and recovered 6 bodies from *Kuttabul* wreckage.'

Lance Bullard's account, by contrast, is extraordinarily vivid. He was the senior rating in the dive team that day, and it fell to him to compile a report. 'I will never forget the scene when we arrived on the sleeping deck of the sunken ship,' he wrote.

The sun was shining through a gaping hole in the deck head, giving a green glow to the still water. Blankets and clothing were scattered around the deck. Hammocks were still slung with their occupants as if asleep.

There were two men sitting on a locker leaning towards each other as if they had been having a yarn before turning in. There was not a mark on any of them of any kind. The blast from the explosion must have killed them instantly. I think we passed up seventeen bodies before we were called up and ordered down the harbour to Taylor Bay.

Work on the *Kuttabul* continued with trainee divers. The senior team had a new and vastly more dangerous task: Matsuo's midget. Roy Cooté and Lance Bullard stayed suited up as the launch crossed the harbour from Garden Island to Taylors Bay.

◆　◆　◆

The divers were ordered to investigate 'oil slick and bubbles coming to the surface' in Taylors Bay. Neither Bullard nor Roy Cooté gives a time for when this work began. Evidence from Bullard's account and from Roy Cooté's dive log suggests it must have been around midday. Let Lance Bullard continue the narrative:

> When we arrived at Taylor Bay, Lieutenant Whittle dropped anchor about 50 yards upstream from the bubbles as the tide was running out. The depth was about 85 feet. Roy Cooté finished dressing and dropped down. He made a complete circular sweep, trailing his lines. He reported nothing and was called up.
>
> Lieutenant Whittle moved the boat further upstream and I dropped down. While descending, I heard a continual throbbing noise in my helmet, but I assumed it was caused by some boat on the surface. On the bottom I walked to the full extent of my lines and started to sweep. The bottom was about six inches of mud on hard sand. Walking and trailing heavy breast rope and air hose was hard going and stirring up the mud made for poor visibility. After about 10 minutes I stopped to let the water clear and have a breather, and as the water cleared I caught a glimpse of a steel wire stay about 20 yards away.
>
> I walked towards it and saw a submarine lying practically on an even keel and apparently undamaged. I put my hand on the hull, which was quite warm. Suddenly, I realized that the sound I had heard from the time I entered the water was coming from the sub and was quite loud.
>
> I thought she might take off at any minute and I hated the thought of tangling up with her if she did. I reported by phone to

the boat and Lieutenant Whittle asked me to hang on for a while and he would send Roy Cooté down my lines with a buoy rope. While I waited I stepped the length of the sub and made it about 85 feet. I had a good look at the bow and was surprised to see the doors of the two torpedo tubes, one on top of the other, were partly open with the noses of the torpedoes protruding. The top one was out about three feet and the lower about 18 inches.

Soon I felt my lines tighten and heard Roy Cooté say over the phone: 'I can hear the motor running and will be getting out of this as soon as this buoy rope is made fast.'

Roy Cooté's dive log is, as usual, the soul of brevity: 'Dived off Taylor Bay for Jap sub. Found it still alive and moving.'

There is one addendum to this story which is worth recording, though it is not to be treated as cast-iron fact. There is a standard procedure for divers sent down to find and recover stricken submarines. They tap on the hull. If any of the crew is still alive, they tap back. Both Jeff and Kevin Cooté tell the same story. Their father told them more than once that he had tapped on the sub's hull on this dive and got a response from the sub's crew. Cooté's reference in his dive log to the sub as 'still alive' may refer to the crew's response, and not merely to the turning engine. However, Lance Bullard's account makes no reference to this highly significant fact, so it may simply be part of a good yarn.

◆   ◆   ◆

The divers' work was far from finished. Having tied a buoy to Matsuo's submarine in Taylors Bay, they then moved on to the boom net to look for Chuman's midget. Lance Bullard continues: 'We went down harbour to the boom defence net at the Watsons Bay end [Bullard is incorrect here—the sub was found at the Clifton Gardens end of the net] and found another sub hopelessly fouled by her propellers in the steel mesh. I inspected the fore end of this sub on the bottom. There was debris scattered everywhere, but both torpedoes were intact.'

Roy Coomé's dive log at this point becomes positively garrulous. 'Dived for other sub and found it fouled with boom net tangled in screws.'

Coomé's next entry will have the conspiracy theorists leaping to their websites. Still on Monday, 1 June, he records: 'Dived for third sub. Found it off Chowder Bay.'

Matsuo's sub now lay dead in the water in Taylors Bay with a buoy attached, Chuman's sub lay trapped in the boom net, and Ban's sub had been picked up by Inner Loop 12 slipping out of the harbour more than 12 hours ago. Where can this miraculously discovered extra submarine have come from? Reg Andrew and Athol Townley would, of course, have an answer. But the evidence that only three submarines took part in the attack is so overwhelming that we can simply rule out the 'fourth submarine' possibility.

Most false sightings of midget submarines can be traced to paravanes towed by minesweepers. But Roy Coomé was too experienced and too skilled to make this elementary mistake. If he says he saw a midget submarine, we would do well to listen.

The following is simply a suggestion by the author but it would seem to fit the facts. Bullard's account of the dive on the net uses the word 'we' to describe finding the stern of the sub tangled in the net. However, his report of finding the bow section is very much in the first person. He had spent a lot more recent time in deep water in Taylors Bay than Roy Coomé, so it may be that when he arrived at the net he was close to his time limit for deep-water diving, whereas Roy Coomé had dived much earlier and had time to recover. (Coomé's second Taylors Bay dive, to bring down the buoy, was very brief.) When Chuman fired his forward scuttling charge, it blew the bow section off the submarine. The bow came to rest about 6 metres from the main body of the sub in the direction of Chowder Bay. The most likely scenario is that the dive boat tied up at the net and Roy Coomé dived alone and found the stern of the sub tangled there. The dive boat then left its position on the net and moved in the direction of Chowder Bay, perhaps in response to a metallic contact. Both Coomé and Bullard dived again, and found the bow. Coomé's first reaction was that this was another submarine.

Roy Cooté's dive log is a contemporary record of each day's diving, while Bullard's (undated) account was written some time after the event. Cooté never again refers to this Chowder Bay submarine, while there are repeated references later on in the dive log to searches for submarines elsewhere in the harbour, notably near the Heads where *Yandra* claimed a submarine sunk. The most likely explanation, therefore, is that the Chowder Bay submarine was simply the bow of Chuman's sub, and that Roy Cooté realised this soon after. However, for years he would tell his two sons Kevin and Jeff, and his grandson Craig, that he knew where the missing third submarine lay. But he wasn't telling.

◆   ◆   ◆

Incredibly, the divers' day was still not over. They now undertook an operation which took more than usual skill and quite incredible courage. They returned to Taylors Bay with orders to secure two 2½-inch (6-cm)-thick steel cables to Matsuo's sub. Picture the scene. They have just come from a dive on a sub which had fired a devastating demolition charge, blowing itself apart and killing its crew in the process. So the Japanese would have no qualms about doing the same with the Taylors Bay sub. As far as the divers could tell, the Taylors Bay sub was still 'alive'—its hull was warm, the engine was still turning, there may even have been a signal from the crew that they were still alive and capable of doing damage. Two torpedoes were hanging out of the bow, very likely armed and lethal if disturbed.

Muirhead-Gould in his 31 August report on the salvage operation sets out the problems in stark detail.

The preliminary survey by the divers indicated that some form of explosive was attached to the bows. Intelligence reports also indicated that some form of demolition charge might be expected in the tail. The difficulty of divers in ascertaining that the protrusion from the submarine's bow was the warhead of an undischarged torpedo is understandable, considering the operation was in 13½ fathoms [81 feet or 24.7 metres], with the poor light at that depth in the late afternoon. Divers were instructed to shackle on two 30-fathom [180 feet or 55 metre] lengths of 2-inch wire, and to avoid interference with both the tail section and the inside of the bow protector guard. The state of the live torpedoes was unknown and, as the submarine was lying in a line with bows up harbour, it was considered unwise to pass any strops around the forward section at this stage.

Roy Cooté's dive log is as terse as ever. 'Dived again on first sub,' he reports. 'Attached wires for lifting.' This time there was no response to tapping on the hull.

The two wires were attached to the minesweeper HMAS *Samuel Benbow* on the surface. Matsuo's midget was now securely in the grip of the Royal Australian Navy.

◆　　◆　　◆

So who sank Matsuo's submarine? In his 5 October 1948 letter Ric Breydon wrote, basing his words on Townley's action report: 'Townley dropped a marker buoy on the spot, and subsequently secured his anchor to the submarine until divers descended and fixed wire cable to her hull.' That is not how the divers remembered it. If there had been a marker buoy in Taylors Bay on the site of the wrecked submarine, and a patrol boat with its anchor secured to it, then surely that would be the place to start the search? In the divers' view, they found the submarine themselves from a stream of bubbles. The only buoy they refer to is the one tied to the sub by Roy Cooté.

That leaves the question of Townley's submarine being visually sighted, surfacing and under way. As we have seen, Muirhead-Gould disputes this: in his version, Townley attacked a submarine after picking up its location from *Yarroma*'s hydrophone. The point is important because if the submarine was sighted on the surface then it still had plenty of life in it and Reg Andrew's depth charge did not finish it off. If it was merely picked up by hydrophone then it could have been resting on the bottom with its engine still running but otherwise lifeless, the condition in which it was ultimately found. Without being able to read the action reports, it is impossible to make a considered judgement. Whatever special pleading G. Hermon Gill received from the Townley and Andrew camps, he made his final conclusion clear in the official history. Waxing slightly poetic, he wrote of *Yarroma's* and *Steady Hour's* Taylors Bay action: 'Intermittent depth charge attacks were delivered on submarine contacts recorded by detection gear and by visual "sightings" in that deceptive period of twilight and shadow-borne illusion of a growing dawn.' The quote marks around 'sightings' are Gill's. The use of words like 'deceptive' and 'illusion' tell the whole story: when it came to *Yarroma's* and *Steady Hour's* sightings, he clearly didn't believe a word of it.

When Matsuo's submarine was hauled to the surface, it had taken a fearful battering from depth charges. The midget had suffered far more damage than could ever be traced back to Reg Andrew's single charge (or even two charges). However, it should be remembered that Matsuo had spent an uncomfortable night in Sydney Harbour: he was rammed at least once, quite probably twice; *Yandra* had dropped six depth charges pretty close to him; Reg Andrew had hit him squarely with at least one charge; and finally *Yarroma* and *Steady Hour* had dropped no fewer than seven depth charges in his immediate area.

In the nightmare world of nuclear warfare theory, the high priests use a particularly macabre phrase. Referring to the fact that the various nuclear and thermonuclear powers have enough weaponry to destroy the planet several times over, they talk about 'making the rubble bounce'. Matsuo's midget seems to have suffered a similar fate. It was almost certainly taken out of the war by Reg Andrew's first charge. The next eight simply made the rubble bounce.

Part III

AFTERMATH

Chapter 14

No reference whatsoever

Sydney woke up on the morning of 1 June 1942 asking itself the regular party-goer's question: what on earth happened last night? Nobody seemed to know. As dawn broke, the smoke and smell of explosives still hung in the air over the harbour. The all-clear had sounded, and people crept out from their shelters and from under their kitchen tables, turned the gas back on, drained the bath, and put the clothes peg they had been chewing back in the peg basket. What was that all about, they asked each other?

The newspapers and radio stations gave no clue. At 3.30 am on Monday morning, just as Reg Andrew was setting off for Taylors Bay in *Sea Mist*, the Federal Censor in Canberra sent an urgent telegram to all newspapers, radio stations, magazines and wire services saying: 'Pending official statement no reference whatsoever to incident in Sydney Harbour last night.' Foreign correspondents had their stories censored to oblivion. Not even the morning radio news bulletins were allowed to explain the thunderous explosions, pyrotechnic gunfire and swarming naval activity seen and heard by thousands of Sydney's harbourside dwellers.

The censor's edict probably made little difference to the morning newspaper coverage. The main action had taken place too late for a full account to appear there anyway. Instead the *Sydney Morning Herald* led off with news of the first 1000-bomber raid on Germany. However, Brian Penton, the legendary editor of the Sydney *Daily Telegraph*, made a rare mistake. A former *Telegraph* reporter worked the switchboard that night at Naval Intelligence. She overheard what was going on and against all the rules rang her old paper in plenty of time to make the early editions, before the censor's edict came into effect. She tipped off the news desk: Japanese submarines are attacking in Sydney Harbour. Penton told her not to be a silly girl, and spiked the story. Instead the *Telegraph* informed its readers breathlessly, in a report from London, that Princess Elizabeth last night gave a private informal dance in the drawing room of her country home. It was, said the report, the first at which she was hostess since her recent coming out. Social historians might like to note the substantial change which has taken place in the use of the phrase 'coming out'.

The strict censorship was not unusual. All military authorities in similar circumstances tend to start by suppressing the story until they can think of some face-saving formula for describing what happened. The authorities broke their silence at 2 pm on Monday afternoon with a brief statement of more than usual duplicity, cabled from General Headquarters in Melbourne. 'In an attempted submarine raid on Sydney three enemy submarines are believed to have been destroyed, one by gunfire, two by depth charges. The enemy's attack was completely unsuccessful. Damage was confined to one small harbour vessel of no military value.'

Let no one think, after reading this, that Goebbels was the sole trader on the Big Lie stand. Apart from the disservice it did to the 21 dead sailors on HMAS *Kuttabul*, omitting them entirely and dismissing with contempt the fate of 'one small harbour vessel of no military value', the statement was dishonest in almost every respect. The authorities well knew that at least one of the submarines had been destroyed by its own hand, not by depth charges or gunfire. The statement's principal aim was to suppress the brutal truth that luck rather than competence had saved Sydney from a far worse fate. For a while, it served its purpose.

◆　◆　◆

For the 10-year-old Peter Doyle, later to become famous as the owner of Doyle's Restaurant on Watsons Bay, Monday, 1 June was a great day for a young boy living near Sydney Harbour's shores. He had spent a large part of the night under the kitchen table with a peg in his mouth, wearing a pair of improvised ear muffs made from powder puffs. Now, with the arrival of daylight, the harbour shore was littered with desirable souvenirs: bits of floating wreckage, perhaps even the odd spent shell. He remembers people wading out in to the harbour to pick up stunned fish, victims of the depth charges.

◆　◆　◆

There must have been a moment in the course of 1 June 1942 when Rear Admiral Muirhead-Gould realised he was potentially in a lot of trouble. He was in charge of Sydney Harbour's defences, and they had failed badly. No fewer than three enemy submarines had slipped into his harbour, two of them ignored by the indicator loop watch and unmolested by no fewer than six patrol vessels tasked with guarding the harbour entrance. All three submarines had passed effortlessly through the boom defence. It was a miserable performance, suggesting poor discipline and even poorer planning and training. Having further wrong-footed himself by disbelieving the submarine reports when they first reached him, Muirhead-Gould was now in a precarious position. He had publicly made a fool of himself in front of the entire crew of *Lolita*, and there would always remain the suspicion that the dinner party at 'Tresco' was a factor in the Admiral's handling of Sydney's defence. Some kind of inquiry or, worse, a Royal Commission, would be unlikely to leave his career or reputation other than in tatters. The evidence of *Lolita*'s crew alone would be enough to destroy him. To avoid this danger he needed to come up quickly with some plausible narrative which would not leave him too exposed, and which would satisfy those who might otherwise press successfully for some sort of inquiry. A few scapegoats would come in handy, too.

The Australian government's first reaction—and also their final decision—was to share Muirhead-Gould's view. They had already set up a judicial inquiry into the humiliating shambles in Darwin in the face of Japanese air attack. The last thing they needed was a second inquiry revealing shaky defences and poor leadership, this time in Australia's most important port. So there was a common interest in coming up with a credible story which didn't delve too deeply into the flaws in the system or the personal failings of those at the top. Muirhead-Gould would have to provide the necessary account, and quickly.

The submarines themselves were a useful distraction. By the afternoon of Monday, 1 June two of the attacking submarines had been located. If they could be raised from the harbour bottom, they would yield all sorts of useful intelligence. There might be code books and charts with clues to future attacks, as well as a host of useful information about weapons, equipment and tactics. As a bonus, if the newspapers could be induced to focus on the submarine raising instead of conducting an embarrassing post mortem into how they got past the defences and inside Sydney Harbour in the first place, that might buy Muirhead-Gould and the government a little time.

The most urgent need was to establish exactly what happened. How many submarines had got into the harbour? Had any escaped? How many were sunk? Who sank them? After any battle, the commanders are required to write an action report summing up what they did, and when and where they did it. There were plenty of ships playing an active role in the Battle of Sydney Harbour that night, and Muirhead-Gould needed their accounts urgently. The most important reports would come from *Yandra*, *Yarroma*, *Lolita*, *Sea Mist* and *Steady Hour*, all of whom had dropped depth charges on credible submarine contacts. *Yandra* had also rammed a submarine. *Kanimbla* and *Geelong* had opened fire on submarine contacts. The unarmed Nappie *Lauriana* had made close visual contact with a submarine. The anti-submarine specialist *Bingera* had chased submarine contacts around Kirribilli and Cremorne Point. All could help to establish what had happened. Better still, all would have stories to tell which would show the defences in a good light.

The two US Navy ships *Chicago* and *Perkins* would also prepare action reports, but these would be submitted to the US Navy's Pacific command in Pearl Harbor rather than to Muirhead-Gould. As we shall see, they would tell a less flattering story.

◆ ◆ ◆

Muirhead-Gould was not the only commander starved of information on 1 June. Off Port Hacking, the five Japanese mother submarines waited for the return of the midgets. They had seen searchlights roaming the Sydney night sky in an agitated way, suggesting that some sort of attack was under way. They had no idea whether or not it had succeeded, or what had happened to the midgets and their crews. All they could do was sit and wait.

◆ ◆ ◆

Although the last shot in the Battle of Sydney Harbour had been fired at 8.27 am (*Yarroma*'s last depth charge in Taylors Bay), there was plenty of military activity on 1 June. Nobody knew how the midget submarines had been transported to Sydney. They might have been carried aboard a surface vessel, but the chances were they arrived strapped to the deck of a larger submarine, or larger submarines. Whatever the method, there was a near certainty that one or more mother ships were lurking outside Sydney waiting for the return of the midgets and their crews. Eight aircraft were ordered to search the area, while another six stood by as a striking force to attack anything they found. The various warships which had fled the harbour in the early hours of the morning also joined the hunt. The five mother submarines stayed submerged and silent. Nobody found anything.

◆ ◆ ◆

Monday marked the emergence of one of the consistent heroes of the entire saga, a civilian torpedo fitter at Garden Island, Frank Lingard. His widow Ivy Lingard recalled in a television interview her fears for his safety that day when he set off to work. 'I was a bit worried that morning,' she remembered. 'It was wet and miserable. I had visions of him rushing off down the gangplank at Garden Island and slipping.' She didn't know the half of it. If slipping on a wet gangplank had been the worst danger Frank Lingard faced that day, he could have counted himself a lucky man.

There is no record of whether Ban's second torpedo was still resting on the rocks when Frank Lingard first tackled it, or whether it had been moved to a safer place. It had come to rest not far from a munition store, so the risk of a calamitous explosion was very real. The highest probability is that it was moved away quickly, and disarmed later. A contemporary newsreel shows a close-up of Frank Lingard, face untroubled beyond a look of fierce concentration, in a workshop applying a screwdriver to a torpedo which is still very much alive. Some of the explosive had spilled out, but the pistol and detonator were firmly in place, and the fact that it had been fired meant the mechanism was in its most potentially dangerous state. The detonator alone would be capable of killing a man at close range.

Lingard's first examination told him the design resembled British torpedoes with which he was already familiar. This judgement mercifully proved to be correct. The wires and the charges were more or less where he expected them. Gingerly he removed the pistol and primers. Ban's torpedo was now harmless. All this was done entirely voluntarily.

That night Ivy Lingard reacted as any wife might have done. 'I knew nothing about all this until he came home,' she recalled. 'Of course I was horrified to think that he'd taken such a risk when he had two little sons to think about.'

Lingard's heroism that day alone would have been enough to win him a place in the roll of honour in the Battle of Sydney Harbour. He could not know it at the time, but for him it was only a beginning. There was much more dangerous disarming work ahead.

◆　　◆　　◆

What of Sub-Lieutenant Ban and Petty Officer Ashibe? Until November 2006 their midget's fate remained a mystery. Japanese radio broadcasts after the raid reported that no midget submarine crew had been recovered, so the defence knew that both sub and crew must have been lost somewhere. The supposed wreck was 'discovered' on no fewer than 40 different occasions over the next 64 years. Award-winning documentary makers mistook a heap of sand in Broken Bay for a buried submarine. Others triumphantly photographed sunken paravanes, boomerang buoys, old pipes and other plausible junk and waved their pictures aloft before an admiring populace. It fell to a group of engaging and happy-go-lucky weekend explorers called No Frills Divers to find the real submarine in late 2006 in a bit over 50 metres of water, about 3 kilometres off Newport Reef on the northern Sydney beaches. The wreck is largely intact—the scuttling charges have not been fired. However it has taken a battering from professional fishermens' lines and nets and from the ravages of its long years underwater.

In the light of this discovery, what do we know with anything approaching certainty of Ban's and Ashibe's intentions and final fate? We know that at 1.58 am on the morning of 1 June something crossed Inner Loop 12 heading for the open sea, and it must surely have been Ban. Six minutes later Inner Loop 11, which stretched between North Head and South Head, recorded a crossing very likely caused by Ban's midget. Ban had made it to the open sea. What happened next?

A bit of speculation first. Everything Ban did that night suggests that he intended to survive if he could. He was, of course, an exponent of the 'sure to die' warrior's code. But everything points to his wish to live to fight another day. His progress through Sydney Harbour is usually portrayed as fast and furious. It was not. He travelled very slowly from his Inner Loop 12 crossing at 9.48 pm to his sighting by *Chicago* near Garden Island at 10.52—he averaged about 3 knots, his best speed for conserving his batteries. He probably had to put on a bit of speed when *Chicago* opened fire on him, but that will have been for no more than a few minutes. He took 90 minutes to travel from his last sighting near the Harbour Bridge to his firing position at Bradleys Head, a distance of about 3 kilometres. He then took another 90 minutes to travel from Bradleys Head to Inner Loop 12, again a distance of about 3 kilometres. So the idea that his batteries were close to exhaustion by the time he crossed the loop outbound will not hold. He still had between 4 and 8 hours useful battery time left.

We are also entitled to attach some significance to the fact that his torpedoes were set to 60-degree left deflection. As discussed earlier, this is a tactic used by a submarine commander who intends to play hard to catch. The torpedoes' wakes told the eyewitnesses on *Perkins* and *Chicago* that they had been fired from the direction of Bradleys Head. But Ban's heading will have taken him quickly away from this firing line and thus improved his chances of survival. All the evidence points to an intention to survive the night.

So what happened? If he intended to return to the agreed rendezvous point with the mother submarines, Ban should have turned right and headed for Port Hacking to the south of Sydney. However, he clearly turned left and headed north. Why?

The most commonly touted theory is that he turned away from the rendezvous point to avoid giving away the position of the mother subs, waited until his batteries were exhausted, then committed suicide. At the time of writing, there has been no attempt to enter the submarine, so we have no idea of the final fate of the two submariners inside—if, indeed, that is where their remains lie. However, we should not rush to judgement. The scuttling charges were not fired, and the crews of *Toku-tai* submarines that took part in earlier raids did not always choose suicide.

At Pearl Harbor, Sakamaki and Inagaki both abandoned their wrecked submarine and attempted to swim to shore. Inagaki drowned, but Sakamaki made it to safety. While Sakamaki later asked to be allowed to commit suicide, it is significant that he did not attempt suicide when his submarine was finally trapped on a reef. He chose instead to swim for it.

Another of the Pearl Harbor submarines was discovered in shallow water in Keehi Lagoon in 1960, damaged by depth charges. The remains of the crew were not aboard. Japanese midget submariners wore a uniform that closely resembled the flying suits worn by Japanese pilots. The most sensible explanation is that the crew escaped successfully from their sinking submarine but subsequently drowned. Their bodies were then mistaken for the bodies of downed Japanese pilots. Scraps of

Japanese naval uniform were found in Pearl Harbor after the raid, lending support to this theory.

At Diégo Suarez the midget submarine that attacked HMS *Ramillies* and sank *British Loyalty* escaped from the harbour. However, the sub had rudder problems and grounded on a reef shortly afterwards. The two submariners escaped from their stricken midget and managed to reach the shore. They set off on foot for the rendezvous area. After a tip-off from a local resident, British forces moved out to capture them. Both Japanese sailors were killed, along with a British soldier, in the ensuing gunfight. The fact remains that both Diégo Suarez sailors made it to shore and attempted to rendezvous with their mother submarines. Suicide does not seem to have entered their calculations.

So a clear pattern emerges from previous midget submarine missions: the crews generally set out to survive. A further argument against a planned and lonely suicide by Ban and Ashibe is the obvious one—they might have done more damage if they had remained inside Sydney Harbour. If they were determined to die, they would have done better to creep underneath *Chicago* or *Canberra* and fire their scuttling charges, in the hope that they could take one of their targets with them.

Finally, Ban and Ashibe were in an entirely different position from their fellow submariners in the Sydney raid. Chuman and Omori suicided while trapped in the boom net and under attack. Matsuo and Tsuzuku were cornered in Taylors Bay with depth charges raining down on them. The crews of both midgets were doomed, and knew it. They chose suicide rather than hand victory to their tormentors. Ban and Ashibe had made it to open water, where they were in no way cornered and were not under attack. Suicide was not an obvious response to their situation.

So what *did* happen? Despite the discovery of the wreck and subsequent examination by the divers who found it and by a Royal Australian Navy remote submersible camera, the midget leaves plenty of unanswered questions. Did Ban's submarine take battle damage? The sunken hull has lost its bow and stern cages, the bow casing above the upper torpedo tube and half of the upper torpedo tube itself, the casing around the conning tower, the net cutter, most of its rear horizontal and vertical rudders, the conning tower hatch and the top half of the periscope. This damage is readily traceable to the various fishing nets and lines snagged on the bow and conning tower of the wreck and wrapped around its hull. Some of the missing parts can be seen amongst the debris on the seabed alongside the wreck, showing that this damage took place long after Ban had left Sydney Harbour.

The hull has been repeatedly holed, but most of the holes are either part of the design of the sub or are the result of corrosion from its 64 years underwater. They do not show the 'dimpling' effect of bullet strikes. Nevertheless it seems unlikely that Ban escaped entirely untouched by the hail of fire from *Chicago* and *Geelong* when he was caught on the surface near Garden Island and again near Fort Denison. It is possible he was hit by one or more bursts from *Geelong*'s Vickers machine-gun or *Chicago*'s anti-aircraft pom-pom. These hits cannot have inflicted major damage or the submarine would have been crippled there and then. However, they may have inflicted minor damage, leading to slow leaks and other gradually developing problems.

Ban must have been under power and under control for at least three hours, from 10.52 pm to 2.04 am, to carry out his attack on *Chicago*, and to make his way out of Sydney Harbour. So if he had problems, they cannot have been critical until the time he was leaving the harbour. His first problem after clearing the Heads would be the weather. The wind had backed around from south-west to south and increased to 20 knots, gusting to 30 knots. If he turned south towards the agreed rendezvous point, he would be running into the teeth of Sydney's notoriously ferocious southerly. At this point his torpedo tubes would be wide open after firing, so the sub's clumsy bow would be almost totally unmanageable facing into the weather. His best hope for survival would have been to turn north and ride with the wind, leaving the rendezvous for another day.

Did Ban and Ashibe attempt to reach land, like their six fellow midget submariners at Pearl Harbor and Diégo Suarez? The conning tower hatch of Ban's midget was open when the wreck was found, suggesting the crew might have tried to escape. However, video footage recorded by No Frills Divers of the interior of the control room shows the sub's conning tower ladder folded and stowed. It seems unlikely that the crew would tidy the ladder away in the frantic moments after abandoning their submarine. So the highest probability is that the ladder was not used at all. The crew had no other way of exiting the submarine. The only conclusion possible is that there was no escape attempt by the crew. As for the open conning tower, the hatch was found resting on the seabed a few metres away from the wreck of the sub, indicating that it was ripped off and dumped by a passing fishing boat's line or trawl net not long before the sub's discovery in November 2006.

We need to look at one possibility, long championed by the historian and retired judge Dr James Macken. Jim made his first appearance in this book as a Riverview schoolboy watching the raid from the school's rooftop. His subsequent theory on the fate of Ban's midget was enthusiastically taken up by the makers of the 2005 television documentary *He's Coming South*. The documentary-makers have continued to defend it even after the discovery of the wreck of Ban's submarine many kilometres away from the place where they claimed to 'find' it in 2005.

Jim Macken's theory was that in the weeks after the raid there were a number of plausible sightings of a midget submarine around Broken Bay, just north of Sydney's fashionable Palm Beach. The entrance to Broken Bay is about 11 kilometres north of where the wreck was actually found. According to this theory, Ban and Ashibe set their sub to neutral buoyancy before committing suicide. Their submarine then drifted out of control for several weeks in the waters around the entrance to Broken Bay. It rose to the surface and submerged of its own accord, probably as a result of changing water temperatures and salinity, before finally coming to rest. Jim Macken's theory ends there: he has never made any claim to have found the submarine, nor to know its exact location.

The documentary-makers, however, have continued to argue that there is no conflict between this theory and the subsequent discovery of the actual submarine. According to this view, the submarine did indeed drift around Broken Bay before being dragged out to sea by the tide and pushed south by the current to its final resting place off Newport Reef. The fatal flaw in this theory is that the submarine simply did not have enough battery power left to make it to Broken Bay in the first place. Cruising economically, it had somewhere between four and eight hours of battery left when it passed through the Sydney Harbour Heads. Taking the current and wind into account, Ban had between 6 and 12 nautical miles of life if he headed north. He came to rest about 9.7 nautical miles from the Heads.

Additionally, setting the sub to neutral buoyancy and leaving it to drift would go against all of Ban's training and instincts. The midget submarines were still regarded as one of Japan's most secret weapons. Leaving the sub to drift would be an invitation to the enemy to seize it intact. Ban's training would tell him that the sub had to be kept safe from enemy hands. As for the 'sightings' by qualified observers in Broken Bay, these can be referred to William of Ockham for judgement: the highest probability is that they made a mistake.

At this point in the narrative, nothing would make the author's day quite so sunny as a simple answer to the question of why Ban headed north, and what he chose to do when he arrived at the midget's final resting place. Both questions are likely to remain permanently unanswerable. If the wreck is raised, or if the contents are sucked out and examined, then it may be possible to discover if the submariners did indeed perish with their boat, and how they died. At the time of writing, the wreck seems destined to remain undisturbed, clinging to its secrets.

Nevertheless, we can make some intelligent guesses. It seems highly likely that Ban was in some sort of difficulty by the time he entered the open ocean. The sub may have sprung a small leak or two, either as a result of *Chicago*'s and *Geelong*'s attack or as a consequence of the violent manoeuvring inside the harbour. Even a very small leak could build into a major problem over the space of three or four hours. The sub may have become difficult to control, as did the Diégo Suarez sub, or it may have developed an engine problem as a result of a leak or battle damage.

Another strong possibility is that Ban found himself facing the same difficulties as Sakamaki at Pearl Harbor. Battery fumes caused both Sakamaki and his crewman Inagaki to pass out repeatedly, and they frequently lost control of their sub. Ban will have submerged around the time he entered Sydney Harbour, some time before 9.48 pm when his midget set off a trace on Inner Loop 12. He will have spent most or all of his time fully submerged or at periscope depth with the conning tower hatch closed until around 10.52 pm when he was sighted by *Chicago*. The hatch will have remained closed throughout his encounter with *Chicago* and *Geelong*, and for all the time he lay underwater before his torpedo attack at 12.29 am. He probably stayed fully submerged, or at periscope depth but still with the hatch closed, until he reached the open ocean around 2.04 am.

Thus he manoeuvred for five hours, from around 9.30 pm until 2.30 am, with his hatch mostly closed and the engine running for much of that time. The build-up of fumes inside the submarine must have been crippling, and it is possible that by the time they reached open sea Ban and Ashibe were finding life inside their craft impossible. Their problems would increase with every minute they remained sealed and under way. In those circumstances, it would be a matter of wonder that Ban and Ashibe managed to control the submarine at all.

If any or all of these problems—bad weather, slow leaks, loss of control and fumes—gained a grip on the submarine, then Ban's best bet would be to remain on or close to the surface and go where the wind took him. He could do this until his batteries ran out. After that? His position would then be hopeless, and suicide might begin to look like the only option. If his scuttling charges refused to fire as a result of water damage or failed batteries, then opening the conning tower hatch and putting the submarine into a dive would keep it out of enemy hands and make for a clean end for its crew.

For now, all these mysteries will remain unsolved. All we can say with certainty is that the submarine is firmly settled a few miles off the

Sydney coast, with its hull unbroken by powerful scuttling charges left unfired by the crew. Until the wreck is raised, or its contents examined, we will be no closer to an answer to the last great question from the Battle of Sydney Harbour: How did Ban and Ashibe die, and is the newly discovered wreck the final resting place of two brave men?

Chapter 15

Has *everybody* seen a submarine?

The newspapers had a field day on Tuesday, 2 June. 'Enemy subs enter Sydney Harbour—three midget raiders destroyed,' proclaimed the *Sydney Morning Herald*'s front page. There followed pages of pictures and news stories, including pictures of midget submarines from the Pearl Harbor raid. However, the censors set very narrow guidelines on what could be written. They were particularly anxious to conceal the fact that the submarine crews had suicided, judging probably rightly that the Australian public would be even more alarmed by the thought of suicide raiders than they already were by the news of enemy submarines in their beloved harbour.

Meanwhile, the government took the line that everything had gone swimmingly on the night, and would everybody please calm down and congratulate the defence forces on an excellent job done. The Minister for the Navy Norman Makin made a statement on the raid to Federal Parliament in Canberra on 2 June. It was a world-beating piece of effrontery. 'This attempt was unsuccessful,' said Makin.

Its failure was due to the preparedness of our defences for such an attempt and to prompt counter attack carried out by harbour defence vessels and other warships in the harbour.

That the attempt by such midget craft to enter Sydney Harbour in the middle of the night was instantly detected, and that the counter measures were so prompt and so effective reflects credit on those responsible for the harbour defences.

The first alarm was given by a patrol vessel at Sydney Heads shortly before 10 o'clock on Sunday night . . . the alarm having been given, patrol vessels and warships in the harbour were on the alert . . . we have good grounds for satisfaction at the results achieved.

So that's all right, then.

Later that day Prime Minister Curtin continued the reassurance while raising the submarine count from three to four. He said in a radio broadcast: 'Vigilant and prompt action of the naval forces guarding our shores has prevented any material success being achieved by the submarines. After careful analysis of all reports of fighting and attacks it is now confirmed that four midget submarines attempted to enter Sydney Harbour on the night of May 31. At least three of these submarines were destroyed.'

The submarine count remained at four for the rest of the war, and was not reduced to three until much later when Japanese naval documents became available. The four were: Midget 'A' (Ban), which fired the torpedoes that sank the *Kuttabul* and which was thought to have escaped; Midget 'B', sunk by *Yandra* near the harbour entrance; M-14 (Chuman), trapped in the net and scuttled; and M-21 (Matsuo), sunk by depth charges in Taylors Bay. In fact *Yandra*'s submarine was not sunk. Midget 'B' and M-21 were the same submarine.

◆　　◆　　◆

Over in Taylors Bay, the minesweeper *Samuel Benbow* attempted to tow Matsuo's midget to a safer position. In particular *Benbow* wanted to swing the hull so that the bow pointed towards the shore rather than up the harbour. If the jammed torpedoes somehow gained a new lease of life, then it would be better if they ran aground rather than ran amok in the main harbour. However, the sub stubbornly refused to move. The stern was well stuck in the harbour mud, and the *Benbow* simply did not have the strength to shift it.

Roy Cooté's dive log is more than usually terse. 'Diving on first sub. Rough weather broke 4-inch wire strops.' Tomorrow they could try again, this time using a crane.

◆　◆　◆

By the morning of Wednesday, 3 June, something akin to submarine fever had taken over Sydney. There was hardly a fisherman who had not seen a submarine, sometimes as early as 48 hours before the attack. Swirls of bubbles suddenly assumed huge significance. Ferry passengers were convinced they had seen periscopes, conning towers, even whole submarines. One man claimed to have held onto the periscope of a submarine trapped in the net, and walked on its hull. He then rowed flat out across the harbour to Naval Headquarters on Garden Island to recount this remarkable tale, and was told to 'take more water with it next time'.

Everybody had a story. What did you see? What did you hear? How did you spend the night? Mary McCune, then two years old, was close to the action at Whiting Beach in Mosman, next door to Taronga Park zoo. This placed her opposite *Chicago*'s and *Geelong*'s gunfire, not far from *Kanimbla*'s guns, and just 1000 metres from Taylors Bay and the depth charges dropped by *Sea Mist*, *Steady Hour* and *Yarroma*. It was a lively night for any toddler. Mary recalls:

I can't remember any sounds or anything else like that. What I remember most was being woken up in the middle of the night, which was unusual. I remember being dressed in a Chinese black silk dressing gown with red dragons on it and taken off to a garage along the street that was built into the cliff. That was the air-raid shelter for the street.

I think it sticks in my memory because of the dressing gown. It was my first vain memory. I really fancied myself in it. I think it's informed the rest of my life. I've been concerned ever since with what to wear for the occasion.

Donald Dunkley's story speaks for most of Sydney. He was 12 years old and living in Chatswood, a northern Sydney suburb kilometres away from the harbour and the main action. The air-raid sirens went off some time around midnight. The family did not have an air-raid shelter, and had been told to get under a bed or a kitchen table instead, or stand in a doorway arch. The entire family—mother, sister, brother and young Donald—opted to get under the main double bed.

Even before they scrambled into their improvised shelter, they knew there was something different this time. Usually the street's air-raid warden came around beforehand and told them a trial air-raid drill would be carried out that night. The warden would then parade up and down the street, knocking on doors to warn that there was a chink of light coming from this or that window. Not this night. There was no warning before the sirens sounded. 'So we thought: this is the real thing,' Donald remembers.

> We were quite concerned about it. But we could hear no guns, no bombs, and we thought this was very strange. We were waiting for the bombs. We were listening and thinking it'll come soon, it'll come soon, it'll come soon. And nothing happened.
>
> We were under the bed a long time, waiting and waiting. Then the all clear came and we got out. We immediately went to the radio, the ABC, to try to find out what it was all about. We were a bit confused, not hearing any sign of warfare or anything.

The radio told them nothing. The censors made sure of that.

Meanwhile, the newspapers continued to accept the government's version of events. Yes, some submarines had managed to enter the harbour. But look what a great job the defences had done. Sydney had been saved by their alert professionalism.

◆ ◆ ◆

Reg Andrew's first attempt at an action report was not a huge success. He wrote it jointly with a fellow Channel Patrol boat skipper who happened to be a solicitor in civilian life. When he handed it over to Ric Breydon, the flotilla commander, it was thrown back at him across the desk. He was told to go back and rewrite it in the first person. No more 'we'. Action reports had to be 'I'.

◆ ◆ ◆

For the five mother submarines waiting in a disciplined line off Port Hacking, this was an agonising time. Japanese standing orders required a reconnaissance flight after any raid, to assess damage. But with both Glens crashed and sunk, Sasaki and the Eastern Attack Group had no way of finding out whether or not the attack had succeeded, or what damage had been done. They simply had to wait for the return of the midgets. They stayed submerged, resting on the seabed during the day, their ears glued to the hydrophones hoping for the sound of a midget submarine approaching. At night they surfaced, charged their batteries, and listened some more. The radio and the hydrophones stubbornly refused to come up with the good news that a surviving midget crew needed picking up.

Meanwhile, the defence's search for the mother ships continued, still with no result. The pilots explained that it was impossible to see a submarine in deep water even in daylight, unless you happened to pass directly overhead. This time luck was with the submarines.

Some time on Wednesday, 3 June, Sasaki decided that they had waited long enough. Three whole days had now passed with no sign of any of the midgets. Like the crews at Pearl Harbor and Diégo Suarez, all must have been lost. Sasaki ordered the mother submarines to disperse, and to switch their attention to sinking any ships they could find, warships or merchant ships.

The first strike took place on the evening of Wednesday, 3 June. It was a total failure. I-24 fired a torpedo from close range at the small Australian freighter, *Age*. It missed. I-24 now manned its deck gun and fired four rounds at the *Age*. All four missed. The freighter had been manoeuvring using standard evasive tactics, and they worked. It arrived unscathed in Newcastle Harbour some four hours later.

The next attack was far more deadly. Ninety minutes after the *Age* incident, I-24 came upon a second coastal freighter, the 4800-ton *Iron Chieftain*, owned by the Australian mining giant BHP. Two torpedoes later the ship was headed for the bottom, taking 12 of the ship's company with her. The ship's wireless operator stayed at his post and managed to send a signal reporting the attack and giving the ship's position. He was lost with the ship. However, 12 of the crew found safety on a raft, and another 25 survived on a lifeboat. The 12 on the raft were picked up five hours later by the anti-submarine ship HMAS *Bingera*. The lifeboat with its 25 survivors made it to the beach at The Entrance.

The defences now went into overdrive. Sydney Harbour was again closed to outbound shipping. RAAF reconnaissance planes scoured the ocean hunting for the attacking submarine. As before, they found nothing.

Next it was the turn of I-27. Around dawn on Thursday, 4 June near Gabo Island off the south-eastern coast of Australia, the submarine fired a torpedo at the freighter *Barwon*. The torpedo mysteriously failed. It passed under the ship and exploded 200 metres away, causing no damage. I-27 now tried its deck gun, but this too failed to inflict any damage.

That evening I-27 spotted the freighter *Iron Crown*. This time there was no mistake. I-27's torpedo sank its target in less than a minute, taking 37 of the ship's 42 crew with it. The submarine was seen by a patrolling RAAF Hudson which attacked with two anti-submarine bombs. Although both bombs went close, the submarine appeared to survive. It submerged and escaped.

In the space of 24 hours the mother submarines had managed to inflict far more damage than was ever achieved by the midgets. The Eastern Attack Group still had plenty of fight left in it, whatever the fate of the Sydney Harbour attack.

◆　◆　◆

The divers returned to Taylors Bay on Wednesday. Roy Coloté and Lance Bullard went down together and changed the hemp buoy rope for a steel wire rope which they could use to travel up and down. Lance Bullard recalls: 'The weather was bitterly cold with a southerly wind causing a choppy sea. The riggers at Garden Island had been making slings to bring the sub to the surface. They were made of 3-inch wire rope. The harbour crane *Hawk* was placed in position.' Roy Coloté is his usual loquacious self: 'Dived on first sub again. Attached more wires.'

On Thursday morning the serious business of raising the sub began. For the crane to do its job, the divers had to pass two slings under the submarine's hull, one near the bow and one near the stern. This was both difficult and dangerous. Although three days had passed since the sub was sunk, there was still no certainty that the crew were not still alive and capable of detonating their scuttling charges as soon as they heard activity nearby. The divers had to be stealthy as well as thorough.

A lighter had tied up alongside the crane, and dropped the slings over the side. Let Lance Bullard take up the story:

> We left the surface at 1.30 pm, and the first job on the bottom was to find the slings and sort them out. The sub seemed to have sunk deeper in the mud at the stern. We started digging at the bows and after half an hour we met and passed one end of the sling through, leaving half on each side, then hauled the ends up on the sub's deck and passed one end through the eye and laid it on the deck leading aft.

The bow sling had been comparatively easy. The stern was another story. Bullard continues: 'We were using our hands and knives, and seemed to be working a long time, as the hole had to be fairly big to go in head first and leave room to dig and scrape the mud back.' Picture the scene: the divers are 85 feet (26 metres) under water, trying to dig a hole under the buried hull of the submarine using only their bare hands and knives. The hole has to be big enough to allow their huge helmets to pass through. They have to do this while not banging the hull of the sub with their helmets or lead-weighted boots for fear of stirring the sub's crew into violent action. It can't have been easy.

Bullard continues:

Finally, Roy poked his arm through. I backed out and passed one end of the sling through. I walked around to him as he was backing out of his hole. When he stood up I pointed to his breast rope which was still leading into the hole. He pulled but could not clear it. Finally, he had to go back in and clear it. We had the ends of the two slings together and joined them with a big shackle which had to go on the hook of the *Hawk*'s lift.

The big block carrying the wires of the lift was a huge affair, and had to be as she could lift 60 or 70 tons. The weather must have got worse, as now the block was jumping up, down and sideways continually. We were both wet and cold and tired. We could not get our shackle onto the block. The block was swinging too much. We had five minutes spell and then decided to have one more try, as the light was getting bad. I grabbed the big shackle and Roy was trying to steady the block. I lifted the shackle at the same time as the *Hawk* dipped, and it was on. Just like that.

We reported finished and left the bottom, knowing we had four steps on the way up: the first at 50 feet only for about seven minutes, and the last at 10 feet where we had over an hour. These stagings were to decompress and the timetable had to be carried out strictly by the book, otherwise diver's paralysis or bends was the result. We finally got back to the boat at approximately 6.45 pm.

They had been underwater for over five hours, cold, wet and in constant danger. It was too late to try lifting the submarine that evening. The commander in charge of salvage operations decided they would simply tighten the slings and wait until the morning. Bullard was unhappy with the arrangements. If the slings were tightened, he warned, the up-and-down movement of the *Hawk* would make them rub against the serrated net cutter of the submarine, seriously weakening them. Lieutenant Whittle, the senior diver, agreed with Bullard. The commander over-ruled them both.

The salvage team assembled at 7.30 am next morning. The divers were not sent down to check the slings. At 8.15 am the *Hawk* took the strain and began hauling in, watched by a flotilla of launches and small craft on the harbour, and with the shores of Taylors Bay lined with spectators. First the block broke the surface. Everybody tensed. Then the shackle appeared, and the slings. Empty. The sub had cut through both slings and remained firmly on the bottom. Bullard had been proved right. All yesterday's courage and toil had been wasted.

The salvage team now decided the steel buoy rope might be strong enough to do the job. Lance Bullard was sent down to take a look. He arrived on the harbour bed but could not see the sub. Panic stations. Had the sub and its crew somehow escaped? He searched around frantically, then looked up and saw the sub's bows about 12 feet (3.5 metres) off the bottom, swinging backwards and forwards. 'I went up quick smart,' he wrote.

The sub was now dragged along the bottom into shallow water, and lifted using the 3-inch wire rope attached to the bow. More tension. Then the sub's bows broke the surface, followed by the hull, dangling vertically from the wire rope like a big game fish about to be landed. The stern section had broken off during the dragging operation, but the main body of the submarine was clear of the water. Matsuo's midget was now ready for closer examination.

◆   ◆   ◆

First to board the submarine was Lieutenant Percy Wilson, the Garden Island intelligence officer. His most vivid memory is of the seamen's hair. Both Matsuo's and Tsuzuku's hair had turned bright green, the result of leaking battery chemicals.

Now it was the turn of Frank Lingard to display more remarkable courage. His wife Ivy Lingard recalls: 'As the submarines were brought to the surface, Frank went into them and saw that some of the demolition charges had not been used. He took the responsibility of removing them, and the charges from the torpedoes.' As well as the demolition charges, Matsuo's two torpedoes protruded from the bow of the submarine, both in an unknown state of readiness and stability. They might well have both been armed. Lingard had no way of knowing.

Ivy Lingard continues: 'He had to go down into the submarines, but not while they were in the water. They were brought up on land by huge cranes and there were still dead bodies in the submarines.' The bodies of Lieutenant Keiu Matsuo and Petty Officer First Class Masao Tsuzuku, with their neat, single-shot bullet wounds, were removed and transported to the police morgue.

After his experience gained disarming Ban's second torpedo on Garden Island, Lingard had some idea how to tackle the two torpedoes from Matsuo's midget. The demolition charges were a different story. Although the salvaged submarines from Pearl Harbor had given the Allies some idea of where and how to find the charges, the Americans had passed on very little intelligence from their find. So Lingard had little to go on. Nevertheless, he succeeded in disarming both sets of scuttling charges, from the fore and aft ends of Matsuo's midget.

He must have dreaded the thought of Chuman's submarine still to come.

◆　◆　◆

The tail of Matsuo's sub was lifted several days later. Roy Coomé was fulsome. 'Dived while crew lifted Sub 1,' he wrote, followed by: 'Dived on Sub No 2 surveying for lifting.'

◆　◆　◆

While all this was going on, far more important events were taking place in the Pacific to the north. After the score draw in the Coral Sea, Yamamoto still needed his decisive battle with the US Pacific Fleet. In particular he needed to finish off the aircraft carriers. He had enjoyed a flawless six-month run of successes, stretching from Pearl Harbor to the

Java Sea, and he was confident that one more major attack would finish the job. Over-confident, in fact.

He chose the US fleet's base on Midway Island as his target, and set out to lure the American aircraft carriers there for a final, decisive knockout round. But the code-breakers were now into their stride, and they anticipated him well. In fact luck played a major part, too, this time favouring the Americans. A group of American aircraft had set off in the wrong direction, and chanced on the Japanese carrier force with its planes on the deck refuelling and rearming. The next seven minutes were some of the most extraordinary and dramatic in all military history. Quite simply, they swung the Pacific war in the Allies' favour. The Japanese lost four heavy aircraft carriers, one heavy cruiser, 234 aircraft and 2200 men. In the space of seven minutes, the Imperial Japanese Navy became a broken force. The defeat was so total and so humiliating that the Japanese commanders at Midway at first could not bring themselves to tell Tokyo what had happened. The Japanese government did not pass on the information to the remains of their navy, let alone the Japanese public, for several weeks.

Yamamoto finally had the decisive battle he had been yearning for. And lost it comprehensively.

◆　　◆　　◆

In Sydney the newspapers hardly knew which way to turn. They divided their attention between the events in Midway, the submarine attacks on merchant shipping in Australian waters, and the lifting operation on the midget submarines. They also continued to publish eyewitness accounts of Sunday night's excitements. For once, the news from the north was good. The tide of war might be turning the Allies' way. In Sydney, the government and navy story continued to hold. The harbour defences had done a fine, professional job. Very little harm done.

It could not last. And it didn't.

Chapter 16

Caught napping

S*mith's Weekly* occupies an odd corner in the history of Australian journalism. It began its life on 1 March 1919 as a weekly newspaper devoted to the cause of ex-servicemen. It was doggedly in favour of the little bloke. It was also jingoistic, racist, bigoted and small-minded. It missed no opportunity to refer to Italians as Dagoes, Chinese as Chinks and Japanese as Japs or Nips. Its major claim to fame is that, together with its offspring the *Daily Guardian*, it introduced the Packer family to Australian journalism and publishing. The Packer fortune started here, though by 1942 the Packers had long since sold their interest in *Smith's Weekly*.

The paper's coverage of the submarine raid got off to a flying start with a remarkably prescient Donaldson cartoon, reproduced below. The cartoon appeared one day *before* the midgets arrived. *Smith's Weekly* kept up this cracking pace the following week. The 6 June issue devoted the whole of its third page to committing the worst crime any journalist can perpetrate. It is guaranteed to drive governments and military establishments into a state of purple-faced apoplexy, and have them reaching for their gags and rattling their gaol keys. The crime? *Smith's Weekly* got the story right.

This cartoon by Donaldson appeared in *Smith's Weekly* on page 5 of the Saturday, 30 May issue— one day before the midget subs arrived in the harbour.

"It's undersize. Do you think we ought to throw it back?"

Under the headline, 'Battle of Port Jackson'—Whose the Responsibility?', it went into self-righteous overdrive. In large type, its sub-headline set out the key demand. 'How submarines entered Sydney Harbour calls for inquiry and sackings. If it's the navy or the coastal defences that neglected safeguarding the great port of Sydney, the responsibility should be sheeted home.'

The story which followed began by recalling: 'Early in the war at Scapa Flow the Nazis sank a battleship under the eyes of the British Navy. That, and what happened at Pearl Harbor, should have been sufficient warning of what to expect in Australia's greatest port.'

The paper then went on to list the failings of the defence. Precautions at Sydney Heads were believed to have been taken. There should be no possible chance of a submarine entering Port Jackson. Where were the detector devices? Why had the government taken so long to announce the facts? The city was alive with rumours. Most people thought Sydney was under attack from the air. Others thought ammunition aboard a ship had exploded. Why did the government not put a stop to the rumours by telling the truth straightaway?

The paper went on to imply that the defences had been caught napping. 'Suddenness of the incident was underlined by the fact that through it all Sydney Ferries and Manly Ferries continued to run. Watchers saw Manly boats, both outward and inward bound, carry on with their trips and pass across the scene of the action as though nothing were happening.'

'Sole cause for satisfaction', *Smith's Weekly* concluded, 'is that the Japs didn't pull off the trick. But more safeguards and greater vigilance are plainly called for at the entrance to Sydney Harbour.'

The story ended with two provocative declarations. 'After Pearl Harbor, Emperor Hirohito of Japan granted posthumous promotion to the heroes of his suicide squads who manned these pigmy submarines and did not return. They were all named by Tokyo radio. Here's a chance for a few more posthumous promotions. They are brave men without a doubt.'

This was followed by a second declaration, a throwaway line to end the story. 'Incidentally, the part our US allies played in this Port Jackson incident was splendid. We salute them!' As we shall see, this apparently innocuous final pat on the back was delivered with enough force to send a positive horde of unpalatable facts stumbling into the daylight a week later.

◆　　◆　　◆

The mother submarine I-24 continued to lurk outside Sydney Heads, while the I-21 sat outside Newcastle Harbour. In the early hours of Monday morning, 8 June, in what was obviously a coordinated attack, they delivered a few parting shots at the Australian mainland.

At about 14 minutes past midnight, I-24 opened fire with its deck gun from a position 16,000 yards out to sea on a bearing of 142 degrees from the observation post at Dover Heights. The gun flashes were seen from three observation posts, and all agreed on the sub's position. The whole attack lasted between two and four minutes.

The first reaction from Combined Defence Headquarters was that it was an air raid. Don Caldwell Smith, the radar gunner who had picked up the daylight Glen flight on 23 May, had his radar unit stationed on Royal Sydney Golf Course in the southern harbourside suburb of Rose Bay on the night. 'Headquarters were going crook at us,' Don recalls. 'They were saying: "Don't you realise we're being bombed?" But we couldn't find anything.'

The air-raid sirens sounded a full warning at 12.30 am, 16 minutes after the first shells landed. People snapped into their rehearsed air-raid drills. Some had an uncomfortable time as a result. There had been a lot of rain in the preceding few days, and those who pinned their faith in slit trenches in the back garden found themselves up to their knees in icy water. Nevertheless, they stayed in their shelters until the all clear sounded.

Others reacted less well. The chief warden from the suburb of Randwick, a Mr W. McGee, complained to reporters: 'Many people— and those in flats in particular—have yet to realise what an alert means. As soon as the alert sounded, lights went on everywhere as people woke up and got up to see what it was all about. People in the Coogee area were the worst offenders.'

Given that the shelling of Sydney probably caused more alarm among the civilian population than the midget submarines ever managed, it is extraordinary that to this day it is hard to pin down exactly what happened. A report dated 11 June 1942 and headed 'Secret—

Operational Research Report No. 6' says seven shells were fired, of which six failed to explode. The more commonly agreed figure is 10 shells, but after that it is hard to find any two accounts which tell the same story. Nor is there any agreement on the target. Some accounts say the Japanese were aiming at the Harbour Bridge, as was strongly hinted in the newspapers next day. In that case the shells fell kilometres short. Others believe the shells were aimed at the flying-boat base at Rose Bay, which was certainly closer to where they actually landed. Just as likely is the notion that the Japanese were aiming at the midget submarines' original target of Garden Island. Finally, and William of Ockham is likely to nod his head at this suggestion, it is perfectly possible that the Japanese had no target at all in mind, and simply wanted to cause maximum alarm among the citizens of Sydney by lobbing some unwelcome ordnance in the middle of their sleeping suburbs.

For the minute, it is as well to accept the version of events set out on a map supplied to the author by the Australian War Memorial in Canberra. This shows 10 shells, of which six failed to explode, one exploded but did no damage, and three exploded with consequent damage. In the War Memorial's version, two of the unexploded shells had the temerity to plonk themselves into the sacred turf of Royal Sydney Golf Club at Rose Bay. Of the remaining four, one fell in Balfour Road, Rose Bay, one in Beresford Road, Rose Bay, one in Bunyula Road, Bellevue Hill, and one in Simpson Street, Bondi. The shell which exploded but did no damage landed on the corner of Fletcher Street and Small Street, Woollahra, near Cooper Park. Some reports dispute the no-damage verdict, and say it broke a few windows. Contemporary photographs bear this out.

The three shells which did actually explode inflicted no serious injury to people, and only modest damage to property. However, they rattled the citizenry of Sydney as no other event has rattled them, before or since. The sheer speed of the attack meant there was no warning. The first anybody knew was the characteristic whistling of inbound shells over the Eastern Suburbs of Sydney. Contrary to legend, they mostly ignored the mansions of Vaucluse or Dover Heights. Instead they headed unerringly for the red-brick working-class blocks of flats in Bondi and Rose Bay.

The shell which landed at the corner of Manion Avenue and Iluka Street, Rose Bay, near the Cranbrook School playing fields, slammed through a double-brick wall of the Grantham Flats, crossed a bedroom, sliced through two more walls, showered the sleeping Mrs Ernest Hirsch with debris, buried her son under a pile of masonry and fractured his foot, and left the son's wife and baby unharmed in an adjacent room. The Australian War Memorial map credits this as an exploded shell but the author David Jenkins in *Battle Surface!* reports that it failed to explode and instead came to rest on a staircase. In the Jenkins account, three air-raid wardens carried it to a nearby park and buried it. A navy demolition team later recovered it.

The shell which landed in Bradley Avenue, Bellevue Hill, tore apart the back rooms of the home of Mrs M. McEachern, and did some damage to the house next door. Mrs McEachern was wakened by an explosion and rushed out onto her verandah to see what was happening. She heard a second explosion and the whistling of a shell. She rushed back into her house where she heard a 'terrific explosion which shattered every window in the building'. It entirely demolished her kitchen. When help arrived, Mrs McEachern refused to go to a neighbour's house. 'My house is still standing', she said, 'and I don't see why I should go elsewhere'.

The final exploding shell landed in the street outside the Yallambee Flats, on the corner of Plumer Road and Balfour Road, Rose Bay. It destroyed a section of a house, slightly injuring a sleeping woman. She was cut by flying glass.

The War Memorial's version overlooks one shell, which strayed well away from the rest. It landed in Olola Avenue, Vaucluse, where it failed to explode. Given that there were only 10 shells in all, the probability is that one, not two, shells landed on Royal Sydney Golf Club. Don Caldwell Smith remembers digging for only one shell next day.

This time the censors placed no ban on reporting the attack, and it dominated the front pages of the 8 June newspapers. Reporters managed to find that mainstay of all home-front war stories, a battling granny. Mrs J. Reed gave the afternoon editions of the *Daily Mirror* the perfect headline: 'Blow the Japs! Says Woman Sleeper of 91.' Barbara Woodward, aged ten, added a nice touch. 'I heard a bang in the road and grabbed my kitten "Mr Churchill",' she told the *Sydney Morning Herald*. 'I went with the other children to a room at the back of the flat. Mr Churchill was not frightened.'

For Donald Dunkley in Chatswood, it was a repeat of the week before. Chatswood is many kilometres from Rose Bay, and the sound of the exploding shells did not carry that far. At the sound of the air-raid sirens the family obediently dived under the bed again and waited for the bombs to arrive. Again, none came.

When the all clear sounded, the family responded as before by switching on the radio. This time it was a different story. The censors had not had time to block the news. 'We tuned in to the ABC', Donald recalls, 'and after a little while there was a broadcast came from the BBC, over the ABC, saying that Sydney had undergone some sort of a bombing attack from submarines. There was a flat at Bondi. I think there was a fatality there, somebody killed.' (Incorrect, happily.)

The whole attack took less than four minutes. Although the flashes of the I-24's guns were seen clearly by the observation posts which supported the shore batteries on South Head, the submarine submerged before the shore batteries had time to respond. The I-24 slipped out to sea and resumed the hunt for merchant ships.

◆　　◆　　◆

At 2.15 am, almost exactly two hours after the shelling of Sydney, I-21 attacked Newcastle. The submarine fired a total of 34 rounds, eight of them flares to illuminate the target and 26 conventional shells. All were aimed at the shipyards. The attack was a miserable failure. Twenty-five of the 26 conventional shells failed to explode. The only exploded shell fell into a park, where the subsequent shrapnel punched 20 holes in a nearby house but otherwise did no damage. One of the unexploded shells demolished a tram shed.

This attack lasted 16 minutes, and gave the batteries at Fort Scratchley time to fire four rounds back. None hit the I-21. It too now submerged and slipped out to sea in search of merchant ships.

◆　　◆　　◆

On Monday morning the divers switched their attention to the boom net and the remaining submarine. Lance Bullard recalls: 'I inspected the fore end of the sub on the bottom. There was debris scattered everywhere but both torpedoes were intact.

'We had to cut out the stern with underwater cutting gear, and finally shackled a 10-foot patch in the hole, which will give a good idea of how badly her propellers had fouled up with the net.'

Muirhead–Gould, in his account of the salvage operation, records that the salvage party had learned valuable lessons in Taylors Bay. 'In view of previous experience of passing strops round the hull, and hanging the lifts, the operation of lifting the submarine was carried out without any difficulty.' He is free in his praise for all involved.

It is considered that in the early stages of securing wires to the submarine 21 [Matsuo's submarine in Taylors Bay], and during the subsequent lifting operation, the Naval divers, diving party, Maritime Services Board officials and plant staff, also Naval Dockyard riggers, carried out an excellent salvage job, as the possibility of booby traps had to be considered and the potential danger from some form of explosion could not in any way be discounted. Furthermore, the danger of wires parting, or gear carrying away, causing a premature explosion, was a practical possibility.

Roy Cooté was, as usual, less wordy. His dive log for Monday, 8 June, reads: 'Dived and lifted No 2 sub.'

The badly mangled bodies of Lieutenant Kenshi Chuman and Petty Officer Takeshi Omori were taken from the submarine and brought to the police morgue, ready for burial next day.

That left the job of disarming the submarine. This time Frank Lingard knew his way around both torpedoes and midget submarine demolition charges. Chuman's forward demolition charge had already detonated, but the rear charge had failed to explode, so only one set of charges needed Lingard's attention. Chuman had made no attempt to fire his torpedoes, and they remained in their tubes unarmed. It was Lingard's simplest task yet. When the last torpedo pistol and detonator had been gently eased from their mountings, he must have heaved a sigh of relief audible around the harbour.

◆ ◆ ◆

With the benefit of 20–20 hindsight, not every action by Rear Admiral Gerard Charles Muirhead-Gould in the course of the Battle of Sydney Harbour was either wise or adroit. But his next action reflected great credit on him. It was innovative, dignified and humane. It may have contained an element of calculation, but if it did then that too reflects well on Muirhead-Gould. The Admiral ordered that the recovered bodies of the four Japanese sailors be buried with full military honours.

The ceremony at Rookwood Crematorium on Tuesday, 9 June, was brief, simple and moving. It lasted only 15 minutes. The bodies of the sailors were brought to the crematorium in coffins draped with the Japanese flag. Inside the chapel, not a word was spoken. When the coffins disappeared from view, a naval party fired three volleys in salute. A bugler sounded the Last Post.

The ashes of the four Japanese sailors were preserved, and subsequently returned to Japan via a Swiss diplomatic intermediary. It is said that Muirhead-Gould ordered the burial with full honours in the hope of securing better treatment for Allied prisoners. It was intended to show the Japanese the chivalrous way to treat an enemy. If the intention was to help Allied prisoners, it transparently failed. However, the gesture was genuinely and warmly appreciated in Japan, and did much to pave the way for good relations between Australia and Japan after the war.

Muirhead-Gould defended his decision in a radio broadcast of great dignity and humanity.

I have been criticised for having accorded these men military honours at their cremation, such honours as we hope may be accorded to our own comrades who have died in enemy hands: but, I ask you, should we not accord full honours to such brave men as these? It must take courage of the very highest order to go out in a thing like that steel coffin. I hope I shall not be a coward when my time comes, but I confess that I wonder whether I would have the courage to take one of these things across Sydney Harbour in peacetime. Theirs was a courage which was not the property or the tradition or the heritage of any one nation: it is the courage shared by brave men of our own countries as well as the enemy, and however horrible war and its results may be, it is a courage which is recognised and universally admired. These men were patriots of the highest order. How many of us are prepared to make one thousandth of the sacrifice these men made?

The speech was warmly and widely reported in Japan. It is quoted there to this day.

Muirhead-Gould referred to the fact that he had been criticised for his actions, and some accounts refer to 'widespread criticism'. If there was, it is hard to find. A search of the more jingoistic publications, from *Truth* to *Smith's Weekly* to *The Bulletin* turned up no editorials, no letters to the editor, no snide attacks. The same was true of the mainstream newspapers of the day. The only sour note the author could find appeared in the Sydney *Daily Telegraph* on the morning of the ceremony. Any journalist reading this book will smile knowingly at what follows. It is a common and legitimate tactic for a newspaper to work out who is most likely to be offended by whatever is at issue, and ring them up for a 'quote'. The sub-editors then can justify the headline 'Fury over Jap Funeral' or 'Row over Admiral's Jap Flag', even though there was no such thing until the newspaper got on the case. Thus the news is created by newspapers rather than merely reported.

On the morning of the funeral, the *Daily Telegraph* had clearly spoken to Mr H.R. Reading, general secretary of the Australian Natives'

Association, to get a 'quote'. He was not best pleased with the Admiral's plans. The ANA was a loony bunch of ultra-patriots which spoke for nobody much but itself. Mr Reading opined:

> On behalf of the Association, I enter my emphatic protest at the decision to accord full military honours. Apparently the atrocities committed on British men, women and children in Hong Kong, and the maltreatment of Australian soldiers in islands off Australia are forgotten very quickly. I say Australians should not forget these events or the loss of life on the depot ship in Sydney Harbour or last night's attacks. We want a total war effort. Well, let us have it without cant or hypocrisy.

In general, the Admiral's decision was widely welcomed and seen as both chivalrous and shrewd. Rightly so.

Chapter 17

The nightwatchman's tale

The 6 June story in *Smith's Weekly* put the government and particularly the Minister for the Navy on the back foot. The newspaper had demanded an inquiry. Norman Makin would have none of it. However, he issued a statement on Wednesday, 10 June, which went some way towards acknowledging that all had not been right on the night. 'A thorough investigation has been made into the entry of Japanese midget submarines, and this has proved the defences are up to the mark,' Makin began. He continued disarmingly: 'It must not be forgotten that the defences are not yet complete. It was the first time they had been tried out, and the experience gained of the enemy's methods and of any shortcoming in the defences will be valuable. Steps have already been taken to tighten them up.'

Smith's Weekly pounced. If the powers-that-be were irritated by the paper's first entry into the fray, they went ballistic in the face of the next week's issue, dated 13 June. This was genuinely fine popular journalism, exposing the smug cant of the official version of the story and getting right to the heart of it. The paper blazoned across the top of its front page: 'With War at the Door—Our Navy Must Never Be Caught Napping.' The story below was headlined: 'Conflicting

Statements on Sydney Harbour Raid—There Should Be a Public Inquiry.'

On page three the paper warmed to the subject with a story headlined: 'Submarines Attack in Sydney Harbour—Story of the Night-Watchman.' As we have seen, the official version of events was that a well-trained, highly disciplined and professional defence force sprang instantly and effectively into action, quickly detected the intruders and sank the attacking submarines before much harm resulted. Not so, said *Smith's Weekly*. Far from the navy picking up the submarines using all its high-tech detectors and weapons, the first alert had come from a civilian nightwatchman in a rowboat. Worse, the navy would not believe his story when he tried to warn them.

The *Smith's Weekly* story did not name Jimmy Cargill, and the odd incorrect detail makes it unlikely that he was the source. However, the story was essentially correct, and profoundly embarrassing. 'About 10 o'clock he [the nightwatchman] noticed unusual movement in the water not to be accounted for by tidal or other natural influences,' *Smith's Weekly* wrote. 'He thought he detected a dark object submerged at a point where the disturbance was most evident. He at once rowed to an auxiliary naval vessel on duty not far distant. There he reported what he had seen, and was told he was talking nonsense and had better go home and get to bed, or words to that effect.'

Smith's Weekly had discovered that the nightwatchman was employed by the Maritime Services Board. When they tried to get confirmation of the story from his employers, a Board spokesman told the paper to contact the navy. A reporter duly called the Naval Establishments Office, where a spokesman said: 'We won't make any statement on anything you publish.' When it was pointed out to him that this was serious, he said after some hesitation: 'I will see the admiral's secretary and see what he thinks about it.' Later the spokesman called back. 'The admiral will not make any statement on that. If you wish to make any inquiry on that you must address it to the secretary of the Naval Board.' The newspaper promised to do just that.

But if the story of the nightwatchman irritated the navy, the paper's front-page story sent them apoplectic. According to *Smith's Weekly*, the newspaper had been handed a statement on the sequence of events by 'a Sydney resident, a businessman of standing, a public figure, a man of calm judgement, of unquestionable repute, and of military experience'. To this day we have no idea who this insomniac paragon of truth and excellence might have been, but we do know he had a fine view of the action. 'His residence is on one of the harbour points overlooking the scene of the focal point of the battle,' *Smith's Weekly* reported. 'From his balcony he had a dress circle view of what happened, and he observed closely.

'He states that it was near 11 o'clock when the first shot was fired. This was from an Allied warship in the harbour.' The term 'Allied warship' is highly significant. In other words, the first shot was not fired by an Australian ship, but by a ship from some other navy. The story continued:

Immediately afterward, tracer bullets were cutting the water, were ricocheting nearby. Pom-poms were firing. In a searchlight beam, about fifty yards from the Allied ship, the conning tower of a submarine was half showing. It travelled on a course parallel with the side of the ship and from the bow towards the stern. One or two shots were fired from the five-inch gun of the warship, the submarine then being slightly astern of the vessel. When the smoke cleared the conning tower was no longer visible.

So far, this was a pretty good account of *Chicago*'s prompt response to sighting Ban's submarine. *Smith's Weekly* then came to the nub of its story. 'The eye-witness further states that there was also an Australian warship in the harbour and not far distant from that of our ally. But it was fifteen or twenty minutes before our vessel showed any sign of life or before it used a searchlight.'

So the Australian defences, far from springing smartly into action at the first hint of a threat, simply sat with their arms folded while the Americans did all the reacting. More was to follow. 'Again', said the paper, 'if Garden Island batteries fired any shots at all, they must have synchronised perfectly with those from the Allied warship, since no sound from the island was distinguishable.

'Question, did Garden Island fire any shots? If not, why not?'

The paper then pointed out that the torpedo which wrecked the *Kuttabul* was fired 90 minutes later.

This means that for an hour and a half one of the submarines at least had the run of the inner waters of Port Jackson.

The eye-witness further states that in the upper part of the harbour no depth charge was fired until 6 am.

He also declares that two or three nights previously, an aeroplane flew over Sydney. It came from the direction of the sea, with lights showing, and subsequently, with lights out, flew between the Allied warship and Garden Island.

It was supposed to have been identified, but was it? If so, and if it was recognised as one of our own planes, why was it that an alert which took place at that time, at an air force camp, was continued for four hours, with personnel dispersed throughout that time?

The foregoing are statements too well grounded to be dismissed.

This was an astonishingly good piece of reporting. It also committed the unforgivable crime of making the navy look silly, and the navy responded accordingly. The Director of Naval Intelligence, R.B.M. ('Cocky') Long, had an early sight of the article and decided it was time for the full majesty of the law to descend on the impertinent hacks. He drew up a charge sheet of the newspaper's crimes and presented it to the Navy Board on 12 June. His minute paper was accompanied by a draft letter which he suggested the Board should send to the Attorney General's Department, setting out the basis for a prosecution. *Smith's Weekly's* crimes? There were two: (a) under National Security (General) Regulation 42 for endeavouring to influence public opinion in a manner likely to be prejudicial to the defence of the Common- wealth; and (b) under National Security (General) Regulation 17 for publishing—in a manner prejudicial to defence—information with respect to measures for the defence or fortification of a place on behalf of the Commonwealth.

The essence of Cocky Long's complaint, in his own words, was that *Smith's Weekly* had 'deliberately attempted to foster public disquiet by discrediting and belittling counter-submarine measures taken by the Royal Australian Navy, by drawing odious comparisons between the efficiency of Allied ships and ships of the RAN, to the detriment of the latter, and by insinuating that neglect and inefficiency characterised one of the RAN's ships and one of the RAN's shore establishments.' The article had also 'disclosed the alleged presence of fixed defences on Garden Island and the presence of Allied warships and RAN ships in Sydney Harbour, publication of which was forbidden by regulation'. So off to prison, then.

Cocky Long's draft letter and minute paper are addressed to the Chief of Naval Staff, his deputy, and to the Minister for the Navy. The circulated version has been well scribbled on and annotated by no fewer than nine signatures and sets of initials. The scribblers' signatures are mostly impossible to decipher, but one looks very like Norman Makin, the Minister for the Navy. He wrote in longhand: 'I am afraid there is no chance of a conviction under Reg 42, and very little hope of one under Reg 17. Smith's will state that their motive was the highest. All papers referred to warships and shore defences & Smith's has done little more. There is no harm in asking A.-G. [the Attorney General] for an opinion, however.' This note is dated 15 June. A quite heroically indecipherable set of initials has added below it the single word: 'Concur.' Whoever concurred did so on 18 June. The next set of indecipherable initials, dated 22 June, is appended to a scribbled note to the effect: 'C.N.S. [Chief of Naval Staff] has decided that no further action should be taken in this matter.' At the bottom of the page is a final, laconic instruction dated 23 June: 'File.'

The cat was now well and truly out of the bag. The government and the navy could no longer pretend that all had gone well on the night of the submarines. They had already acknowledged that lessons had been learned, and defences had been tightened. *Smith's Weekly* continued to call loudly for an inquiry. The paper pointed out that the American government had instantly set up an inquiry into Pearl Harbor, presided over by a Supreme Court judge. The Australian government had done the same when Darwin was bombed. Surely a submarine attack *inside* Australia's most important port warranted an inquiry, if only to answer public unease. Not necessary, said Makin. The Admiral's report would do.

♦   ♦   ♦

By the week beginning Monday, 15 June, a fortnight after the first submarine attack, the air was positively sulphurous with the smell of serious trouble. The usual government tactic of dismissing newspaper stories as the ill-informed musings of over-excited hacks would not work in this case. Too many people had seen from behind parted curtains that the enemy had managed to evade the defences and wreak havoc inside Sydney Harbour. Any doubts that Sydney's defences were leaky were settled with the shelling of the Eastern Suburbs. The public was now well and truly alarmed.

Then a new and vastly more dangerous critic entered the arena: the United States Navy. As early as 2 June the executive officer of the destroyer USS *Perkins*, G.L. Ketchum, had filed a brief action report to his skipper. The following day *Perkins'* skipper, W.C. Ford, filed a full report, including a sketch showing two torpedo tracks passing either side of and chillingly close to USS *Chicago*. On 5 June, Captain Bode followed up with *Chicago*'s action report. Both reports went to the US Navy's Pacific headquarters in Pearl Harbor, Hawaii. Both reports were highly critical of the defences of Sydney Harbour.

Perkins' commanding officer Ford wrote:

The fact that there is no net at the entrance to the harbour and ferries were continually coming through this entrance made it a very simple matter for the submarines to get into Sydney Harbour. The torpedo which sank the ferry passed close aboard CHICAGO's stern and close aboard PERKINS' bow and only had a small chance of missing. It was good fortune rather than good harbour defence which prevented great damage.

The USS *Chicago*'s captain was equally scathing. Bode had a fair bit to hide about the night's proceedings, but that did not prevent him from sticking it to the Sydney defences. 'The necessity for protecting harbours', Bode wrote, 'requires submarine nets, or the new type of torpedo nets, backed by at least two Light Indicator Nets. These must be provided with positively operated gates. All other electrical devices such as electric loops, asdics, sono buoys, mine fields, etc., should be considered ancillary to such positive closure and not substitutes therefore. Until such positive measures are provided, the danger will be great.'

To put it mildly, the US Navy did not like what it saw. The Commander of the US Navy's Destroyer Division Nine, F.X. McInerny, added his own damning assessment when he concluded a report to the Commander of US Naval Forces, South-West Pacific (Admiral Chester Nimitz) with the following words:

From personal observation, entering Sydney during daylight and darkness, the control over entering ships leaves a great deal to be desired. Apparently there are many ships, merchant and naval, that do not have private signals for entering, and still are not prevented from entering until properly inspected. I believe that an enemy surface ship, flying false colors and making false signals, could enter the harbour during daylight or darkness, under present conditions.

The US Navy demanded action. On 12 June the Commander of Allied Naval Forces, South-West Pacific Area, Vice-Admiral H.F. Leary, wrote to Sir Guy Royle, the Chief of Naval Staff of the Royal Australian Navy, enclosing copies of *Perkins'* action report and sketches plus McInerny's scathing assessment. Leary concluded his letter to Sir Guy with a stark demand: 'It is requested that necessary action be taken to provide maximum protection to vessels in Sydney Harbour from enemy submarines.'* The implications for the Australian government and the Australian Navy were horrendous. If Sydney Harbour was not properly protected, then US ships could not safely anchor there. Australia's whole defence strategy of 'looking to America' was under threat. Indeed, given that Japan's objective was to cut off the sea routes between Australia and America and thereby make Australia untenable as a base for an American counterattack, Leary's letter shows that the Sydney raid had taken the Japanese some way towards success. The Naval Board's regular meeting was due to take place on Monday, 15 June. The meeting was delayed a day to make way for the King's Birthday celebrations, and the full Board met on 16 June. It cannot have been a happy meeting.

There was now an urgent need to come up with a narrative which could be defended against the likes of *Smith's Weekly* and which would convince the US Navy that it was safe to tie up ships in Sydney Harbour. Sir Guy Royle wrote in hand on Leary's memorandum: 'I will answer this after I receive NOCS [Naval Officer in Command, Sydney—in other words Muirhead-Gould's] report and his reply to my letter of today 16/6.'

The Chief of Naval Staff then wrote sympathetically, if somewhat elliptically, to Rear Admiral Muirhead-Gould: 'I am afraid you have been having a very hectic time and are competing very ably with the many problems that arise.' He probably meant coping very ably with the many competing problems that arise, but that is only a guess. Sir Guy's letter ranged over a number of topics, from the possible court martial of the skipper of *Yarroma* to the posting of the Free French destroyer *Le Triomphant*. Where it is relevant, it has been quoted in other parts of this narrative. However, the key section amounted to a demand for some kind of explanation from Muirhead-Gould for the failure of Sydney's defences.

---

* This was a nice piece of hypocrisy on Leary's part. His failure to pass on the warning implicit in the 30 May FRUMEL decrypt, discussed in Chapter 5, was at least a contributory factor in the less than maximum protection Sydney Harbour offered its guest vessels.

'Leary and I are still rather disturbed', Sir Guy wrote, 'by thoughts such as the following:-

'Three submarines were able to pass through a gap which was supposed to be under observation by the "YARROMA".

'That the Loop Officer failed to recognise the signatures of the midget submarines. This you have already explained.

'That there is sufficient close liaison between the Loop Officer or X.D.O. [External Defence Officer] and the searchlights and the patrol boats.'

Muirhead-Gould needed to come up with something fast. On 17 June he responded to Sir Guy with a two-page report. It amounted to not much more than a brief account of the action, and fell far short of Sir Guy's need for some way to reassure the Americans. It also gives a fair idea of how much confusion still surrounded the whole story more than two weeks after the event. Muirhead-Gould accepts Reg Andrew's three submarines, and tentatively raises the sub count to five taking part in the raid. He lists them by loop crossing.

2001   Sighted in boom net at 2130 approx by Maritime Services watchman and reported by him to YARROMA. Self destroyed at 2230. (No 1)

2148   Sighted off Garden Island Ferry Wharf at 2252 by CHICAGO and many other craft. Fired two torpedoes from direction of Bradleys Head at 0030 at CHICAGO. Sank KUTTABUL. Other torpedo on rocks near gun wharf steps unexploded. Sighted in Taylor Bay or Chowder Bay 0500 approx. by SEA MIST's crew and possibly sunk. (No 2)

——   2254 sighted by YARROMA and LAURIANA (at inner Heads). Rammed by YANDRA and attacked by six depth charges at 2307, before crossing the loop. Probably destroyed. Not reported till next day. (No 3)

0159   Not sighted until seen with two others in Taylor Bay or Chowder Bay, at 0500 approx. by SEA MIST. (No 4)

0301   sighted by CHICAGO at Heads at 0250 approx. Sighted in
Taylor Bay at 0500 approx. by SEA MIST. (No 5)

He then gave the result of the attacks.

No 1)   Self-destroyed. Hull has been recovered.
No 2)   Two of these were probably sunk in Taylor Bay but only
one has been found.
No 4)
No 5)
No 3)   Is considered unlikely to have survived YANDRA's attack.
If it survived, it could have been identical with No 4 or No 5.

This brief document was hardly going to do the job of satisfying a
seriously restless US Navy. Sir Guy needed more, and five days later it
was forthcoming. The 22 June report was a different matter. This time
Muirhead–Gould set out to address some of the failures of the defence,
and to allocate blame for what had gone wrong. All his ire was directed
at juniors, of course. The watch keepers at the Loop Station were first in
the firing line. There had been a 'regrettable failure' to identify the 2001
and 2148 crossings. 'I consider that the Loop system fully justified itself',
wrote Muirhead–Gould, 'though, naturally I must deplore the fact that
the human element failed'.

Next in the blame game was Jimmy Cargill. 'A midget submarine was
in the harbour for about two hours,' said Muirhead–Gould. 'It was seen
by Mr James Cargill of the Maritime Services Board Staff who took
some time to collect a friend and to communicate this vital information
to the Channel Boat on patrol.' This was simply untrue, and Muirhead–
Gould must have known it.

Eyers and *Yarroma* were next. '*Yarroma* did not open fire because he
thought it might be a mine,' said the report. 'This is deplorable and
inexplicable.' Well, yes. But it might have been more honest to add that
Yarroma and not Jimmy Cargill was the principal cause of the two-hour
delay.

The report credited Townley's *Steady Hour* with sinking the submarine in Taylors Bay, adding: 'Further investigation shows that *Yarroma* and *Sea Mist* were equally concerned in this attack, and *Yarroma* thus to some extent made up for her previous indecision.'

It also accepted Reg Andrew's count of three submarines, going into some detail on the point. 'Although *Sea Mist's* report, at 0500, that she had seen three submarines in Chowder Bay sounded at that time fantastic, it is now considered that this was actually possible,' Muirhead-Gould wrote.

> Examination of the captured charts shows what may have been the position of the submarine in this area. *Sea Mist's* subsequent reports give great promise of a successful attack in Chowder Bay. Members of her crew drew a most convincing sketch of the stern cage of the submarine which they claim to have seen. At this time, no one was aware that these submarines had tail cages. It is unfortunate that all efforts to locate this submarine have failed.

They failed because the submarine did not exist. Reg Andrew and the crew of *Sea Mist* saw the tail cage of Matsuo's submarine, already accounted for in Taylors Bay.

Muirhead-Gould then went on to list the lessons learned. First, the signal chaos had to end. Channel Patrol boats would have proper radio telephone sets as soon as possible. Arrangements were being made to stop ferries immediately at the request of an authorised naval officer. The night movement of tugs and barges would be kept to a minimum to reduce confusion at the Loop Station.

Some actions had already been taken. The Naval Auxiliary Patrol boats had all been armed with depth charges. A new depth charge detonator able to function in less than 42 feet (about 13 metres) of water had been developed and was now being supplied to Channel Patrol boats and Nappies. Garden Island's operations room was being provided with a radio telephone set. No more would the Admiral communicate with his fleet by sending a hapless Lieutenant in a speedboat around the harbour delivering messages.

It was not all bad news. The report concluded by commending 'the general good conduct, zeal and determination of all who took part in a very exciting operation'. Muirhead-Gould recommended to the notice of the board: Mr James Cargill, for his vigilance and initiative and for his personal efforts to report a suspicious circumstance to proper authorities; and to a lesser degree Mr W. Nangle who helped him; Lieutenant A.G. Townley RANVR and the crew of HMAS *Steady Hour*; Sub-Lieutenant J.A. Doyle RANR(S) and crew of HMAS *Sea Mist* (note: not Reg Andrew); Lieutenant J.A. Taplin RANR(S) and the crew of HMAS *Yandra*; Engineer Captain A.B. Doyle CBE RAN, Commander (E) C.C. Clark RAN; and Bandsman M.N. Cumming. The last three were commended for rescue work on *Kuttabul*.

In his 16 June letter to Muirhead-Gould, Sir Guy Royle says in part: 'I am sorry you have been unable to locate the *Sea Mist*'s midget submarine. I will certainly send congratulations to Lieutenant Taplin [note: poor old Reg misses out again—Taplin was the skipper of *Yandra*, not *Sea Mist*], but I propose to wait a little longer as I understand you intend carrying out some sweeping operations in his area. I haven't settled any award yet, but DSC would seem to be about the right standard.'

So it is clear that at this stage the Chief of Naval Staff did not regard the whole affair as a catastrophe, and was of a mind to hand out medals at the comparatively high level of a Distinguished Service Cross to Reg Andrew and presumably to others who had performed well. There is something of an unofficial scale for these awards, and the usual reward for sending a submarine to the bottom was the slightly lesser Distinguished Service Order. Sir Guy intended to be more generous. Yet, as we shall see in the next chapter, somewhere along the line the medal list sank as surely as the submarines.

Chapter 18

The Admiral's report

It is a nice area of speculation to ask why Muirhead-Gould's 22 June report did not satisfy the Naval Board and why the Admiral felt obliged to write further. The chronologies attached to the two reports are identical. The information in the appendices to the 16 July report is more elaborate than the information in the 22 June version, but otherwise the story is much the same. There is no correspondence to be found in any of the archives ordering Muirhead-Gould back to the drawing board, but the Admiral nevertheless felt obliged to pick up his pen again. The most striking difference between the 22 June report and the final 16 July report is that 16 July omits much of the criticism of junior officers contained in the 22 June version. It may be that the Naval Board felt the 22 June report would do little to reassure the Americans. They needed something soothing rather than probing.

As far as reassurance of the public was concerned, a blander report was essential. The Australian government steadfastly refused to set up an inquiry, whether open or behind closed doors, into the midget submarine raid. The Admiral in charge of Sydney Harbour was preparing a report, they said, and that would have to do. After all, Rear Admiral Muirhead-Gould had been judged capable enough to sit on the

Royal Navy's Board of Inquiry into the sinking of HMS *Royal Oak* by a German submarine in Scapa Flow. So who better to look into the sinking of HMAS *Kuttabul* by a Japanese submarine in Sydney Harbour? This really was an appalling decision. If heads were to roll, then the most likely first head on the block would be that of the person in charge of Sydney's harbour defences. To put the entire inquiry into the hands of the man most likely to be its first victim was about as sensible as asking the average working criminal to conduct his own trial single-handed, and decide his own sentence. Muirhead-Gould must have accepted the challenge with relish.

Politically, the report had to fulfil two functions. It had to supply the navy and the Australian government with a defensible narrative, a story they could tell to the public without having it torn apart by the likes of *Smith's Weekly*. It also had to satisfy the US Navy that Australian harbours were now safe places to anchor American ships. Finally, it had to get Muirhead-Gould off the hook. It needed to give the impression that Sydney Harbour's defences had been, in Norman Makin's phrase, 'up to the mark'. Given these objectives, Muirhead-Gould made a fair fist of it with his 16 July account. The report is not marked 'SECRET'. However, it was never intended to be made public, at least not at the time. It contained a lot of military information which the navy, very reasonably, wished to keep to themselves. It was declassified on 2 February 1965.

The report is reproduced in its entirety in Appendix III. At this point in the narrative it is sufficient to look at how Muirhead-Gould put the best spin he could on the story to reassure the government, the Australian public and—most important of all—the US Navy.

The report, addressed to the Secretary, Naval Board, Melbourne, runs to 16 pages and some 4000 words. It begins with a four-page narrative, followed by six appendices. The first appendix is a detailed chronology of events, starting with the first loop crossing, which Muirhead-Gould times at 8 pm, and ending with *Yarroma* dropping her final depth charge at 8.27 am the next morning. The second appendix deals with the documents and maps recovered from Matsuo's sub. Next comes an analysis of the recovered torpedoes, two from Matsuo's submarine, two from Chuman's, and the unexploded torpedo from Ban's midget, which grounded itself on the rocks of Garden Island. The Admiral then deals with the indicator loop crossings and their tell-tale traces. After that come two pages of hand-wringing under the heading: lessons learnt— mistakes made and remedies. However, it was not all bad news. The final appendix is headed: 'Recommendations for recognition of personnel', and offers what is clearly a medals list.

The report puts the midget submarine count at four. 'Of these,' Muirhead-Gould wrote, 'two are known by their actual Japanese numbers (No. 14 and No. 21). The other two unknown midgets are referred to as "Midget A" and "Midget B" respectively.' The Admiral then went on to get the number of mother submarines right. 'It is considered that the force which attacked Sydney consisted of five "I" class submarines, four midget submarines, and one, possibly two, float planes,' he wrote.

However, he began to stray from the straight and narrow when describing Ito's spy flight. 'The attack was possibly preceded by aerial reconnaissance, which may have been carried out on 29th, 30th and 31st May,' the Admiral wrote. 'A reconnaissance of Sydney Harbour, especially the Naval Anchorage area, was carried out by one biplane single float plane at approximately 0420K/30 May.' This is, of course, incorrect. The Glen was not a biplane, it had two floats and not a single float, and Ito's flight took place on 29 May, not 30 May. Otherwise Muirhead-Gould has got everything right.

His inaccurate reporting of Ito's flight did not end there. He continued: 'The plane, which was burning navigation lights, approached the harbour from a northerly direction, flew over the Naval Anchorage, circled USS *Chicago* twice, and departed in a due east direction.' This is not how Ito remembers it. The account given in Chapter 6 is based on Ito's own sketches. Given that Muirhead-Gould got the date and the plane's description comprehensively wrong, it is probably safer to stick to Ito's version. However, the Muirhead-Gould version appears in most accounts of the raid, including the official history.

Next came a really serious whopper. 'Allied warships in Sydney Harbour at the time included the following,' wrote Muirhead-Gould.

'No. 1 Buoy—HMAS *Canberra*; No. 2 Buoy—USS *Chicago*; No. 4 Buoy—USS *Perkins*; No. 5 Buoy—USS *Dobbin*; No. 6 Buoy—HMAS *Bungaree*; Birt's Buoy—HMS *Kanimbla*; Off Robertson Point— HMAS *Australia*.'

This is outrageous. The weasel words 'warships . . . included' allow Muirhead-Gould to slide over the fact that he had many more warships and much more useful firepower at his disposal than he cared to admit. He does not list the two anti-submarine specialists HMAS *Yandra* and HMAS *Bingera*, nor does he list the 10 Channel Patrol Boats, all of which carried anti-submarine depth charges and some of which carried the latest ASDIC submarine detection equipment. Muirhead-Gould's great tactical failure on the night of the raid was his abysmal use of his available resources. By his own account, he issued only three orders, all of them vague and general. Throughout the entire night he failed to direct his forces in any coordinated way. For the record, HMAS *Australia* was not in the harbour at the time, and was therefore not tied up off Robertsons Point. If any ship could be said to be moored off Robertsons Point, it was the armed merchant cruiser HMAS *Westralia*. Most accounts, including the official history, place *Westralia* in Athol Bay. However, she was moored well off the Athol Bay shore, placing her somewhere between the shoreline and Robertsons Point.

Muirhead-Gould's account then moves on to the midgets themselves. 'The first attempt at an entry was made by Midget No. 14 [Chuman], and was unsuccessful', he wrote. 'She crossed the loop at 2001 and, by 2015, was caught in the nets (centre portion, close to the Western gate). She was unable to free herself, and blew herself up at 2235.'

Muirhead-Gould is being a bit economical with the truth here. He describes Chuman's entry as 'unsuccessful', then says he was caught in the net, implying that the net did its job and prevented Chuman's entry. But Chuman did in fact succeed in entering the harbour. After he had made it past the net, he backed into it, tangling himself in the net on the harbour side. This may seem like hair-splitting, but it is part of the general pattern of Muirhead-Gould's report to say things worked well when they didn't.

Muirhead-Gould's next error is scarcely his fault. He accepts that *Yandra* attacked and probably sank a submarine near the Sydney Harbour heads, outside the boom net and indicator loop. He wrote: '"Midget B" made an unsuccessful attempt to enter the harbour but failed to reach the effective loop (No. 12) or, consequently, the boom. She was sighted by *Yandra* (the Duty A/S Vessel on patrol within the Loop Area) and later by *Lauriana* who illuminated her until intercepted between the Heads, at 2254, by *Yandra*. Two separate attacks were carried out by *Yandra* on "Midget B" during a period of 9 minutes, starting from the time she attempted to ram the submarine at 2258 until her second attack—a full pattern of six depth charges—at 2307. It is considered that "Midget B" was destroyed by this second attack, in a position 023° 3.6 cables* from Hornby Light.'

This is, of course, incorrect though that is no fault of Muirhead-Gould's. In fact Midget B (Matsuo's submarine or Midget No. 21), survived *Yandra*'s attack. She was eventually sunk by *Sea Mist* in Taylors Bay six hours later. However, this error is part of the general pattern of the report, which repeatedly says the defences worked when they didn't.

The Admiral's narrative now moves to the Taylors Bay attack. He wrote:

Midget No. 21 entered the harbour at 0301, at which time she crossed No. 12 Loop. She proceeded up harbour unobserved until she reached Bradley's Head vicinity. Here she was sighted by *Kanimbla* and fired on at 0350 and gave rise to the unconfirmed contact made by *Doomba* off Robertson Point at 0450.

She was detected in Taylor Bay and attacked with depth charges, first by *Sea Mist* at 0500, then by *Yarroma* and *Steady Hour* until 0827. The effect of these attacks was clearly shown in the great amount of damage done to Midget No. 21, which was evident in the wreck when it was recovered. It is probable that the

---

* A 'cable' is a regular nautical measure of distance. It is equal to 200 yards or approximately 180 metres.

first attack caused the submarine to run into the bottom, because the lower bow cap was damaged and both caps were jammed, although set to release. The torpedo tubes had both been fired, although the bow caps had jammed on release. The lower tube had been fired with the external adjustment fittings engaged, and these had sheared off when the torpedo moved in the tube. This suggests that an attempt was made to fire in a hurry, and was prompted by, or interrupted by, the depth charge attacks.

Muirhead-Gould's conclusion that Matsuo's submarine damaged its bow cage and torpedo caps while crash diving in Taylors Bay and subsequently failed to launch its torpedoes is reasonable within the logic of the report, but is almost certainly incorrect. Muirhead-Gould's problem is that he believes Matsuo's midget was sunk by *Yandra*, when in fact it survived *Yandra*'s attack and made it into the harbour. However, it is also fair to point out that this version suited Muirhead-Gould nicely. Far better to say the torpedoes failed after Reg Andrew's depth charge attack in Taylors Bay than to admit that an Allied ship like *Canberra* had a lucky escape from a torpedo attack an hour earlier. Again, the defences are portrayed as working when they didn't.

There is a curious little blip in the chronology section. At 10.30 pm, according to Muirhead-Gould, *Yarroma* reported—'Object is submarine. Request permission to open fire.' It is hard to reconcile this with 'Tubby' Anderson's account, supported by Jim Nelson, that it was *Lolita* which initiated the attack, not *Yarroma*. However, *Yarroma* had been the source of all earlier communications, and this may simply be a slip of the pen on Muirhead-Gould's part. Note that there is no record of the order to open fire being given.

The chronology records that at 11.14 pm Muirhead-Gould ordered: 'All ships to be darkened.' However, there is no trace in the 16 July report of his earlier order that ferries and other harbour traffic should continue to run, fully lit. In his 22 June report he defended this by saying: 'The more boats that were moving about at high speed the better chance of keeping the submarines down till daylight.' Sometime between 22 June and 16 July he must have realised that this was not the brightest order he had ever issued, so he air-brushed it out of the final report.

The chronology then comes up with another whopper. At 11.15 pm, according to Muirhead-Gould, 'USS *Perkins* slipped and was ordered back to buoy by *Chicago* securing again at 2340 to No. 4 Buoy.' This account of *Perkins*' movements is a monstrous slur on her blameless crew. Muirhead-Gould is simply covering up for the inadequacies of *Chicago*'s Captain Howard Bode, and for the role of the 'Tresco' dinner party in the night's proceedings. The Admiral manages to imply that *Perkins* had somehow taken it upon herself to leave her buoy, and had to be dragged back to it by *Chicago*. As we have seen, *Perkins* slipped under direct orders from Lieutenant Commander Jimmy Mecklenberg, then senior officer aboard *Chicago*. Mecklenberg correctly wanted *Perkins* to screen *Chicago* until the cruiser could get under way. Bode foolishly ordered *Perkins* back to her buoy because he did not believe the submarine story.

However, Muirhead-Gould's 2315 entry does give better insight into the timing of Bode's movements. His mendacious 2220 entry read: 'Captain Bode, *Chicago*, left Tresco with suggestion that he should go to sea with *Perkins*.' Bode cannot have been aboard *Chicago* before 11.15 pm, when *Perkins* slipped. And he must have been aboard before 11.40 pm, when *Perkins* returned to her buoy; 11.30 pm seems about right, not 10.20 pm.

The author has every sympathy with the Admiral by the time the chronology moves to 5 am next morning and the attack on Matsuo's submarine in Taylors Bay. To this day there is no agreement on the exact sequence of events there, and Muirhead-Gould has simply let each skipper have his say. The first entry says: 'Red Verey's Light seen in Taylor Bay by *Yarroma* and depth charge explosion heard. *Yarroma* proceeded to scene at full speed and en route saw 3 more Verey Lights and heard further detonations.' Clearly this is *Yarroma*'s version of events.

Muirhead-Gould now moves to Athol Townley's version. '*Steady Hour* sighted suspicious object. Whilst proceeding up West Channel *Sea Mist* attacked and fired Verey Light (red). *Sea Mist* reported 3 submarines.'

Goonambee now takes over. '*Sea Mist*, at request of *Goonambee*, investigated suspicious object in Taylor Bay. Fired 2 depth charges on each occasion firing a Red Verey Light before so doing. Aldis Lamp was used to illuminate target.'

The report does not include a version which exactly matches *Sea Mist*'s account. However, Muirhead-Gould can hardly be blamed for this. Everyone involved in Taylors Bay that morning told a very different version of the same story. Muirhead-Gould has simply picked out three versions and recounted them, albeit briefly. Chapters 12 and 13 of this book attempt to separate fact from fiction, and medal-seeking from honest reporting.

There is one rather odd entry at 5.40 am: 'Rear-Admiral-in-Charge and Chief Staff Officer proceeded down harbour.' This second venture onto the harbour by Muirhead-Gould and his chief staff officer is no-where documented except in this brief sentence in the official report. There is a later reference to the chief staff officer proceeding down the harbour at 7.30 am and to *Winbah*'s arrival at Taylors Bay between 7.30 am and 7.55 am. It would seem that Muirhead-Gould and his CSO commandeered the harbour launch *Winbah* and set off down the harbour together at 5.40 am to check up on proceedings. The Admiral was presumably delivered back to Garden Island at some point, leaving the CSO to head off alone at 7.30 am to Taylors Bay and talk to Townley and *Steady Hour*. As the depth charge attack in Taylors Bay was still under way, it cannot have been helpful to either *Steady Hour* or *Yarroma* to have the CSO prowling about in an unarmed launch while they were busy trying to finish off Matsuo's midget.

The report concludes with 'recommendations for recognition of personnel'. This section is worth quoting in full.

> The following are recommended to the notice of the Naval Board
> for their display of zeal and determination throughout the operation:-
> (1) <u>Mr. J. Cargill</u>.   For vigilance and initiative in his personal
>   efforts to report a suspicious circumstance to
>   the proper authorities.

> (It is for consideration whether this man has merited an award under the provisions of A.F.O. 1464(1) of 1941.)

and

(2) <u>Mr W. Nangle</u>   who, to a lesser degree, assisted Mr Cargill.*

(3) <u>Lieutenant A.G. Townley, R.A.N.V.R.</u>
> and the crew of HMAS *Steady Hour.*

(4) <u>Sub-Lieutenant J.A. Doyle, R.A.N.R. (S)</u>
> and the crew of HMAS *Sea Mist.*

(5) <u>Lieutenant J.A. Taplin R.A.N.R. (S)</u>
> and the crew of HMAS *Yandra.*

(6) <u>Engineer Captain A.B. Doyle, C.B.E., R.A.N.</u>
and

(7) <u>Commander (E) G.C. Clark, R.A.N.</u>
> These officers arrived on the scene minutes after the explosion which sank *Kuttabul*, and displayed commendable fortitude in searching the vessel for any man who might be trapped. In doing so, they had to wade in deep water, under hazardous conditions, in darkness, as it was not known at the time which portion of the decks had been rendered dangerous by the explosion. They lent assistance to a number of men who had been shocked by the suddenness and force of the action.

(8) <u>Bandsman M.N. Cumming, Official No. 20501.</u>
> This rating, who was onboard *Kuttabul* at the time of the explosion, showed determination in diving into the water from the vessel, swimming a few yards and assisting a rating on to *Kuttabul*'s deck. He also again dived

---

* The words 'to a lesser degree' have been crossed out in ink.

into the water into *Kuttabul's* wreckage in order to see whether anyone needed assistance. Although no great courage or endurance was necessary, he displayed considerable initiative.

(9) Mr F.J. Lingard (Torpedo Fitter).

For the removal of pistols and primers from torpedoes, and demolition charges from submarines, this work being carried out entirely voluntarily.

The Skipper and crew of Naval Auxiliary Patrol Boat, *Lauriana*.

For prompt action in illuminating the submarine.

The Captain and crew of HMAS *Yarroma*.

For their part in the sinking of Midget 21. It is considered that this action redeemed, to some extent, their earlier failure.

All personnel of the Dockyard First Aid Party.

For their efficient handling of casualties.

Muirhead-Gould's final appendix was, of course, a list of recommendations for medals. It differs from the 22 June list only by the very welcome addition of the name of the torpedo fitter Frank Lingard. As we have seen, as early as 16 June the Chief of Naval Staff Sir Guy Royle was of a mind to award medals at the high level of Distinguished Service Cross (DSC). That is not what happened, however.

Dealing with the medals list first, I have no quarrel with any of the names on it. However, I would be inclined to add a few more. 'Tubby' Anderson and the crew of *Lolita* displayed cool and ready aggression when they found Chuman tangled in the net. Their depth charges may not have been effective, but their actions undoubtedly led to the scuttling of the midget submarine. They sank a submarine as surely as Reg Andrew did, and rather more surely than Athol Townley. But Muirhead-Gould had made a fool of himself in front of the whole crew of *Lolita*, and the Admiral must have felt it would be too much of a climb-down to include them now in any awards. The other glaring omission is the divers. Lance Bullard and Roy Cooté displayed astonishing courage in securing Matsuo's submarine in Taylors Bay. As far as they could tell, the submarine was still 'alive' when they tackled it. They knew that the Japanese had explosive charges aboard which would surely have killed them both if they had detonated while the divers were anywhere nearby. Bullard's and Cooté's courage was not brief and furious in the heat of battle: it was cool, unwavering and sustained over more than a week. It has gone unrecognised until the publication of this book.

The Battle of Sydney Harbour is unique in Australian military history in that no medals were awarded to any of the participants. Every other major action dating back to the Boer War brought a crop of medals for those who took part. The consensus among those involved in Sydney is that somewhere along the line the government and the navy decided that the whole battle had been a complete fiasco, and the best bet would be to draw a line under it and move on. No courts martial. And no medals. It is a monstrous injustice, and it is not too late for the Royal Australian Navy and the Australian government to do something about it. (If the United States government wanted to do something for Jimmy Mecklenberg, that would be a further piece of belated justice.)

◆　◆　◆

In the National Archive in Melbourne there is an undated letter from the Secretary of the Naval Board addressed to the Naval Officer in Charge, Sydney. From other sources it is possible to date the letter as being sent on 3 October 1942, four months after the attack and 11 weeks after the submission of Muirhead-Gould's 16 July report, to which it refers. The letter is headed 'Midget submarine attack on Sydney Harbour'. It is worth quoting in full.

I am directed by the Naval Board to refer to your letter of 16th July, 1942, No. B.S.1749/201/37, appendix VI, in which you bring to notice the names of certain officers, ratings and civilian personnel for recognition in regard to operations against enemy midget submarines in Sydney on May 31st–June 1st, 1942.

The Board have read with pleasure your report and commendation and have directed that appropriate notations are to be made in the records of the following officers and ratings:-

Engineer Captain A.B. Doyle, C.B.E., R.A.N.
Commander (E) C.C. Clark, R.A.N.
Lieutenant A.C. Townley, R.A.N.V.R.
HMAS *Steady Hour*
Lieutenant J.A. Taplin, R.A.N.R. (S)
HMAS *Yandra*
Sub-Lieutenant J.A. Doyle, R.A.N.R.
HMAS *Sea Mist*
Bandsman M.N. Cumming, O.N. 20501.

They desire also that the thanks and congratulations of the Naval Board be communicated to Mr. F.J. Lingard (Torpedo Fitter) and to the Dockyard First Aid Party.

The Naval Board further request that their congratulations be communicated to the crews of HMA Ships *Steady Hour*, *Sea Mist* and *Yandra*, and to the skipper and crew of the Naval Auxiliary Patrol Boat *Lauriana* for their efficient work, and to the captain and crew of HMAS *Yarroma* for their part in the sinking of Midget 21.

The Naval Board have recommended that a monetary reward of £40 be made to Mr. J. Cargill and £10 to Mr. W. Nangle, and desire to express their appreciation of the vigilance shown and prompt action taken by them.

Signed
Secretary.

In the margin alongside the name of Sub-Lieutenant J.A. Doyle and *Sea Mist*, an anonymous hand has scribbled: 'Should be Lieut. Andrew.'

That was the sum total of all awards and commendations made to Australians for their part in the Battle of Sydney Harbour: 'appropriate notations in the records' of five officers, one of them incorrectly named; a pat on the back for the crews of five ships; thanks and congratulations for Frank Lingard; and 40 quid for Jimmy Cargill and a tenner for his mate Bill Nangle. At least the Imperial Japanese Navy promoted their submariners two ranks. Though their sailors had to die first.

Chapter 19

Final rest

The story of the midget submarines of the Eastern Attack Group was never other than bizarre. Their path to their final rest proved to be every bit as exotic.

Within days of the raid, two submarines had been recovered: Matsuo's from Taylors Bay, and Chuman's from the net. Both had broken in two. Chuman's submarine snapped just forward of the conning tower, with the separated and largely demolished bow section flung towards Chowder Bay by the blast from his scuttling charges. Matsuo's submarine had lost its tail section from just behind the rear battery compartment, broken off while the sub was being dragged to shallow water before being raised. The two sections of each submarine were lifted from the harbour bed. The broken remains were carried to Clarke Island, not far from Garden Island in the middle of Sydney Harbour.

First they were thoroughly searched for any intelligence they might yield. The harvest was good, particularly from Matsuo's submarine. His midget had taken less internal damage than Chuman's scuttled wreck. As we have seen from Muirhead-Gould's report, there were copies of British Admiralty charts, with rendezvous points and entry tracks neatly drawn. And there was more. There were bundles of photographs, mostly aerial pictures of Sydney and Newcastle, together with cuttings from 1938 Australian magazines and newspapers showing the various features of Sydney Harbour, including Garden Island, Cockatoo Island and the Harbour Bridge. The Japanese had cast their net wider than the harbour itself: there were also references to Sydney's Government House, Central Railway Station and the Town Hall. Other cuttings dealt with the city of Wollongong, the Hawkesbury Bridge, Newcastle Harbour and Airfield, the BHP steelworks and the steelworks at Port Kembla. The Japanese had prepared well.

The submarines contained the personal effects of their crew: ceremonial swords, Matsuo's 1000-stitch *senninbari* (stomach protector), even a red umbrella. The navy released very few details of these finds: best not tell your enemy how much you know about him. On 25 June the Navy Office in Sydney sent a teleprinter message to the Department of Naval Intelligence in Melbourne: 'Press have got information that crews of midget S/MS [submarines] were shot in mouth. They also bringing up report of red umbrella. Suggest facts should be released in order to prevent imaginative stories being published.' The Naval Intelligence department would have none of it. They cabled back: 'Your 0231Z/24 [02.31 am Zulu time on 24 June, meaning 12.31 pm on 25 June, Eastern Australian Time] have requested publicity censorship forbid any reference personnel or equipment midget submarines unless officially released Navy Melbourne.' The navy was particularly anxious to suppress any hint that the Japanese had arrived on a suicide mission.

By the end of June the submarines had been thoroughly examined from top to bottom. Engineers drew up detailed plans and diagrams. They were able to estimate the subs' speed and endurance. Intelligence officers concluded from the food supplies and other evidence that these were not suicide missions. The engineers also examined the five disarmed torpedoes, two from Chuman's submarine, two from Matsuo's, and one unexploded torpedo aground on Garden Island. The Dutch Navy conducted extensive tests on the torpedoes. They were particularly interested in the unexploded torpedo fired by Ban. Why had it missed? Why had it not armed? (Their findings, largely overlooked, have been incorporated into earlier chapters of this book.)

Once the submarines had given up their secrets, there remained the question of what to do with them. The navy had been thinking about this right from the beginning. Sir Guy Royle's 16 June letter to Rear Admiral Muirhead-Gould mostly dealt with the consequences of the attack. However, it contained two revealing paragraphs. 'The charts and other relics you obtained from the midget submarines have been most valuable,' Sir Guy wrote. 'I am looking forward to seeing the ceremonial sword which is on its way to Navy Office. I will have it transferred to the National Museum.' At the end of the letter Sir Guy added a handwritten postscript: 'I should like the midgets to be used eventually to obtain funds for Navy House Sydney i.e. after all official investigations are completed.' The word Sydney had been underlined by Sir Guy. God forbid that any money should find its way to Navy House Melbourne.

Sir Guy had his way. The navy prepared the submarines for a grand tour of Australian cities. Chuman's bow section had been well and truly detached from the rest of the midget by the blast of his scuttling charge. The navy completed the job of shortening the submarine by removing the tail section as well. That left about two-thirds of the submarine, including the conning tower and forward and rear battery compartments, ready to be mounted on a large trailer. The forward battery compartment was a key element. It had taken most of the force of Chuman's scuttling charge, and the navy left the ripped and jagged hull section on display for all to see. The trailer and its battered submarine were then hooked up behind a heavy truck, and began a 4000-kilometre publicity tour. Although this was primarily a fund-raising venture, the tour clearly had a secondary purpose. The navy had a morale-boosting message to sell to the Australian public, and a warning for the Japanese: mess with the Australian Navy and you'll finish up looking like this. The truck drove inland to Canberra, then continued down the Hume Highway to Melbourne, crossed to Adelaide, and finally made its way back to Sydney. It stopped at towns along the way, and hordes of the curious gathered around to marvel at this exotic sight. The crowds were invited to make donations to the Navy Fund, which supported seamen and their widows and families. There is no record of the amount raised, but it was probably substantial.

The navy now set about creating a composite submarine for display. They sliced cleanly through Matsuo's submarine on either side of the conning tower, and detached Matsuo's bow section. This bow, together with its highly visible dent where the steel cable had cut into the hull while the midget was being raised from Taylors Bay, was matched up to the centre section of Chuman's submarine, fresh from its triumphant road tour of all points south. Chuman's tail section, which had been removed to make the submarine fit the touring trailer, was now reunited with the centre. All three sections were moved to Canberra and put on open-air display on the west lawn of the Australian War Memorial. At this point the three sections were supported on blocks but remained separate, with the public able to peer inside the submarine from the gaps between the sections.

Matsuo's sliced-off conning tower remained on Garden Island, awaiting further orders.

◆　◆　◆

When war broke out between Japan and Australia, each country still had diplomats in place. They remained there until August 1942, when an exchange was agreed through Swiss intermediaries. On 13 August 1942, over 10 weeks after the attack, Tatsuo Kawai, the Japanese Minister at the Legation of Japan in Melbourne, wrote to the Swiss Consul-General in Sydney to say:

> I have the honour to inform you that the ashes of the four Japanese officers and men, whose bodies were recovered from submarines sunk in Sydney Harbour, were duly delivered to me this morning by the Swiss Consul in Melbourne, Mr Pietzcker, in person.
>
> In acknowledging the receipt of same, I hasten to express to you my sincerest thanks for your whole-hearted assistance given to this matter. I am grateful to the Australian authorities, too, for their handing over to me of the ashes for return to Japan.

Next day Kawai and his mission sailed home, carrying the ashes with them. They followed a convoluted route, via the port of Lourenco Marques in Portuguese East Africa (now Mozambique). When the diplomats and their sad cargo finally arrived in Yokohama, thousands turned out to greet the return of the remains of the four submariners. Matsuo's fiancée Toshiko was in the crowd.

The results of the Sydney attack became known in Japan some time around 4 June 1942, at about the same time that Japanese aircraft carriers and cruisers were sinking in horrific numbers in the Battle of Midway. There had been no inclination to and no opportunity for the crowing and myth-making which followed the midget submarine attack on Pearl Harbor. The Sydney funeral with its full military honours and Rear Admiral Muirhead-Gould's broadcast had been widely reported in Japan immediately after the event, but very few details had been released to the Japanese public of the raid itself. Japanese commentators interpreted the funeral and Muirhead-Gould's defence of it as evidence of Australian admiration for Japan.

However, on 8 December 1942, the first anniversary of Pearl Harbor, Admiral Yamamoto announced a citation for the midget submariners of the Eastern and Western Attack Groups, for 'brilliant results at Sydney Harbour and Diégo Suarez'. Full recognition did not come quickly. It was not until 27 March 1943 that the Japanese Navy gave any details of the raids. They also announced that Yamamoto's citation had been 'brought to the attention of the Emperor'. All submariners who had taken part in the Sydney and Diégo Suarez raids were posthumously promoted two ranks. Unlike their Pearl Harbor colleagues, however, they were not publicly proclaimed as war gods, although they were unofficially worshipped along with other war gods at the Yasukuni shrine. There was a curious parallel in the lack of honours for both the Japanese and the Australian heroes of the Battle of Sydney Harbour.

◆　　◆　　◆

In Australia, a modest little industry now sprang up. The navy sold souvenirs. Even after constructing the composite submarine, the navy had plenty of leftover material. Bits of brass pipe from the submarines, together with a certificate of authenticity confirmed by the printed signature of Muirhead-Gould, went for sixpence each. So did a piece of electrical cable, similarly authenticated. A 25-mm square of copper with an indecipherable Japanese character on it was a much more substantial purchase. That would cost the buyer a shilling. All proceeds went to the Royal Australian Navy Relief Fund.

The navy organised the production of 313 dozen (3756) tiny lead submarines and 25,000 postcards. Some of these were handed over to the Department of Information, which shipped them off to the United States for sale there. Metal from the submarines—very likely from the bow of Chuman's submarine and leftover parts of the centre section of Matsuo's—was melted down or beaten and converted into ashtrays, together with an inscription confirming to the buyer he was stubbing his cigarette in a genuine bit of a Japanese submarine sunk in Sydney Harbour.

The navy now had to consider what to do with whatever had been left behind by the souvenir industry. In August 1944 the Department of Supply informed the navy that it was of a mind to accept a tender of £30 from Kallion Brothers for the scrap metal which hadn't been converted into ashtrays. However, Kallion Brothers withdrew their offer when the navy insisted that the submarines must not be cut up and sold for souvenirs. This was, of course, a nice bit of hypocrisy on the navy's part. But it saved what remained of the submarines for posterity.

Meanwhile, the composite submarine gathered rust and graffiti outside the Australian War Memorial in Canberra. In 1966, in the middle of Beatlemania, a group of university students painted it yellow. They were ordered to pay for the paint's removal.

In 1968 Matsuo's 86-year-old mother accepted an invitation to come to Australia and visit the War Memorial. She climbed into the submarine and sprinkled some *sake* in the conning tower area, a traditional Japanese salute to the dead. Nobody told her that this was Chuman's conning tower, not her son's. She read aloud a poem she had written on the first anniversary of her son's death. Amid some controversy, the War

Memorial presented her with Matsuo's lightly blood-stained 1000-stitch *senninbari*. She was not told her son had died by his own hand. The Australians allowed her to believe he had been killed by depth charges after putting up a hard fight.

The composite submarine remained on the lawn, its condition continuing to deteriorate. By the beginning of the 1980s the War Memorial's trustees were forced to recognise that their prize exhibit's problems went beyond the attentions of pranksters with cans of yellow paint. They decided to send the submarine to the naval dockyard on Cockatoo Island in Sydney for restoration, including the removal of 40 years of graffiti.

The restored submarine is now the centrepiece of the Australian War Memorial's special section devoted to the raid. It remains one of the most popular exhibits in the entire collection. Instead of displaying the submarine in three separated sections, the Cockatoo Island restorers welded it together to create a more convincing replica of the original. The black-painted hull hovers menacingly in a dimly lit room, rippling light playing over it to simulate the movement of water. The brightest light shines inside the devastated sides of Chuman's forward section, still dramatically flayed open by the blast of a scuttling charge fired a lifetime ago. The crushed bow cage and damaged bow caps from Matsuo's submarine have been lovingly repaired and restored. They gleam in the soft light.

The tail of Matsuo's submarine is also kept at the War Memorial, not far from the special exhibit. It can be found in the Pacific War room of the Second World War section.

The sliced off conning tower of Matsuo's submarine was kept for years at Garden Island in Sydney. It was finally restored by students from the Wagga Wagga Technical and Further Education College, who undertook the work as a training exercise. The restored conning tower is now back on Garden Island, mounted on a special plinth in the café of the new and excellent Naval Heritage Centre there. Garden Island is, of course, no longer an island. The graving dock under construction during the raid has filled the gap between the original island and the mainland at the foot of Macleay Street, Kings Cross. The salvaged wheelhouse of the *Kuttabul* for years served as the gatehouse to the still-active naval shore base there, renamed HMAS *Kuttabul* in honour of the old ferry. In November 2000 the wheelhouse moved to the Australian War Memorial in Canberra, where it now sits close to the composite submarine whose fellow midget did it such an injury all those years ago.

♦　　♦　　♦

The ultimate fate of Ban's midget, resting on the seabed in a bit over 50 metres of water off Newport Reef, Sydney, has yet to be decided. It is in water controlled by the Australian state of New South Wales. Both the state and the Commonwealth of Australia have set up overlapping legal protection for the site. No one may enter a zone with a radius of 500 metres around the position 33 degrees, 40' 21" south and 151 degrees 22' 58" east. Fines for disturbing the wreck could reach $1.1 million under New South Wales law, while Commonwealth law provides for further hefty fines plus immediate confiscation of boat and dive equipment.

The wreck is not without its dangers. The Sydney submarines carried two sets of scuttling charges, each of 135 kg of TNT, packed in round canisters fore and aft. There is no record of exactly where these charges were stored on the subs, or of whether the canisters were watertight. Each charge had two detonators, one electric (connected to the batteries) and one non-electric (fired by lighting a 'match' fuse). While the TNT would be hard to set off without a detonator, the state of the detonators themselves remains unknown. They are certainly being given the benefit of the doubt by all divers approaching the wreck.

After proclaiming their legislative controls, the authorities proceeded to set up sophisticated monitoring systems to guard the wreck against intruders. These include a shore-based fixed camera trained permanently on the wreck site, plus camera-mounted buoys with permanent lights stationed over the wreck, and a sonar listening device on the sea bed nearby, all connected directly to and monitored by the New South Wales Water Police. Any unauthorised boat or diver approaching the midget can expect brisk attention from the authorities.

The wreck has settled to about the depth of a metre into the sandy seabed. It has filled inside with sand, again to the depth of about a metre. Although the hull is largely intact, the effect of corrosion over the years has made it fragile and vulnerable. Any attempt to raise it would run the substantial risk of destroying the very object it set out to save.

If Ban and Ashibe died with their boat, then any remains would very likely be found buried in the sand at the bottom of the control room, or in the nearby access areas. It would be technically feasible to place a large pipe through the open conning tower hatch into the control room, suck out the contents and draw them to the surface. However this would be a grotesque and indefensibly brutal approach to a delicate problem. Drawing the hull contents up to the surface would badly disturb the wreck, destroying any archaeological clues the remains might offer. Quite simply, this will not be allowed. Recovery of any human remains will take place only through a complete recovery of the hull. Such an operation would cost tens of millions of dollars as well as risking the destruction of a major heritage site.

At the time of writing, something of a consensus was beginning to emerge between the Japanese and Australian authorities, the families of Ban and Ashibe, and the various heritage offices involved. This is likely to mean that the sub and its contents will be left entirely undisturbed on the seabed, at least in the short term. However, there is some precedent for the idea of constructing a metal cage around the wreck, after which divers will be permitted to dive to visit the cage to view and photograph the submarine inside. Such cages are not cheap to build: the cost could run into millions of dollars. Under this scheme, the cage would need to be maintained and access to it controlled, with permits issued to parties of divers approved to approach the wreck. The cage could include a lockable door, so that authorised entry to the submarine would still be possible.

For the time being, the New South Wales Heritage Office, assisted by other heritage agencies and industry, is carrying out detailed surveys of the site, trying to determine the condition of the structure and to unlock its secrets. This information will be needed before any new steps are taken to protect and manage the wreck, perhaps even to design a cage.

◆　◆　◆

There is one other collection of midget submarine memorabilia known to the author. It is a clear plastic bag full of odds and ends, and it lives under the desk of John Perryman, the Senior Naval Historical Officer at the Royal Australian Navy's Sea Power Centre in Fyshwick, Canberra. The Sea Power Centre holds navy archives and conducts research for the navy. John very kindly invited me to help myself to a couple of pieces from the bag and I chose two circular wooden seals, one about 11 cm across and the other about 5 cm across. The larger one was once painted white, but the paint has faded over the years and some of it has been replaced by scorch marks, possibly from the scuttling charges which destroyed Chuman's midget. I had them mounted and framed, together with their certificate of authenticity signed by John. They hang over my desk in London, and they kept an eye on me while I wrote this book.

Epilogue

Whatever happened to . . .?

A remarkable number of the men and ships who took part in the Battle of Sydney Harbour lived to tell their tales. Many of those who emerge well from this story, particularly officers from the US Navy, had their abilities recognised and were promoted. Others fared less well. I hunted high and low for a photograph of Captain Howard Bode, but could not find one anywhere. His tragic story, recounted below, no doubt accounts for the fact that he has been air-brushed from history.

THE MEN
Warrant Officer Herbert 'Tubby' Anderson moved on from the Channel Patrol boats to a shore posting in the port of Darwin. He left the navy on 24 April 1946, and returned to Adelaide, where he rejoined the fire service. For years he was coxswain of *Fire Queen*, the only floating fire-fighting vessel protecting the port of Adelaide. He retired in 1964, but continued his love affair with the sea, building his own 34-foot racing yacht, *Ghost*. He died of a stroke in 1966 at the age of 63. His son Harold, at the time of writing entering his eighth year as mayor of the city of Charles Sturt in Adelaide, recalls that his father often said

without bitterness that those Australians who took part in the Battle of Sydney Harbour had never received the recognition they deserved.

Lieutenant Reginald Andrew remained in command of HMAS *Sea Mist* for nine months before transferring to HMAS *Lolita*. He never enjoyed a comfortable relationship with navy authority, and after 18 months with the Channel Patrol boats he was moved to menial and routine shore jobs, first in Cairns in northern Queensland and then to Milne Bay in New Guinea. He left the navy as soon as he could after the war. For a time he worked in the petrol industry, first as Queensland sales manager of the long-disappeared oil company Purpull, then with his own independent petrol station. Reg Andrew died in 1984, survived by his remarkable widow Jean, who celebrated her 100th birthday in April 2006. For the rest of his life Reg clung tenaciously to his story of sinking two submarines in Taylors Bay. In correspondence with the author Steven Carruthers, Steven tried to persuade Reg that only three submarines entered Sydney Harbour that night, and Reg had sunk one of them. Reg would have none of it. He wrote dismissively to Steve: 'If only three midgets came, then I am a bloody hero!' He was.

Captain Howard D. Bode of the USS *Chicago* is ultimately one of the tragic figures of this story. His personal inadequacies caught up with him a few months after the Battle of Sydney Harbour. On 9 August 1942, he was aboard *Chicago* in command of one of two mixed battle groups of British, Australian and American ships escorting troop carriers near Savo Island in the Solomons. Contrary to normal naval practice, Bode chose to lead his battle group from the rear. They were 'jumped' by a more agile Japanese group, and *Chicago* took some serious but far from fatal damage in the early exchange of fire. Although Bode was in command of the group, he decided to withdraw, taking *Chicago's* long-range guns with him and leaving his group to their fate. Bode then compounded this tragedy by failing to warn the second Allied battle group of the presence of a powerful and aggressive Japanese force in their area. They too were taken by surprise. The resulting carnage was appalling, leading to the sinking of three heavy American cruisers, USS *Vincennes*, *Quincy* and *Astoria,* and the heavy Australian cruiser HMAS *Canberra*. The Allied death toll was 1024, with a further 709 wounded. The Japanese lost no ships, and confined their casualties to 35 killed and 51 wounded. It was the worst blue-water defeat in the US Navy's history, and they set up an inquiry under Admiral Hepburn into the causes. The report of the inquiry was not intended to be made public at the time, but on the eve of its delivery Bode learned he had been singled out for censure. On 19 April 1943, he shot himself. He died next day.

Lance Bullard left the Australian Navy on 30 January 1946. After the war, he never dived again. He worked on a farm near Muswellbrook in the Hunter Valley of New South Wales, before retiring. He then indulged a passion for sketching. His account of the divers' work raising the two midget submarines, written decades after the event, is sharply observed and fluently written. If he had combined his writing with sketching, he might have produced a classic book. He died in 1978 at the age of 76.

Jimmy Cargill remained with the Maritime Services Board, though not always as a nightwatchman. He became involved with general security on the wharves at a time when militant industrial action made this job no sinecure. He retired from the Maritime Services Board in 1953 and died in 1986, aged 96, largely forgotten despite his key role in the events of 31 May 1942. The only mention of his passing was a single-paragraph story in a free suburban newspaper, the *Wentworth Courier.*

Roy Cooté left the navy on 31 March 1946. Like his comrade Lance Bullard, he never dived again after the war. He bought a general store in remote country north of Mildura, and for years lived an amiable life dispensing petrol and general supplies to a handful of surrounding landholders. He eventually sold the store and retired to Melbourne. A combination of heavy smoking and years of wear to his lungs from diving took its toll. He died of emphysema in 1984, aged 83.

William Floyd, *Chicago*'s gunnery officer who read the riot act to his anti-aircraft crews after they missed Ito's flight, was later promoted to Rear Admiral. He survived the war and retired to Coronado, California.

Warrant Officer Susumo Ito survived the war. He did well to do so: by the end of hostilities he had flown over every Australian capital city. He returned to the skies over Sydney on 19 February 1943, where he was fired on by anti-aircraft batteries and chased by fighter aircraft. He managed to evade his attackers. In the last months of the war he had the appalling task of dispatching *kamikaze* pilots to their certain death. The process so sickened him that he would have nothing to do with aviation after the war. In the peace, he set up his own electronic business in the Japanese city of Iwakuni. He was 'discovered' in the most extraordinary way. There were plenty of Australian occupation forces stationed in Iwakuni after the war, and the mayor organised a dinner for visiting Australian journalists. He cast around, desperate for someone local who knew something about Australia. Ito shyly admitted that he had indeed visited Australia several times, though without ever actually making contact with Australian soil. He did subsequently manage a visit to Australia, this time at ground level. He was slightly surprised by how big Australians were, and by the fact that many of the women had moustaches. He is still alive at the time of writing, probably the only Japanese survivor of the Battle of Sydney Harbour.

Jimmy Mecklenberg, the quick-thinking officer whose prompt attack on Ban's submarine saved *Chicago* from early destruction, was later promoted to Captain, USN. He survived the war and returned to civilian life where he worked in the fledgling telecommunications and IT industry in Alexandria, Virginia.

Rear Admiral Gerard Charles Muirhead-Gould remained at his post as Naval Officer in Command, Sydney, for most of the war. However, as the Allies advanced into Germany, his knowledge of that country and his language skills in German meant he could be better employed in Europe.

He was transferred to Wilhelmshaven in September 1944 as Officer in Command of the former German naval base. While serving there, the heart problem that kept him away from active service finally caught up with him. He died of a heart attack in Wilhelmshaven on 26 April 1945, only 11 days before Germany's surrender ended the war in Europe.

Lieutenant Athol G. Townley had the most glittering subsequent career of all the participants in the Battle of Sydney Harbour. On the night itself he had shown commendable leadership skills and a talent for quick thinking, and both these attributes stood him in good stead after the war. He entered Federal Australian politics, and rose to be Minister for Defence in the Menzies government. In 1960 he accepted the job of Australian ambassador to the United States, but died suddenly of a heart attack before he could take up the post. Sadly, it has been impossible to find in any public archive his action report on the events in Taylors Bay on the morning of 1 June 1942. It might have helped settle the question of who did what.

THE SHIPS

USS *Chicago* was damaged during the Battle of Savo Island (see entry for Captain Howard Bode, above). She was sunk by Japanese land-based bombers on 30 January 1943 during the Battle of Rennell Island. Although there were few American casualties from *Chicago* (62 dead while 1049 of her crew were rescued), her sinking was seen as potentially a major blow to American morale. Admiral Chester Nimitz, Commander of US Naval Forces, South-West Pacific, threatened to 'shoot' any of his staff who leaked her loss to the press.

HMAS *Lauriana* went on to greater glory. On 31 May 1942 she was part of the Naval Auxiliary Patrol fleet, and still owned by Harold Arnott. The navy bought her from Arnott on 27 August 1942 and fitted her with a 20-millimetre Oerlikon anti-aircraft gun, a Vickers machine-gun and 10 midget depth charges. She frequently travelled to New Guinea, where she acted as sleeping quarters for General Douglas

MacArthur. *Lauriana* is credited with shooting down two Japanese Zero fighters. She still carries bullet holes from strafing attacks by Japanese aircraft. She was returned to Arnott on 27 November 1945. She then changed hands several times before being bought by her present owner, a Sydney dentist. She is now being refitted in loving detail after coming to grief when a rope fouled her propeller, cracking her engine's gearbox, and forcing a complete re-build of her decking and superstructure. She is expected to re-emerge some time in 2007, and take her rightful place as one of the most beautiful yachts on Sydney Harbour.

HMAS *Lolita* did not make it. The Channel Patrol boats were inclined to accumulate petrol vapour in their bilges, and each boat was equipped with ventilating exhaust fans to remove it before it reached a dangerous build-up. In Madang Harbour on 13 June 1945, with the war almost over, an attempt was made to start *Lolita*'s engine while fumes had been allowed to gather. The immediate explosion led to the death of two crew members and the total destruction of the veteran patrol boat.

USS *Perkins* had the most tragic end of all the ships involved in the Battle of Sydney Harbour. While on convoy escort duty on 29 October 1942, she was involved in a collision with the Australian troopship HMAS *Duntroon* in darkness at sea. The impact cut her in two. She sank immediately, with the loss of four lives. Ian Mitchell, the young signalman who manned Garden Island signal station on the night of the midget submarine raid on Sydney Harbour (see Chapter 8), was a signalman on *Duntroon* on the night of the disaster.

HMAS *Sea Mist* still appears on the register of the Australian Maritime Safety Authority, though without her HMAS label. Immediately after the war she was bought by the Sydney radio station 2GB and made available as a 'perk' to the radio personality Jack Davey. She changed hands several times and underwent major refits. She is said to be in excellent condition today. AMSA lists her home port as Sydney. However, she is believed to be based in Queensland.

HMAS *Steady Hour* did not survive the war. She was destroyed by fire on 3 March 1945, while stationed in Darwin.

HMAS *Yandra* survived the war. She was paid off at Port Adelaide on 25 March 1946 and returned to her original owners, the Coast Steam Ship Company of Adelaide, in July 1946. She does not appear on the current Australian Maritime Safety Authority list of registered ships.

HMAS *Yarroma* also does not appear on the current Australian Maritime Safety Authority list. The last traceable entry in the Royal Australian Navy register of requisitioned ships, dated 18 May 1945, shows that her engines had been condemned and that she was awaiting the arrival of reconditioned engines. According to the Royal Australian Navy's publication *A–Z Ships, Aircraft and Shore Establishments* she was sold on 15 December 1945. The *A–Z* does not name the buyer. After that the trail goes cold.

Appendix I

Genuine seller

One of the great legends of the submarine raid is the crash of house prices which followed it in Sydney's harbourside suburbs. While researching this book, the author was repeatedly told about an uncle/cousin/neighbour/grandparent who knew of a house sold for £25 in Rose Bay in the days immediately after the shelling of that suburb. Urban myth. It never happened. However, there was some genuine if brief impact on house prices, and some genuine action from people who saw the raid as the possible forerunner of an invasion. The reality is that a lot of people had already made plans to get out of the cities and into the country if ever the Japanese arrived, and the shelling of Sydney's suburbs made these plans seem more urgent. In particular, people looked to the Blue Mountains, an hour's drive west of Sydney, for sanctuary. Why they would do this remains a mystery to the author. It hardly seems likely that the Japanese, having taken the trouble to invade Sydney, would lose heart 50 kilometres inland and leave the rest of the country to its own devices. It is fair to acknowledge, however, that the genteel mountain hideaways of Leura and Katoomba would be unlikely to suffer the kind of heavy bombing and shelling which Sydney could expect if the Japanese arrived in serious numbers.

So what actually happened? The classified advertising section of the Saturday edition of the *Sydney Morning Herald* is the traditional bulletin board for Sydneysiders wishing to sell anything, from their car to their house. If there were a property crash, it would be evident here. A host of new properties would appear on the market, average prices would plummet, and the scent of desperation would be strong in the air. An examination of the *Herald*'s advertisements for 'Flats, Residential' and 'Houses, Land for Sale' in the weeks before and after the raid tells the story, and punctures the myth.

On Saturday, 30 May, the day before the raid, there were 26 flats advertised in the *Herald* with Rose Bay addresses, and four houses. The rentals for the flats were generally between £2 and £3 a week. The four houses ranged in price from £1050 for a brick cottage with four rooms and a tiled bathroom to £2100 for a modern bungalow with two bedrooms, sunroom, lounge, dining room, hot water service, refrigerator and harbour views. No price was given for a rather more splendid gent's new residence in Wallangra Road, Rose Bay Heights, with four bedrooms, three reception rooms, two bathrooms, three toilets, a ball-room and a double garage. The *Herald* also carried a 'Houses and Land Wanted' advertising section, and Rose Bay appeared there once: a cash buyer was willing to pay up to £3000 for a cottage or bungalow, new or old, in Rose Bay Heights.

So how were house prices two weeks later, on 13 June, when the submarines had been and gone and the shells had fallen all around? The number of Rose Bay flats on offer had fallen slightly from 26 to 21. Rentals stayed between £2 and £3 a week. No houses were offered for sale in Rose Bay. However, in 'Houses and Land Wanted' there was one buyer offering up to £3000 for a four-bedroom modern home in Rose Bay Heights. In other words, no change.

A week later there was some sign of movement. On 20 June the *Herald* listed 25 flats in Rose Bay. This time the cheapest was £1.12.6 a week, down from the £2 lowest price of the week before. There were only two houses for sale, including the gent's residence in Wallangra Road, still unpriced. However, a tone of mild hysteria crept into the wording of the second ad. 'Rose Bay, convenient Tram, Bus and Shops', it began enticingly. 'Commodious bungalow home, 3 reception rooms, 4 bedrooms, all conveniences, Refrigerator, Garage. The OWNER is a GENUINE SELLER and is prepared to SACRIFICE for a QUICK SALE. PRICE £2200 or near offer.'

By the following week, GENUINE SELLER had to face the fact that he was in trouble. His price dropped to £1930 or near offer. There were now six houses for sale in Rose Bay, the largest number yet. The prices were: £1030, £1450, £2330, £2330, £3100 and GENUINE SELLER's £1930. Far from dropping, the average price had actually risen microscopically, whatever the travails of GENUINE SELLER. The only real change was in flat rentals. Flats could now be had for as little as £1.10.0 a week, a 25 per cent drop from the £2 minimum before the attack.

This pattern continued through July and into August. GENUINE SELLER appeared for the final time on 4 July with the price still set at £1930 or near offer. He dropped out of the running on 11 July, presumably because he had genuinely sold. By the end of August it was all over. After the Battle of Midway, the threat of Japanese invasion had evaporated, and the threat of further attacks on Sydney had diminished to vanishing point. Property prices, whether for sale or rental, were emphatically back to pre-attack levels. Instead, the myth of the property crash became part of estate agents' hype. On 8 August the *Herald* carried an ad for a Rose Bay property: 'Pair maisonettes £4350 sacrificed hundreds below cost. Brand new ultra-modern home and investment combined. Beautiful texture brick building, each home contains two reception, 3 b'rooms, beautiful Modern Bathroom, Shower Recess, sep toilet, h.w. service throughout. Garage.' As readers can judge for themselves, it was offered for about the same price as it would have fetched on 30 May, before the subs came. On 15 August the *Herald* carried a similar advertisement for a two-storey home in Rose Bay Heights priced at £2800. The ad was placed by the Laton Smith estate agency and declared: 'It's seldom we are privileged to offer a home of this quality at this price.' Again, the price was no different from the pre-raid price. By 22 August landlords were asking £3.7.6 a week for flats. It was business as usual, if not better than usual.

David Goldstone was a seven-year-old schoolboy living in a block of flats in Old South Head Road near the corner of O'Sullivan Road, Rose Bay. O'Sullivan Road runs parallel to and one block away from Balfour Road, which was hit by two of the I-24's shells. One of the Balfour Road shells exploded, seriously damaging a house and injuring a sleeping woman with flying glass. So the Goldstone family lived pretty much on the front line.

David attended the nearby Scots College, one of Sydney's eight elite GPS schools, as a day boy. Scots had a country campus near the town of Bathurst, about 150 kilometres west of Sydney. In David's words, his parents did 'a minor flip'. They rapidly switched young David from day boy to boarder, and packed him off to the country campus. 'I was pretty upset about it,' he recalls. 'I wanted to know were my friends coming with me. Of course, they weren't.' The whole experience left him scarred to this day: he still can't bear the taste of rhubarb. 'They had fields full of rhubarb,' he recalls. 'They gave it to us for breakfast, lunch and dinner.'

By the end of the year, the Goldstone parents were confident the invasion threat was over. The Australian school year begins in January, not September. When the new school year started in January 1943, David was back to the Sydney campus of Scots College as a day boy, with the menace of both invasion and rhubarb now a thing of the past. To his huge relief, everything in Sydney was as he had left it. The same families lived in the same blocks of flats. His friends hadn't moved. Life could get back to normal.

However, whole families did at least lay plans to move. Donald Dunkley remembers:

A lot of families were ready to go to relatives up in the country. If an invasion actually did take place, we had some relatives living in Harden, the Riverina part of New South Wales. We were advised to contact relatives in the country and see if they were willing to take us if we had to evacuate. They said yes, by all means, we're happy to take you. So, had there been an invasion, I don't know how on earth we would have got there, but we did have this place earmarked that we could have gone to.

I think a lot of other families around the place had relatives in the country, and they were all ready to go if necessary.

Did he have any friends or neighbours who actually moved as a result of the raid? 'I don't know of any.'

The raid did produce one bizarre scramble. Jim Macken's ability to bob up in unexpected places in this narrative will now be apparent from his Riverview and missing submarine contributions. His final appearance in the story flows from the fact that, at the time of the submarine raid, his father managed the fashionable Hydro-Majestic Hotel in the Blue Mountains near Leura, 100 kilometres west of Sydney. He recalls:

I was living at the Hydro with my father and family. He'd been deluged with phone calls from people wanting permanent bookings at the hotel for the duration of the war. He said, we're not doing it because it would preclude ex-servicemen from coming up here. We don't want permanent bookings. We're looking after people who want a holiday. So he knocked them all back with one exception, a man who'd been there before the war, an old colonel who'd been a permanent resident before 1939.

None of this rush for permanent bookings happened before the submarine attack. The submarines and the shelling of Sydney's eastern suburbs triggered it off. Why did people want to move into the Hydro-Majestic?

They all wanted to get out of Sydney. They wanted to rent their houses, or try to sell their houses. But houses were very hard to sell. They wanted to get out of what they saw as the danger area in Sydney. Although they couldn't get to the Hydro, they were buying houses up all over the Blue Mountains.

It petered out after a while. After Midway and the Coral Sea the panic went out, and people stopped buying and went back home. The fear of a Japanese land invasion faded.

So what is the reality of the Great Sydney Harbourside Property Crash? The core truth is that it never happened. Property prices trembled for about eight weeks, and a few people saved 10 shillings a week—$26 a week in today's money—on the rent they might otherwise have paid if the subs had not come. But there was no rush, no widespread panic selling, and certainly nobody bought a house in Rose Bay for £25.

Finally, there is an unpleasant little lie which needs to be held up to the light and then stomped on and consigned permanently to the rubbish bin. A lot of the stories of the property price crash and the subsequent rush for bargains are told by anti-Semites. The eastern suburbs of Sydney have always been attractive to Sydney's Jewish population, just as they are attractive to the *goyim*. It's as nice a place to live as you would find anywhere in the world. The legend would have you believe that jittery gentiles sold their houses off cheap, and the Jews craftily bought them up at bargain prices. That, says the legend, is why there are so many Jews in Sydney's eastern suburbs today.

It is the purest claptrap. Apart from the non-existence of the property crash, so that there were no bargains to be had anyway, there is no evidence that the mix of population in Sydney's Eastern Suburbs altered one jot after the raid. The truth is that most families were in the same houses and flats six months after the raid as they were before the subs and the shells arrived. Ask David Goldstone.

Appendix II

Other gentlemen's mail

One of the enduring controversies of World War II revolves around who knew what, and when. Given that the British at Bletchley Park were reading Germany's most secret diplomatic and military signals, did Churchill know in advance about Pearl Harbor and fail to tip off the Americans because he wanted them in the war? Did Roosevelt know, too, but fail to act for the same reason? Did the Americans know in advance about the midget submarine raid on Sydney Harbour but fail to tell the Australians through carelessness or malice?

These questions still cannot be answered with absolute certainty. However, it is possible to make some reasonable judgements on the basis of what is already known.

Australian Naval Intelligence built a formidable reputation for itself in World War I. It operated as part of British Naval Intelligence, with responsibility for the whole Pacific area. Wireless telegraphy was now an established means of communication, and embassies and armed forces around the world used it to send messages to each other and to their respective governments and headquarters. As these radio broadcasts could be overheard by anybody, messages had to be sent in code.

Cracking the other side's code is a massively time-consuming process, and the intelligence revealed after hundreds or even thousands of hours of analysis often comes too late to be of any practical use. Rather than employ some of the finest brains in the country to go without sleep while trying to crack codes, by far the better tactic is simply to pinch the other side's code books, taking great care to make sure they don't know you have done it (or they will change the code).

In this matter, Australia got off to a flying start in World War I. On the third day of the war an Australian boarding party seized the unsuspecting German ship *Hobart* in Port Phillip Bay, Melbourne. The German captain was caught trying to remove the code books, which the Australians promptly grabbed, along with the captain. The captain was locked up, and the books were sent to the Admiralty in London. They were used throughout the war to decrypt German signals. Intelligence from this source was critical in tipping off the British of the whereabouts of the German Pacific Fleet, leading to its destruction in the Battle of the Falklands on 9 December 1914.

For the rest of World War I, the Australians concentrated on the two forms of intelligence they did best. They set up a chain of informants throughout the Pacific to report on shipping movements. And they set up powerful listening stations to gather what would now be called SIGINT, intelligence gleaned from listening in to the other side's signal traffic. They made several breakthroughs reading German naval codes, and were roundly praised by the British for their efforts.

The end of hostilities in 1918 brought no let-up in the hunt for SIGINT. The Japanese, who had been allies of the British and Americans, proved to be particularly vulnerable. As early as 1919 their codes had been targeted by American cryptanalysts. In 1921 American agents broke into a Japanese consulate, probably New York, and copied the current Japanese Navy codes, producing what came to be known as the 'Red Book'.

The first major intelligence coup followed in the same year. The Washington Naval Conference was set up to agree a limit on peacetime naval strengths. Japan demanded a navy with 70 per cent of the strength of the British and American navies—the so-called 10:10:7 option. The Americans wanted to limit Japan to 60 per cent or 10:10:6.

The American Office of Naval Intelligence, led by Herbert Yardley and known to insiders as the 'Black Chamber', succeeded in cracking the Japanese diplomatic codes. The American Secretary of State Charles Hughes went to the conference chamber knowing from decoded signals that the Japanese were willing to settle for 10:10:6. He simply sat tight until the Japanese capitulated. A treaty was signed in 1922.

Naval intelligence boomed. The Americans set up listening stations in Guam, the Philippines and Shanghai. A stream of cryptanalysts sailed for Japan on three-year language courses, including Lieutenant Joseph Rochefort, the brightest and best of the US Navy code-breakers.

However, back in the US the character flaws of Herbert Yardley, the head of the Black Chamber, led to disaster. Yardley was a brilliant cryptographer but he was not, to put it mildly, an ideal employee. He was a gambler, a drunk, a womaniser and an opportunist. Uncle Sam's interests were allowed to languish while Yardley played poker (he wrote two books on the subject), ran his unsuccessful property business, sold codes commercially, and offered consultancy services on codes to private companies. This left somewhere between little and no time for the job at hand.

It all had to end. In 1929 the Signal Corps began an investigation, and didn't like what it found. At the same time the American Secretary of State Henry Stimson discovered to his horror that Americans were sneakily prying into other people's private communications and issued his famous decree: 'Gentlemen do not read one another's mail.'* The Black Chamber was closed down.

Yardley responded to this indignity by writing a best-selling book, *The American Black Chamber*, published in 1931, which gave chapter and verse of all the American codebreaking efforts, including the coup at the

---

* There is some doubt as to whether Stimson actually said this. It may be apocryphal, rather like the famous Humphrey Bogart line 'Play it again, Sam', which is never actually uttered in *Casablanca*. However, the closure of the Black Chamber was real enough.

Washington Naval Conference. This is about as big a betrayal as any intelligence officer ever committed, making the *Spycatcher* publication rows of the 1980s look small time. The Japanese were furious, accusing the Americans of bad faith. There is evidence, but no proof, that Yardley had earlier sold the same information to the Japanese for $7000, delivering it to them privately before the publication of the book. The facts were bad enough, the Japanese might have reasoned, but to pay $7000 for information which they could have had for $1 by buying a book a few months later was treachery beyond imagination.

Yardley then tried to publish a follow-up book, *Japanese Diplomatic Secrets*, in 1933. Congress passed a special Act banning its publication, the first and only time such action has been taken. Yardley disappeared, working briefly for Chiang Kai-shek while the Japanese planned to invade China, and later for the Canadians, who quickly dumped him.

The upshot was predictable. The Japanese changed their codes.

The SIGINT battle now entered a new phase: the era of the code machine. Enigma, the machine used by the Germans, was largely mechanical, with a series of rotating wheels and drums controlling flashing lights. The wheels were swapped every 24 hours, as were the code keys. The Japanese developed a slightly more sophisticated version, using electrical telephone switching gear in place of the cogs and wheels.

Enigma first saw the light of day in 1919, when it was sold commercially in Holland. The Germans began using it in the 1920s, and continued to develop and improve it until the end of the war. Enigma was first broken by the Polish secret service. They managed to reconstruct an Enigma machine and successfully read German coded traffic between 1932 and 1938. However, the Germans constantly added new twists and variations to Enigma, to the point where the Poles could no longer unscramble the messages. They handed over two of their reconstructed Enigma machines to the British and French secret services, and briefed the British as best they could on how the system worked.

The British were slow to realise the potential of Enigma, and left it to a single cryptographer in 1938. In 1939, the year war broke out, the Enigma team doubled in strength . . . to two cryptographers. But by 1940 the British had seen the light, and a veritable army of cryptographers worked on the German codes. This first proved its mettle in the Battle of Britain, between July and September 1940, giving the British a lot of information about German squadron locations and strengths. The British named their new source of information 'Ultra'.

The Americans continued to lead the way in the attack on Japanese codes. By 1926 navy code-breakers had broken into the main Japanese naval code, and by 1929 they had the entire code in two red buckram binders. This was known as the Red Code. On 1 December 1930 the Japanese switched to a new code, but the Americans broke this quickly too, naming the new model Blue Code.

So far the US Navy had led the way. Now the US Army entered the fray, having taken over the files from Yardley's Black Chamber. They set about tackling the machine-encrypted codes produced by the Japanese version of the German Enigma machine, and by 1937 they were reading Japanese machine-coded messages reasonably easily, using traditional decrypt techniques. They called the Japanese machine Red (no relation to the Red Code).

However, in 1939 the Americans began to intercept messages encrypted on a new and more sophisticated machine, which they called Purple. These turned out to be brutishly difficult to crack. By August 1940 the US Army SIS (Signals Intelligence Service) began to make progress, and in September 1940 they had the breakthrough they needed. The code was solved. Decrypts from this source were known as 'Magic'.

The next step was extraordinary. No one in America had ever seen a Purple machine, nor did anyone have the faintest idea what it looked like. Nevertheless, the Americans built their own version of Purple. They had been using telephone switching gear as a way of speeding up the decryption process, and they now based their Purple machine on the telephone kit. Incredibly, the switching system they chose was the exact same brand and model as the one used by the Japanese in the real Purple. No Purple machine was ever captured during the war, and the first sight of it was some damaged remains found in the Japanese embassy in Berlin in 1945. The real machine looked remarkably like the American cobbled-up version.

Eight Purple machines were built, and they captured a stream of invaluable information throughout the war. There was a major difference between Purple and Enigma. The Japanese version of the Purple machine had two hefty electric typewriters attached to opposite sides of the central machine. An operator typed in the message to be encoded on one typewriter, and the coded version emerged from the other. This made Purple bigger and heavier than Enigma, to the point where it was too bulky and clumsy for operational military use. While the Germans regularly carried Enigma machines on ships, submarines and even tanks, Purple could only be used in embassies and consulates. So it carried diplomatic traffic only, and diplomats did not receive operational military information. In the last days before the outbreak of war Roosevelt and his cabinet had plenty of warning via Magic that war was imminent and that the Japanese were playing for time. However, Magic produced no coded message saying: 'We are attacking Pearl Harbor on 7 December, using planes and midget submarines.' The timing and target for the attack were never revealed to the diplomats.

When the bombs rained down on Pearl Harbor, the urgent need was for operational rather than diplomatic information. There are two ways intelligence services approach intercepts. The simplest, and often the only option, is traffic analysis. How busy are the airwaves? If there is a lot of traffic, something big is brewing. Direction-finding equipment to track the origin of the signal can be equally revealing. Who sent this message? Who replied? Patterns begin to emerge. 'A' in Tokyo sends a message to 'B' in Java about once a week, and 'B' replies straightaway. Every time this happens, a massive air raid is launched from Java next day. So next time 'A' talks to 'B', get ready for an air raid. Knowing the exact content of the message would be nice, but the mere fact that it was sent tells the traffic analyst what he needs to know.

The Holy Grail remains the full decrypt . . . read the enemy's messages and you are reading his mind. So the spies began a double attack on

Japanese naval signals, analysing the traffic and attempting to crack the code.

Highest priority was given to a decrypt of the Japanese naval code known as JN-25. This code was introduced by the Japanese in June 1939 and had been a major target for US Navy code-breakers ever since. It was another brute to decrypt. There were 45,000 characters in the code, each of which could be rendered in 18,000 different ways, giving 810 million possibilities to unscramble.

On 10 December 1941, three days after Pearl Harbor, a team led by an American Navy cryptanalyst, Lieutenant-Commander Joseph John Rochefort, joined the attack on JN-25. There should be a statue in his honour in every Australian town: he and his team at Station HYPO, as the Pearl Harbor spy base was known, played an important part in the Battle of the Coral Sea and a vital part in the Battle of Midway, which finally turned the tide of war against the Japanese.

The cryptographers at Station HYPO were scruffy, eccentric and generally distrusted by the regular navy. Joe Rochefort fought his entire war in carpet slippers and a red smoking jacket. However, their dedication was total. Rochefort worked 20-hour days, and his team pitched in with equal zeal. By February they began making inroads into the code, to the point where they could read between 10 and 15 per cent of an intercepted message. On 16 March 1942 the combined efforts of HYPO and the US Navy spy base on Corregidor (Station CAST) produced the first complete decrypt of a JN-25 message.

Throughout this period, British and Australian code-breakers had not been idle. They had independently made huge inroads into the JN-25 code. Now the two forces were to combine. Corregidor code-breakers were evacuated to Melbourne in February and March 1942, and formed the American contingent at FRUMEL (Fleet Radio Unit Melbourne). FRUMEL was a joint US–Australian SIGINT unit which became a vital link in the intelligence-gathering chain now surrounding Japan.

Nevertheless, the situation was still dire. John Winton, in his 1994 book *Ultra in the Pacific: How Breaking Japanese Codes and Ciphers Affected Naval Operations against Japan, 1941–45* estimates that by 26 May 1942, five days before the midget submarine attack on Sydney, the US Navy was intercepting about 60 per cent of Japanese messages, and reading about 40 per cent. The decrypts were usually incomplete, sometimes as little as 10 per cent of the message. If all you have is five words of a 50-word cable, the result is not usually enlightening.

With a combination of traffic analysis and decrypt, however, Rochefort and his team had managed to piece together a picture of Operation Mo, as the Japanese had rather unenterprisingly called their attack on Port Moresby and its Australian air base. Rochefort even had the dates right. On 3 May the Japanese would attack Tulagi in the Solomon Islands; on 10 May they would attack Port Moresby. If they won, Australia would be cut off and vulnerable. Thus did Rochefort arm Admiral Frank Jack Fletcher, with vital information to fight the Battle of the Coral Sea, on 6 to 8 May 1942.

Within a month Rochefort scored a second triumph, generally recognised as the turning point in the Pacific war. JN-25 traffic analysis and decrypts pointed to a major Japanese attack on a target they called 'AF'. Where was AF? The 'A' indicated an American base. But which one? Pearl Harbor again? The Aleutians? The American mainland? Midway? From traffic analysis and partial decrypts, Rochefort and his team were already convinced that AF was Midway. However, they needed to persuade the top brass of the US Navy before the admirals would commit scarce resources to a major battle at a specific location on a specific date. How could the brass be made to believe that the decrypts were accurate and Midway was the target? Rochefort arranged for the commander on Midway to send an uncoded radio message to the effect that Midway's water-processing plant had been damaged and the island was running out of fresh water. Sure enough, a few days later Rochefort intercepted and decoded a Japanese message saying: 'AF is short of water.' The target was now confirmed, as was the date of the attack—4 June.

Admiral Nimitz had fewer overall resources than the Japanese, but Rochefort's intercept enabled him to position them with devastating effect. The Japanese Navy suffered a crushing defeat, from which it never recovered. Until 4 June the Japanese had never lost a major strategic battle. After 4 June, they never won one. The tide of war had turned.

So if the spies could get good advance warning of the Port Moresby attack and Midway, did they have advance notice of the midget submarine attack on their ships in Sydney Harbour? There is no evidence that they did. The Sydney attack was planned in early March 1942, and the orders to mount it went out to the submarine commanders on 1 April. The first submarine sailed from Truk Lagoon on 27 April. It is very unlikely that much of this was directed by radio, so there would have been little or nothing to intercept up to that point. Nor would Magic intercepts of diplomatic traffic have raised the alarm. The Imperial Japanese Navy was not in the habit of informing its diplomats about where it would strike next.

Direction-finding and traffic analysis from New Zealand did lead to a submarine warning to Sydney, issued on 29 May, two days before the attack. Although the fix was pretty accurate—40 nautical miles from Sydney—the report warned of one submarine, not five, and certainly did not mention midget submarines. The decrypt which should have set the alarm bells ringing was the FRUMEL digest of 30 May, which was only partly decrypted but which was clearly a reconnaissance report identifying targets in Sydney, particularly ships *inside* Sydney Harbour. The biggest 'what if . . .' of the Battle of Sydney Harbour revolves around this message. If, instead of simply passing the FRUMEL decrypt on to Washington, Admiral Leary had also alerted the Australians then things might have turned out differently.

Suppose Leary had sent a message to 'Cocky' Long, the Director of Naval Intelligence, Australia, along the following lines:

Further to New Zealand warning of May 29 reporting submarine presence in vicinity Sydney. Intelligence from a most secret source [the standard cover phrase for intercepted and decoded Japanese signals] indicates Japanese submarine which attacked *Wellen* on May 15 carried out reconnaissance, possibly aerial, of Sydney Harbour and Mascot airfield on or around May 25. Reconnaissance identified naval targets inside Sydney Harbour.

If such a message then led to an anti-submarine alert, Muirhead-Gould might have reacted quite differently to *Yarroma*'s and *Lolita*'s claims to have located and attacked a submarine in the harbour itself, and Captain Bode might have been less sceptical of his officers' sightings of a midget submarine. The Port War Signal Station might have added a few hands to their watch, and might have responded more effectively to the traces given by Chuman's and Ban's submarines. The end result might still have been the same, but Leary's failure to pass on his intelligence surely diminished Sydney's chance to react promptly and well.

However, even a full decrypt of this signal would not have told much about the exact nature of the Japanese threat. The only messages which might have given a clear warning of the timing and nature of the attack were Sasaki's two signals, reported in Chapters 5 and 6, and there is no evidence that either of these was ever decrypted. This was a time when all SIGINT resources were concentrating on the looming attack on Midway. Summaries of naval intelligence by Arthur McCollum, at the Office of Naval Intelligence in Washington, for the period from 15 May to 4 June 1942, are dominated by decrypts of messages setting out Japanese preparations for this major attack, and the diversionary attack on the Aleutian Islands. All intelligence efforts throughout the Pacific focused on Midway, and rightly so. The Sydney raiders were under orders to keep radio transmissions to a minimum, so there was very little radio traffic to excite even the traffic analysts. Any intercepted signal from a single submarine off Sydney may well have been legitimately passed over as low priority for full decryption. The Midway attack was the main intelligence target.

Nor does it make sense to suggest, as some have, that the Americans knew about the raid but kept the information away from the Australians for fear of revealing they had broken into the Japanese codes. FRUMEL was a joint American–Australian operation and, while there was plenty of tension between the Australian and American contingents, the fact that Japanese codes were being broken was well known to the Australians. The Americans were not remotely squeamish about using signal intelligence to fight the Battle of the Coral Sea, and later the

Battle of Midway, so they would surely have been equally brisk about the Sydney raid.

No, like so many conspiracy theories the suggestion that the raid was known about in advance and that knowledge became the subject of a massive cover-up will not stand examination. When things go wrong the question always arises: conspiracy or cock-up? There can be no doubt about the answer in the case of the midget submarine raid on Sydney Harbour. Cock-up wins.

Appendix III

The Admiral's report

Ine of the joys of researching this book is the opportunity it gave the author to return to the forgotten world of manual typewriters and carbon paper. Terms like 'top copy' have left the language now that computers and word processors can churn out 20 immaculate and identical copies of a document in under a minute. In the world of 1942, documents were typed on six or seven pages at once, with carbon paper between the pages. The top copy would be easily readable, but anyone so low on the pecking order that they were destined to receive copy seven could expect to wrestle with fuzzy and often unreadable type, laced with barely readable corrections. After a day in an archive ploughing through a succession of seventh copies, any researcher can be forgiven for hoping his next project will be set in a time when the computer has taken over. However, there is a softness and a vulnerability about manually typed documents which the computer can never match, and it gives them a special charm.

Happily, the top copy of Rear Admiral Muirhead-Gould's report is available in the Australian National Archive in Melbourne. I have tried to capture its flavour by setting it out here in a form as close as I could get to the original. The first page of the top copy is littered with initials and dates as it circulated around the Navy Board. The first set of initials, dated 16 July, probably belong to Sir Guy Royle. The last set of entirely indecipherable initials is dated 31 July. Occasionally someone has scribbled a note on the National Archive's top copy, but the identity of the author of these jottings remains a mystery, as does the timing of their musings. Other copies have been more heavily annotated but it is impossible to tell by whom or when. The annotations on the other copies tend to be a bit more sceptical: one anonymous scrutiniser has tried to work out in the margin which submarine did what, clearly not accepting Muirhead-Gould's version at face value.

Royal Australian Navy

From .....The ~~Commodore~~-in-Charge, H.M.A. Naval Establishments, Sydney

Rear-Admiral

To .... The Secretary, Naval Board, Melbourne

Date ......16th July, 1942.   No. ...... B.S.   1749/201/37.

Subject ...<u>MIDGET SUBMARINE ATTACK ON SYDNEY HARBOUR</u>
<u>MAY 31st – JUNE 1st, 1942</u>

1.   Submitted for the information of the Naval Board is the following report on the Midget Submarine Attack on Sydney Harbour, May 31st — June 1st, 1942:-

2.   Appendices supporting the narrative are attached:
> Appendix   I — Chronological sequence of events.
> Appendix II — Sources of information.
> Appendix III — Submarine and torpedo particulars (operational only).
> Appendix IV — Loop indications and signatures.
> Appendix   V — Lessons learnt.
> Appendix VI — Recommendations for recognition of Personnel.

3.   It is considered that four midget submarines participated in the raid. Of these, two are known by their actual Japanese numbers (No. 14 and No. 21). They are thus referred to in the following narrative. The other two unknown midgets are referred to as "Midget A" and "Midget B" respectively.

4.   It is considered that the force which attacked Sydney consisted of five "I" class submarines, four midget submarines, and one, possibly two, float planes. These were:

"I" 21 (Float plane)
"I" 24
"I" 22
"I" 27
"I" 29 (Possibly float plane)

Midget No. 14
Midget No. 21
"Midget A"
"Midget B".

5.   The attack was possibly preceded by aerial
reconnaissance, which may have been carried out on 29th,
30th and 31st May.

6.   A reconnaissance of Sydney Harbour, especially the
Naval Anchorage area, was carried out by one biplane
single float plane at approximately 0420K/30 May.

7.   Allied warships in Sydney Harbour at the time
included the following:

No. 1 Buoy	–	H.M.A.S. "CANBERRA"
No. 2 Buoy	–	U.S.S. "CHICAGO"
No. 4 Buoy	–	U.S.S. "PERKINS"
No. 5 Buoy	–	U.S.S. "DOBBIN"
No. 6 Buoy	–	H.M.A.S. "BUNGAREE"
Birt's Buoy	–	H.M.S. "KANIMBLA"
Off Robertson Point	–	H.M.A.S. "AUSTRALIA"

8.   The plane, which was burning navigation lights,
approached the harbour from a northerly direction, flew
over the Naval Anchorage, circled U.S.S. "CHICAGO"
twice, and departed in a due east direction.

TACTICS

9.   The contents of Midget No. 21 (ample food supplies,
first aid kit, charts, lists of call signs etc.)
suggest that this was by no means regarded as a
"suicide" venture.

10. The establishment of "picking up dispositions", rendezvous at which midgets were to rejoin their parents, had been made. Five of such rendezvous were spaced at fairly regular intervals (an average of 18 miles apart) two to the northward and three to the southward of Sydney.

11. The waiting parent submarines were in each case spread 2 miles apart on a line of bearing at right angles to the coastline.

RECONSTRUCTION OF EVENTS OF MAY 31st/JUNE 1st

12. Weather conditions were reported outside the heads at 1900K as — rough sea, moderate swell, wind S. by W. force 4, dark and overcast. The moon was full and rose at 1813K. Dawn on Monday, 1st June, was at 0545K; high tide 2125K, height 6 feet.

13. Four midget submarines (Midget 14, Midget 21, "Midget A" and "Midget B") were released (from "I" submarines 22, 24, 27 and 29) off Sydney Heads, a short distance to seawards, but outside the Loop area, during the afternoon of Sunday, 31st May.

MIDGET NO. 14

14. The first attempt at an entry was made by Midget No. 14, and was unsuccessful. She crossed the loop at 2001 and, by 2015, was caught in the nets (centre portion, close to the Western gate). She was unable to free herself, and blew herself up at 2235. Her propellers were thickly covered with grease when the wreck was recovered. No food had been touched, neither had any sanitary utensils been used.

"MIDGET A"

15. The second entry was made by "Midget A". She crossed the loop at 2148, and entered the harbour unobserved.

16. "Midget A" was not sighted until 2252. She was then sighted by "CHICAGO" and a ferry in the proximity of Garden Island. She was also sighted by Dockyard Motor Boat "NESTOR" and an officer on Ferry Wharf, Garden Island, at the same time. She was then close to Garden Island (200 yards off) and proceeding towards the Harbour Bridge.

17. "Midget A" was fired on by "CHICAGO" and apparently turned towards North Shore instead of proceeding further up the harbour. She was next sighted at 2310 from the Oil Wharf at Garden Island (by H.M.S.[*] Vessels "WHYALLA" and "GEELONG") in the direction of Bradley's Head. They fired at her and kept the area under observation for half an hour.

18. "Midget A" fired two torpedoes from the direction of Bradley's Head at 0030. One of these failed to explode, after running ashore at Garden Island. The other passed under the Dutch Submarine K9 which was lying alongside "KUTTABUL" at Garden Island, hit the sea bottom and exploded, sinking "KUTTABUL".

19. It is presumed that these torpedoes were fired at "CHICAGO" at No. 2 Buoy, who was about to slip and proceed. The dock floodlights, which would have silhouetted "CHICAGO", were extinguished just before the torpedo was fired. "Midget A" then escaped, passing over the loop on her exit from the harbour at 0158.

"MIDGET B"

20. "Midget B" made an unsuccessful attempt to enter the harbour but failed to reach the effective loop (No. 12) or, consequently, the boom. She was sighted by "YANDRA" (the Duty A/S Vessel on patrol within the Loop Area) and later by "LAURIANA" who illuminated her until intercepted between the Heads, at 2254, by "YANDRA".

---

[*] It should have been H.M.A.S.

21. Two separate attacks were carried out by "YANDRA" on "Midget B" during a period of 9 minutes, starting from the time she attempted to ram the submarine at 2258 until her second attack — a full pattern of six depth charges — at 2307.

22. It is considered that "Midget B" was destroyed by this second attack, in a position 023° 3.6 cables from Hornby Light.

MIDGET NO. 21

23. Midget No. 21 entered the harbour at 0301, at which time she crossed No. 12 Loop. She proceeded up harbour unobserved until she reached Bradley's Head vicinity. Here she was sighted by "KANIMBLA" and fired on at 0350 and gave rise to the unconfirmed contact made by "DOOMBA" off Robertson Point at 0450.

24. She was detected in Taylor Bay and attacked with depth charges, first by "SEA MIST" at 0500, then by "YARROMA" and "STEADY HOUR" until 0827. The effect of these attacks was clearly shown in the great amount of damage done to Midget No. 21, which was evident in the wreck when it was recovered. It is probable that the first attack caused the submarine to run into the bottom, because the lower bow cap was damaged and both caps were jammed, although set to release. The torpedo tubes had both been fired, although the bow caps had jammed on release. The lower tube had been fired with the external adjustment fittings engaged, and these had sheared off when the torpedo moved in the tube. This suggests that an attempt was made to fire in a hurry, and was prompted by, or interrupted by, the depth charge attacks. The tubes can be fired only from the Control Room; the release of the bow caps can be carried out only from forward; other operations in the tubes may be carried out from the Control Room or the forward compartment.

25. Both members of the crew were shot through the head; the demolition charges had been fired but the fuzes were drowned. It is possible that the junior member of the crew had attempted to escape, as he was found with his boots off. The Captain was wearing boots. This suggests that an early depth charge attack damaged the midget, and later ones progressively wrecked her.

SUMMARY

26. It is, then, considered that four midget submarines attempted to enter the harbour, of which only two —
      "Midget A"
      Midget 21

succeeded in passing the boom, and of which one —
      "Midget A"

got away again.

27. The other three midget submarines were destroyed:
      Midget 14 in the net at 2235/31.
      "Midget B" between Heads at 2307/31.
      Midget 21 in Taylor Bay between 0500 and
      0827/1st June.

                             G.C. Muirhead-Gould
                                 Rear-Admiral

JAPANESE MIDGET SUBMARINE ATTACK —
31st MAY — 1st JUNE, 1942
CHRONOLOGICAL NARRATIVE

TIME (K)	EVENTS
2000	Recorded crossing on No. 12 Loop
2015 approx	Watchman sighted suspicious object in nets near Sheerlegs — Western Channel. Watchman and mate proceeded in skiff to investigate.
2130 approx	Watchman proceeded to "YARROMA" and reported suspicious object. ("YARROMA" was duty Channel Patrol Boat at West Gate) "YARROMA" would not approach for fear that object was a magnetic mine.
2148	Recorded crossing on No. 12 Loop.
2152	88"YARROMA" reported "Suspicious object in net" and was told to close and give a full description.
2210	"YARROMA" reported object was metal with serrated edge on top, moving with the swell. "YARROMA" was ordered to give full description.
2220 approx	Stoker from "YARROMA" sent in Maritime Services Board skiff to investigate and reported object as submarine. "LOLITA" closed "YARROMA". Captain Bode, "CHICAGO", left TRESCO with suggestion that he should go to sea with "PERKINS".*
2227	N.O.C.S. to All Ships, Sydney — "Take A/S precautions." Port closed to outward shipping.

* A likely story!

2230   Watchman sent back to work.
        "YARROMA" reported — "Object is submarine.
        Request permission to open fire."

        "GOONAMBEE" ordered to proceed forthwith to
        investigate object at West Gate. 2nd Duty Staff
        Officer proceeded to Channel Patrol Boats not
        duty. ("GOONAMBEE" was duty M/S Vessel in
        Watsons Bay.)

2235   "YARROMA" reported submarine had blown up.

2236   N.O.C.S. TO GENERAL —
        "Presence of enemy submarine at boom gate is
        suspected. Ships are to take action against
        attack."

2252   "LAURIANA" noticed flurry on water ahead to port,
        investigated with searchlight which showed conning
        tower of submarine, distance 60 feet to 80 feet.
        Signalled Port War Signal Station, Channel Patrol
        Boat and Minesweeper entering harbour and Channel
        Patrol Boat at boom. ("LAURIANA" was one of four
        duty Naval Auxiliary Patrol Boats.)*
        No response.
        "CHICAGO" to N.O.C.S. — "Submarine periscope
        sighted about 500 yards off our starboard bow,
        heading up the channel."

2250   U.S.S. "CHICAGO" at No.2 Buoy switched on
to   searchlight and opened fire towards Fort Denison
2253   — red tracers (pom-pom).
approx Dockyard Motor Boat "NESTOR" halfway between
        ferry wharf and No.2 Buoy noticed disturbances
        in water 40 yards ahead. "CHICAGO'S" searchlight
        then illuminated periscope of submarine coming
        towards "NESTOR". Submarine was steering towards

---

* In fact there were three, not four.

harbour bridge 200 yards off Garden Island. Officer on Ferry Wharf saw periscope in "CHICAGO'S" searchlight. Shots falling all round it.

2254   "YANDRA" sighted conning tower 400 yards away 028° - 3 cables from Hornby Light. ("YANDRA" was duty A/S Vessel on patrol within Loop Area.)

2255   "YANDRA" approached to attack.

2258   "YANDRA" attempted to ram submarine which reappeared 100 yards astern, damaged, and slowly turning to starboard. Position 283° 2.5 cables from Hornby.

2259   "YANDRA" ordered to carry out A/S Sweep. Negative result.

2300   "GOONAMBEE" proceeded from Watson's Bay to Gate in West Channel. Patrolled Bradley's Head to Gate. "YANDRA" at West Gate.

2303   "YANDRA" sighted conning tower 600 yards away.

2304   A/S contact obtained. "YANDRA" prepared to attack.

2307   "YANDRA" fired pattern of 6 depth charges set to 100 feet. Position 023° 3.6 cables from Hornby Light. Submarine was not seen after explosions.

2310   "GEELONG" fired at suspicious object in line to left Bradley's Head and, with "WHYALLA", swept with searchlights for half an hour. ("GEELONG" was A.M.S.* refitting alongside oil wharf. "WHYALLA" was A/S vessel self refitting alongside "GEELONG")

---

* An Australian Mine Sweeper.

2314   N.O.C.S. signal — "All ships to be darkened."

2315   "BINGERA" ordered to immediate notice.
        ("BINGERA" was Stand Off A/S vessel at No.7
        Buoy.)
        U.S.S. "PERKINS" slipped and was ordered back to
        buoy by "CHICAGO" securing again at 2340 to No.4
        Buoy. ("PERKINS" at 4 hours notice at No.4 Buoy)

2330   "BINGERA" to N.O.C.S. — "Ready to proceed."

2334   "BINGERA" ordered to "slip and carry out A/S
        search in harbour. Submarine reported passing —
        proceeding towards harbour bridge."

2336   "BINGERA" reported — "Ready to proceed."
        Rear Admiral and Chief Staff Officer proceeded
        down harbour.

2340   "PERKINS" secured again No.4 Buoy. "BINGERA"
        slipped and proceeded up harbour.

0000   Rear Admiral and Chief Staff Officer boarded
        "LOLITA".

0025   Flood lights new dock extinguished by orders
        N.O.C.S.

0030   "KUTTABUL" hit by torpedo. All lights on Island
        were extinguished by the explosion and the
        telephone went out of order.

0034   Lights and telephone switchboard, Garden Island,
        come into service.

0045   "BOMBAY" "WHYALLA" ordered to raise steam.
        ("BOMBAY" was A.M.S. at 4 hours notice at No.9
        buoy.)
        "PERKINS" slipped.

0103   "BINGERA" ordered to slip between Bradley's Head and Garden Island.

0110   N.O.C.S. — General — "Enemy submarine is present in the harbour and "KUTTABUL" has been torpedoed."

0120   Submarine K.9 slipped and proceeded up harbour in tow. (K.9 was alongside "KUTTABUL")

0121   "ADELE" ready. Told to remain at Buoy. ("ADELE" was Stand Off Examination Vessel at Watson's Bay.)

0125   "SAMUEL BENBOW" reported — "Crew at action stations raising steam." ("SAMUEL BENBOW" was Stand Off M/S Vessel at Watsons Bay.)

0158   Crossing reported on No.12 Loop.

0214   "CHICAGO" to N.O.C.S. — "Proceeding to sea."

0230   "WHYALLA" to N.O.C.S. — "Slipped and proceeding to sea."

0230   Staff Officer, Channel Patrol Boats, received
to   orders to proceed and patrol when ready vicinity
0245   Bradley's Head.
         "TOOMAREE" — East Boom Gate.
         "MARLEAN" — West Boom Gate
         "SEA MIST" - "   "   "
         "STEADY HOUR" to contact duty C.P.B's at boom —
         "LOLITA" and "YARROMA".
         (Stand off Channel Patrol Boats at Farm Cove.)

0243   "PERKINS" to sea.

0245   "STEADY HOUR" ordered "SEA MIST" to patrol
approx   Bradley's Head — Boom.

0256   "'CHICAGO' to sea" reported by P.W.S.S.

0300   "CHICAGO" reported — "Submarine entering harbour."

0301   Crossing reported on No. 12 loop.

0305   "'WHYALLA' to sea" reported by P.W.S.S.

0307   N.O.C.S. ordered "BINGERA" — "Carry out A/S
        patrol in vicinity of 'CANBERRA'."

0320   "BOMBAY" reported — "Ready to proceed."

0335   C.P.B's proceeded on patrol
        Lieutenant Adams embarked in H.M.I.S. "BOMBAY"
        and proceeded to sea on A/S search as per
        N.O.C.S. 1735z/31.*

0340   L.F.B. 92 reported sighting submarine 5 miles
        off Port Hacking at 0105k/1.

0350   "KANIMBLA" switched on searchlight and opened
        fire. "BINGERA" searched area. ("KANIMBLA" was
        12 hours notice at Birts Buoy.)

0450   "DOOMBA" signalled "BINGERA" about submarine
approx contact off Robertson Point. This was
        investigated without result.
        "CANBERRA" signalled unconfirmed sighting
        torpedo track from Bradley's Head at 0440.
        ("CANBERRA" at 4 hours notice at No 1 Buoy.)‡

---

* It is a bit of a mystery why Muirhead-Gould, with his reference to 1735z/31, should suddenly
  slip into Zulu time, commonly known as Greenwich Mean Time. Throughout the report he
  uses Kilo time, usually known as Australian Eastern Standard Time. There is a
  ten-hour difference between the two. The order referred to was therefore issued at 3.35 am
  on Monday morning Sydney time, and presumably is the same order as the one which sent
  the Channel Patrol boats into action.

‡ An anonymous hand has scribbled 'at immediate notice from 0115' below this entry.

0500   "YARROMA" and "SEA MIST" and "STEADY HOUR" all
        patrolling.

0500   Red Verey Light seen in Taylor Bay by "YARROMA"
approx and depth charge explosion heard. "YARROMA"
        proceeded to scene at full speed and en route
        saw three more Verey Lights and heard further
        detonations.

0500   "STEADY HOUR" sighted suspicious object. Whilst
approx proceeding up West Channel "SEA MIST" attacked
        and fired Verey Light (red). "SEA MIST" reported
        3 submarines.

0500   "SEA MIST", at request of "GOONAMBEE",
approx investigated suspicious object in Taylor Bay.
        Fired 2 depth charges on each occasion firing a
        Red Verey Light before so doing. Aldis Lamp was
        used to illuminate target.

0511   N.O.C.S. stopped all sailings from Newcastle and
        Port Kembla.

0532   "BOMBAY" to sea.

0540   P.W.S.S. reported 2 Red Flares, apparently from
        ship anchored on bank.
        Rear-Admiral-in-Charge and Chief Staff Officer
        proceeded down harbour.

0545   "BOMBAY", "WHYALLA", "YANDRA" on patrol outside
        Heads.

0640   "STEADY HOUR" dropped depth charge ("STEADY
        HOUR", "SEA MIST" on patrol Chowder Bay —
        Bradley's Head.)
        "STEADY HOUR" dropped second charge and marker
        buoy in same place.

0658   "YARROMA" picked up A/S contact of submarine —
        confirmed dropped one charge.

0718   "YARROMA" — second attack — one charge. Brown
to   oily tinge in disturbance — oily smear arose.
0721

0725   "STEADY HOUR" reported attacking definite Asdic
        contact — oil and air bubbles.

0730   "WHYALLA" and "BOMBAY" joined company and
        conducted search.
        C.S.O. proceeded down harbour.

"WINBAH'S"   Reported by Commanding Officer, "STEADY
arrival at   HOUR" that his anchor had caught up in
Taylor Bay   submarine and light oil film and large
                bubbles clearly visible.

0755   "YARROMA'S" third attack — same attack
        0718-0721. (Then stationary.)

0827   "YARROMA" — 4th and last attack — Oil and air
        bubbles continued to rise.

APPENDIX II
SOURCES OF INFORMATION

(a) Documents recovered from Midget 21 (translated at
    Navy Office, Melbourne).
    These disclosed the existence of an "Advanced
    Detachment" comprising:

Four Surface Vessels.

Eleven "I" Class submarines: I 10
                                                 I 16
                                               I 18
    I 20
    I 21
    I 22
    I 24
    I 27
    I 28
    I 29
    I 30

Eight "Midgets"   9
    21
    22
    23
    25
    26
    27
    28

Call signs for aircraft attached to I 10, I 21,
I 29, I 30.

It is interesting to note that Midget No. 14 is
not mentioned.

(b) <u>Charts recovered from Midget 21.</u>

   (i)   "Picking up dispositions" apparently placed five "I" class submarines at various rendezvous North and South of Sydney.

          These were —

                    I 21
                    I 22
                    I 24
                    I 27
                    I 29

          Two of the above, I 21 and I 29, were allotted aircraft call signs.

   (ii)   The courses from Sydney to the rendezvous off Broken Bay (shown on the Photostat portion of Chart attached) led to four "I" class submarines (I 22, I 24, I 27 and I 29), leaving I 21 apparently free to act as leader and possibly with her aircraft in lieu of, and not in addition to, a midget.

   (iii)   A working chart showing fixes due East of Sydney Heads, the seaward one being marked "1625".

          These fixes (marked on attached Photostat of portion of Chart) were :

          Outer South Head Light 260° 7.2 miles
          Outer South Head Light 253° 4.1 miles
          Outer South Head Light 247° 3.6 miles
          Outer South Head Light 260° 1.7 miles

   (iv)   Courses were marked on a Sydney Harbour chart recovered from Midget No. 21.

APPENDIX III

SUBMARINE AND TORPEDO PARTICULARS

(operational only)

	Submarine No. 14	Submarine No. 21	"Midget A"
Depth set on Midget's Depth Gear.	46′		
Maximum depth which can be set on submarine.	30 metres.		
Depth set on torpedoes:			
Metres:	6m./6m.	6m./6m.	5m.
Feet:	19.5′/19.5′	19.5′/19.5′	16.3′
Angle set.	Zero.	Zero.	60° left.
Torpedoes:			
Stop Valves:	Shut.	Open.	
Bow Caps:	On.	Half off, levers moved to "release"	
Air Vessel pressure:	2810 lb/sq.in 2810 lb/sq.in	Nil. Nil.	
Demolition charges:	1 fired. 1 fuze drowned	2 fuzes drowned	

APPENDIX IV
LOOP INDICATIONS AND SIGNATURES

Although two loops were in operation (No. 11, laid in 14/15 fathoms, and No. 12, laid in 6/7 fathoms) signatures were registered on No. 12 only.

Four signatures were observed on this loop, at 2001, 2148, 0158 and 0301.

At first these were all believed to indicate inward crossings.

Subsequently, however, it was decided that the 0158 signature could have recorded a crossing in the opposite direction from the other three.

It has accordingly been taken as an outward crossing.

Prints of signatures are attached.

APPENDIX V

LESSONS LEARNT

MISTAKES MADE AND REMEDIES

(a) Unidentified loop crossings at 2001 and 2148 were not recognized. Considerable confusion is caused by traffic over loops.

Remedies

(i) Manly Ferry Service has been curtailed and arrangements have been made to stop it at short notice.

(ii) Port will be closed to small boats at night.

(iii) Loop Indicator Signal Apparatus is being fitted to Local Defence Vessels.

(iv) Searchlight illumination of the loop area has been improved.

(v) Maritime Services Board is stopping trips by spoil lighters and tugs at night.

(b) "YARROMA" failed to engage the submarine.

Remedy

All officers commanding Channel Patrol Boats have been given more definite instructions.

(c) Depth charges were not capable of exploding in depths under 42 feet.*

Remedy

All depth charge pistols issued to Channel Patrol Boats and Naval Auxiliary Patrol have been modified to fire at 25 feet.

---

* An anonymous hand has written below this entry: 'The charges were dropped in greater depths than 7fm.' Seven fathoms is, of course, 42 feet.

(d) <u>Communications</u> through the Port War Signal Station were very slow. The correct R/T transmitter at Port War Signal Station was not fitted as it was not completed. The improvised set was not satisfactory. The F.S.6.R/T in the Channel Patrol Boats was unsuitable and could not be used when engines were running.

<u>Remedies</u>

A suitable R/T Teleradio Set has been tried out and is being recommended for fitting in Channel Patrol Boats and Naval Auxiliary Patrol boats.

It is recommended that R/T Sets be fitted in Examination Vessels, and the Staff Office, Pott's Point. This will save personnel in Examination Vessels and permit control of Channel Patrol Boats from Staff Office, if required.

It is recommended that W/T Set ex Port War Signal Station be fitted in Staff Offices, Pott's Point, for use as Port Wave W/T Station. This will reduce delay in working Local Defence Vessels and save overloading telephone lines between Port War Signal Station and Staff Office. (See also Lt.Cdr Cox's AC/5?42 on 3rd June, 1942, to D.N.I. & D.S.C.)

(e) Naval Auxiliary Patrol vessels were not armed.

<u>Remedy</u>

Naval Auxiliary Patrol Vessels are being supplied with depth charges, machine guns, Verey Pistols and Aldis lamps.

APPENDIX VI
RECOMMENDATIONS FOR RECOGNITION OF PERSONNEL

The following are recommended to the notice of the Naval Board for their display of zeal and determination throughout the operation :-

(1) Mr. J. Cargill. For vigilance and initiative in his personal efforts to report a suspicious circumstance to the proper authorities.
(It is for consideration whether this man has merited an award under the provisions of A.F.O. 1464(1) of 1941.)
and

(2) Mr W. Nangle who, to a lesser degree, assisted Mr Cargill.*

(3) Lieutenant A.G. Townley, R.A.N.V.R. and the crew of H.M.A.S. "STEADY HOUR".

(4) Sub-Lieutenant J.A. Doyle, R.A.N.R. (S) and the crew of H.M.A.S. "SEA MIST".

(5) Lieutenant J.A. Taplin R.A.N.R. (S) and the crew of H.M.A.S. "YANDRA".

(6) Engineer Captain A.B. Doyle, C.B.E., R.A.N.
and

(7) Commander (E) G.C. Clark, R.A.N.
These officers arrived on the scene minutes after the explosion which sank "KUTTABUL", and displayed

---

* The words 'to a lesser degree' have been crossed out in ink.

commendable fortitude in searching
the vessel for any man who might be
trapped. In doing so, they had to
wade in deep water, under hazardous
conditions, in darkness, as it was
not known at the time which portion
of the decks had been rendered
dangerous by the explosion. They
lent assistance to a number of
men who had been shocked by the
suddenness and force of the action.

(8)   Bandsman M.N. Cumming, Official No. 20501.
This rating, who was onboard
"KUTTABUL" at the time of the
explosion, showed determination
in diving into the water from the
vessel, swimming a few yards and
assisting a rating on to
"KUTTABUL'S" deck. He also again
dived into the water into
"KUTTABUL'S" wreckage in order to
see whether anyone needed
assistance. Although no great
courage or endurance was necessary,
he displayed considerable
initiative.

(9)   Mr F.J. Lingard (Torpedo Fitter).
For the removal of pistols and
primers from torpedoes, and
demolition charges from submarines,
this work being carried out
entirely voluntarily.

The Skipper and crew of Naval Auxiliary Patrol Boat,
"LAURIANA".
For prompt action in illuminating
the submarine.

<u>The Captain and crew of H.M.A.S. "YARROMA".</u>
> For their part in the sinking of
> Midget 21. It is considered that
> this action redeemed, to some
> extent, their earlier failure.

<u>All personnel of the Dockyard First Aid Party.</u>
> For their efficient handling of
> casualties.

Acknowledgements

Every author owes a debt to those who have tackled his subject before him, and I am happy to acknowledge the huge debt I owe to others. My old boss Charles ('Hank') Bateson's magisterial work *The War with Japan: A Concise History* remains the definitive account of Japan's role in World War II, and was an invaluable insight into Japanese motives and plans. *Total War: The Causes and Courses of the Second World War* by Peter Calvocoressi, Guy Wint and John Pritchard provided a detailed chronology of the war, and some new perspectives.

Australia Under Siege: Japanese Submarine Raiders 1942 by Steven L. Carruthers is the first full account of the midget submarine raid on Sydney, and challenged the bland reassurances of the official version. Steve did all the hard work of obtaining previously hidden documents, using the Freedom of Information Act. An expanded and revised version of the first book was published in 2006 under the title *Japanese Submarine Raiders 1942: A Maritime Mystery*. My debt to Steve goes deeper than the pleasure of reading his two books: he generously gave me access to all his tapes and files accumulated over 25 years of living with this story. Steve's and my priorities are different, and our accounts are very different in style and emphasis. However, much of the first-hand material in this book about Reg Andrew and the events in Taylors Bay, and also the events aboard the USS *Chicago*, comes from Steve's files, including the taped interviews with Reg Andrew. In some 39 years in the publishing business, I have never known an author to be so uninhibitedly generous to a fellow scribe.

The Coffin Boats: Japanese Midget Submarine Operations in the Second World War by Peggy Warner and Sadao Seno broke new ground by telling the Japanese side of the story in detail. David Jenkins' *Battle Surface! Japan's Submarine War against Australia 1942–44* is a fine work of scholarship and sets a standard against which all subsequent books on this subject will be judged. It is currently out of print. The same author's *Hitting Home: The Japanese Attack on Sydney 1942* is a briefer account, but equally sound, and happily now available again. *Curtin's Gift* by John Edwards is by far the most authoritative account of Curtin's role in the war, and neatly skewers a lot of myths surrounding Curtin's wartime leadership. Dr Steven Bullard's *Blankets on the Wire: The Cowra Breakout and its Aftermath* takes the reader as close as any Westerner can come to understanding the Japanese warrior's acceptance of death, and shame at the thought of surrender. Dr Bullard is the grandson of Lance Bullard, the diver who played so large a part in the raising of the midget submarines. I confess to a soft spot for *Toku Tai: Japanese Submarine Operations in Australian Waters* by Lew Lind. The author and I have often come to very different conclusions from the same set of facts, but his book is distinguished by an entertaining scepticism when confronted with an official account, and I enjoyed every word of it.

The staff at the Public Records Office in Kew, England, were endlessly helpful as I ploughed through war cabinet records. Veteran submariners at the Submarine Museum in Gosport, England, gave valuable advice on the vexed question of how and why torpedoes miss. The staff at the Australian War Memorial in Canberra were unsparing in their help, as were the staff of the State Library of New South Wales in Sydney and the State Library of Victoria in Melbourne. The Australian National Archive collection in Melbourne gave me superb access to original documents. I confess to a hair-prickling moment as I handled the original typed top copy of Rear Admiral Muirhead-Gould's 16 July report on the incident, neatly signed in his blue fountain pen ink.

The staff of the Naval Historical Foundation in Washington and the Modern Military Records Branch of the National Archives and Records Administration in College Park, Maryland, were endlessly and cheerfully helpful. My particular thanks to Laura Waayers and Jodi Foor.

In Sydney, the National Maritime Museum oral history collection gave me some excellent first-hand accounts of the night of 31 May 1942. Dr David Stevens and John Perryman of the Sea Power Centre in Canberra guided me through fascinating day-to-day original documents from cash account books to ships' histories. David's investigation into torpedo tracks, published in the *Australian War Memorial Journal* in April 1995, was the first account I read which made sense of why Ban's torpedoes missed *Chicago* and found *Kuttabul* instead. Commander Shane Moore, director of the Naval Heritage Collection at Spectacle Island in Sydney, was tirelessly patient as I plied him with layman's questions on subjects as diverse as how torpedo engines work to the prevailing sea currents off Sydney Heads. Sue Thompson, deputy curator of the Naval Heritage Collection, went to endless trouble to dig out and scan historic photographs. Tim Smith, Senior Heritage Officer at the New South Wales Heritage Office, patiently explained the niceties of dealing with historic wrecks. John Darroch's encyclopaedic knowledge of Sydney ferry history was patiently offered, and willingly accepted. Rodney Champness gave invaluable help unravelling the mysteries of 1942 military radio sets, especially FS6.

David and Kristin Williamson generously allowed me to share their research for *The Last Bastion*, a television mini-series setting out the political background to Australia's entry into World War II, which David co-wrote with Denis Whitburn. Kristin's book *The Last Bastion* rises well above the television tie-in category, as befits the holder of a first-class honours degree in Australian history.

My French friend Vanessa Pigeon translated original Japanese documents into English from her home in Monterey, Mexico, thereby demonstrating that the global village has well and truly arrived. Roger Doyle used his spectacular talents as a sound engineer to resuscitate Reg Andrew's 30-year-old audio tapes. Without Roger, they might have been lost to posterity.

My special thanks go also to Google and the World Wide Web, whose 24/7 services were particularly helpful in the early stages of my research. There cannot be a single crackpot theory without its web page, and a Google search of some of the key words in this book will take you on a magical mystery tour through irrationality, hysteria, fantasy, paranoia and plain old-fashioned nuttiness, relieved by some wonderfully erudite and helpful material.

Nelson Mews, Steven Carruthers and Helen Young all read the manuscript and saved me from my many sins. All remaining errors are, of course, mine alone. There would have been more of them without Nels, Steve and Hellie.

I cannot find words of praise enough for my publishers Allen & Unwin, who were endlessly encouraging (Rebecca Kaiser, managing editor), then stylish, meticulous, sympathetic and patient (Angela Handley, my editor) throughout the whole process of creating this book. It is a measure of A&U's personal commitment to the project that the cover features a picture of Angela's family preparing for the worst in Sydney in 1942. In an age when the cultures of book publishing and factory farming seem to be converging, A&U is an oasis of flair, good humour and professionalism.

I owe a debt to friends and family who gave me bed and food while I was researching in Sydney: Leigh and Jenny Virtue, Mary and Van McCune, Karma Abraham and Lenore Nicklin, and my brother-in-law Selwyn Owen; elsewhere in New South Wales, Kristin and David Williamson, and Annie and Barry Knight; in Victoria, Sheryl and Craig Cooté, Robert Foster and Jack Bell.

John and Cabby Gunter patiently ferried me around Sydney Harbour in *Delta Skelter*, while I pored over charts trying to find the *exact* location of long-disappeared torpedo tracks, boom nets, indicator loops, and the like. My brother Doug handed over his venerable and dogged Ford

Fairlane, and it shuttled me flawlessly between Sydney and Canberra. Without their generosity, support and good company the task of writing this book would have been much less enjoyable.

Official reports are inclined to skim over unpalatable facts. Their first purpose is often to win medals or to protect the writer's backside, rather than to record the truth. For that reason, in these pages I have often parted company with the accepted version of events. I have also tried hard to stick to primary sources rather than pick my way through the maze of conflicting stories in books, newspapers and magazines, and in radio and television documentaries. With that in mind, my biggest vote of thanks must go to the people who gave unsparingly of their time and memories while I was researching this book. The heroism of the Japanese sailors who mounted the raid on Sydney Harbour has been widely and rightly recognised. My heroes and heroines are the men and women of Sydney: the under-armed, under-trained and often erratically led soldiers, sailors and airmen who found themselves facing a lethal attack where they least expected it, in their own harbour; and the ordinary citizens of Sydney, fearful of an unfamiliar and apparently invincible enemy, who reacted with characteristic good humour to his sudden arrival on their doorsteps.

Bibliography

I have deliberately avoided peppering the text of this book with a profusion of footnotes and references. The publishers and I readily agreed these would achieve little for most readers while slowing the pace of the narrative. Nevertheless, specialist readers and scholars are entitled to know on what authority the author bases his facts.

My primary sources included taped interviews with Jean Andrew, Don Caldwell Smith, Rahel Cohen, Jeff Cooté, Kevin Cooté, Margaret Coote (*née* Hamilton), Donald Dunkley, David Goldstone, Dr James Macken, Ian Mitchell, and 'Darby' Munro. Copies of these interviews will be deposited with the Naval Heritage Centre, Garden Island, where they will be available to researchers. I also drew on taped interviews with Reg Andrew, and log books and other documents, from the author Steven Carruthers. Steve's material included transcripts of research interviews with officers from USS *Chicago* conducted in 1981 and 1982 for the television documentary *Warriors of the Deep*. The interviews were not included in the broadcast version, and only the transcripts survive. Steve intends to deposit this material with the Sea Power Centre in Canberra, where it will be available to scholars.

Roy Cooté's dive log and photographs were supplied by his grandson Craig Cooté. The original log book is now with the Naval Heritage Centre on Garden Island. Other first person accounts came from publicly available documents lodged in the Australian National Archive, most often with its Melbourne centre, and at the Australian War Memorial, in Canberra. I drew on British cabinet minutes and papers from 1939 to 1942, freely available at the Public Records Office in Kew, and on intelligence digests and summaries for April, May and June 1942, lodged with the Naval Historical Foundation in Washington. Contemporary newspapers also provided a host of material. Newspapers are stored on microfilm at the various state libraries around Australia, and I drew heavily from records held at the State Library of New South Wales and the State Library of Victoria.

BOOKS

Bateson, Charles, *The War with Japan: A Concise History*, Ure Smith, Sydney; Barrie and Jenkins, London; Michigan State University Press, East Lansing, 1968.

Bullard, Steven, *Blankets on the Wire: The Cowra Breakout and its Aftermath*, Australian War Memorial, Canberra, 2006.

Burlingame, Burl, *Advance Force Pearl Harbor*, Naval Institute Press, Annapolis, 1992.

Calvocoressi, Peter, Wint, Guy and Pritchard, John, *Total War: The Causes and Courses of the Second World War*, Viking, London, 1972, revised 1989.

Carruthers, Steven L., *Australia Under Siege: Japanese Submarine Raiders 1942*, Solus Books, Sydney, 1982.

—— *Japanese Submarine Raiders 1942: A Maritime Mystery*, Casper Publications, Sydney, 2006.

Edwards, John, *Curtin's Gift*, Allen & Unwin, Sydney, 2005.

Fullford, R.K., *We Stood and Waited: Sydney's Anti-Ship Defences 1939–1945*, Royal Australian Artillery Society, Sydney, 1994.

Gill, G. Hermon, *Royal Australian Navy 1942–1945 Vol. 2*, Australian War Memorial, Canberra, 1968.

Jenkins, David, *Battle Surface! Japan's Submarine War against Australia 1942–44*, Random House, Sydney, 1992.

——*Hitting Home: The Japanese Attack on Sydney 1942*, Random House, Sydney, 1992.

Leasor, James, *Singapore: The Battle that Changed the World*, Hodder & Stoughton, London, 1968.

Lind, Lew, *Toku Tai: Japanese Submarine Operations in Australian Waters*, Kangaroo Press, Sydney, 1992.

Newcomb, Richard F., *The Battle of Savo Island*, Henry Holt and Company, New York, 1961.

Oppenheim, Peter, *The Fragile Forts: The Fixed Defences of Sydney Harbour*, Australian Military History Publications, Loftus, 2005.

Pfenningworth, Ian, *A Man of Intelligence: The Life of Captain Eric Nave, Australia's Codebreaker Extraordinary*, Rosenberg Publishing Pty Ltd, Sydney, 2006.

Reid, Richard, *No Cause for Alarm: Submarine Attacks on Sydney and Newcastle May–June 1942*, Department of Veterans' Affairs, Canberra, 2002.

Royal Australian Navy, *A–Z Ships, Aircraft and Shore Establishments*, Navy Public Affairs, Sydney, 1996.

Stevens, David, *A Critical Vulnerability: The Impact of the Submarine Threat on Australia's Maritime Defence*, Sea Power Centre, Canberra, 2005.

Warner, Peggy and Seno, Sadao, *The Coffin Boats: Japanese Midget Submarine Operations in the Second World War*, Leo Cooper/Secker & Warburg, London, 1986.

Williamson, Kristin, *The Last Bastion*, Lansdowne Press, Melbourne, 1984.

Winton, John, *Ultra in the Pacific: How Breaking Japanese Codes and Ciphers Affected Naval Operations against Japan, 1941–45*, Naval Institute Press, Annapolis, 1994.

KEY DOCUMENT FOLDERS
National Archives of Australia, Melbourne
B6121 Midget Submarine Attack on Sydney Harbour—Signals.

MP138/1 Steady Hour—Sinking of Japanese Midget Submarine.

MP138/1 Japanese Midget Submarine—Sections Stowed at Clark Island.

MP150/1 Naval Auxiliary Patrol.

MP151/1 Awards in Connection with Japanese Midget Submarine Attack.

MP1049/5 Midget Submarine Attack on Sydney Harbour.

MP1185/9 Publicity Contravening Censorship Requests, Midget Submarine Attack.

Australian War Memorial, Canberra

AWM52 Weekly Intelligence Summaries—Submarine Attack Sydney Harbour.

AWM54 Japanese Midget Submarine Attack—Reconstruction of Events.

AWM54 Weekly Intelligence Summaries—Submarine Attack Sydney Harbour, 1942.

AWM54 Plans and Diagrams, Photographs of Midget Submarine.

AWM67 Official History, 1939–45 War: Records of Gavin Long, General Editor.

AWM124 Report of Investigation into Japanese Torpedo.

PR 86/24 Lance Bullard's Account of the Divers' Role.

Sea Power Centre, Canberra

Register of Requisitioned Motor Patrol Boats and Miscellaneous Examination Vessels and Harbour Craft.

Naval Historical Foundation, Washington

SRNS-0001-0078 Summary of Japanese Naval Activities.

SRNS-1517 FRUMEL Daily Digest.

Public Records Office, Kew

Cabinet Minutes and Papers, 1939–1942.

Television documentaries

He's Coming South—Animax Films, 2005.

Sydney at War: The Untold Story—Australian Film Commission, 2004.

Warriors of the Deep—Program Development, 1982.

Index